Aubrey's Game

Marilyn Revill

Aubrey's Game

Aubrey's Game
ISBN 978 1 76041 768 0
Copyright © text Marilyn Revill 2019
Cover image: Marilyn Revill

First published 2019 by
GINNINDERRA PRESS
PO Box 3461 Port Adelaide 5015
www.ginninderrapress.com.au

Contents

Aubrey's Game	7
The Deal	9
Opening the Game	11
Learning the Rules	21
The Sting	41
The Turn of the Game	49
The Twist	63
The Gamble	75
The Trump Card	80
The Joker	93
The Hidden Hand	109
Setting Up the Strategy	120
The Bluff	135
Playing It Out	149
The Wild Card	158
Taking a Trick	163
Testing the Play	172
Rubbish Cards	188
Beating the Odds	202
Playing On	216
The Frozen Pack	234
The Single Hand	239
The Long Game	254
The Tally	270
The Last Bid	274
Epilogue	276
Acknowledgements	277
Author's Note	278

Cassandra and Josh: this book is dedicated to you.
You carry Aubrey's genes on in a way that would make him so proud.

Aubrey Hilton Jury
3 May 1910–19 July 2011

Aubrey with his great-grandchildren, Cassandra and Josh, in 2005

Aubrey's Game

Aub always said, 'You play the cards you're dealt!'

There are all sorts of people in the world, and we've got the lot. There are those who are useful and those who aren't. It all depends on the hand that they appear in. Most of them are ordinary, but occasionally they can become special because of the way they react with others. The ordinary in the hand should never be undervalued; they are the base that enables the rest to be useful, and sometimes the ordinary can shine.

There are Aces that can be good or bad, depending on when they turn up.

There are Kings and Queens, but they are rare and valuable in your life, although you should be mindful that a queen of spades might just turn out to be treacherous.

Then, of course, there are the Jokers. What can you say about them? It probably depends on both the stage of the game and your mindset at the time.

You've got no control over the hand that you're dealt, but you can develop the skills to understand and build your game and to learn as you go along. There's a choice with every hand and a consequence of every choice. You make the best you can of it. And you don't cheat because you don't want anyone else to cheat on you, and if you gamble on it, well, that's just stupid!

Sometimes it's hard to apply the rules properly, and unfortunately some people decide to play by different rules. Of course, it helps when you're playing a two-handed game and you have the right partner.

And there's no point in whingeing about your hand to others; they've all got one of their own.

Just get on with the game!

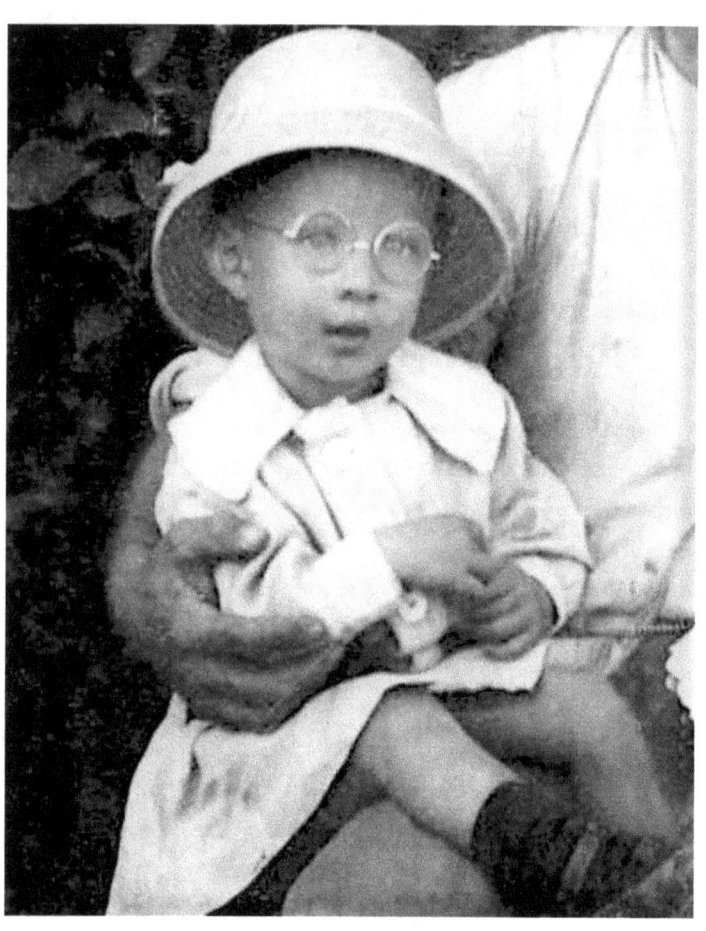

The Deal

1

He slithered over the sand and gravel on his tummy and popped his head up just like he'd seen the blue-tailed lizard do. He hoped Thora hadn't seen him. He had put them behind a big stone and was pleased with himself. He hated them. They were horrible, and they hung off his ears, and the little ends at the back dug into his head, and he wasn't going to wear them ever again.

Later in the day, his mother asked where his glasses were. He stared at her in mute bewilderment. She was very cross and asked several times, but he wasn't telling.

When his father came home, the questions went on, and his dad said, 'It's wrong, you know, Aubrey.'

His mother's piercing eyes stared at him, and he could feel them looking right into the naughty boy deep inside.

Finally, he couldn't keep it in any longer and a big sob crept out and he whispered, 'Under the wouse.'

Then he was lying on the ground with his dad, pointing with his stubby finger at where they were, but no matter how they coaxed, he wasn't going to go and get them. His father was smarter than him, though, and after calculating about where they might be, he pulled some floorboards and retrieved the offending glasses. Henceforth, they were tied on each day, and he really couldn't see much through them with his little cross eyes anyway, because they were always dirty. They were horrible and only made things worse. Right then, he knew that when he was big he was going to do exactly what he wanted to do.

He had been born in the small galvanised-iron house on the blue clay flats at Renmark, a squalling, struggling blue scrap, delivered with the cord around his neck. Nurse Reid had carefully persuaded him to breathe, and his colour had gradually risen to a wan, waxy shade against the swaddling rug. As the first boy born into his family, his name had already been chosen (with Stan's agreement) – Aubrey after Aubrey Payne, and Hilton, being Clarrie's maiden surname.

There were four of them in the family. His father Stanley, his mother Catherine (known as Clarrie), and his big sister Thora. His dad was a barber, skilful with the cut-throat blade, quietly spoken and well liked, and his shop on Holden's corner was a busy meeting place every morning. The men's fashion of the time was to wear a big moustache, and faces needed shaving every day. Aub was fascinated by the motley row of coloured shaving mugs adorning the shelf, because Stan's regulars each kept their own. He liked to go into the shop, but his mother said he was too little and he wasn't allowed in very often.

In April 1911, a fire started in Mr Moller's boot store at about two o'clock one Sunday morning, and the whole shopping block was completely destroyed. Aub trailed through the mess in the ashes looking for the mugs, but there was nothing left, and he got told off because he was so dirty.

Stan was forced to make a new start and worked as a labourer on the fruit blocks until Aub heard that his dad was going to be a policeman. Then there were tea chests and boxes everywhere because they had to pack up as they were going to live in the 'big smoke'. After the fire, Aub was scared of smoke, so he didn't know why they would want to live in it.

They were all really busy, and he was cross because everything was disappearing into a box. He pulled out what he wanted and got a clout on the ears for his effort and they said that what didn't get packed would get left behind. He was very careful to be good in case *he* got left behind.

Opening the Game

2

Stan was tall and dark-haired, and when he tried his uniform on, Mum said he looked 'very distinguished' and 'smart'. Aub and Thora, though, were very quiet, because they thought he looked a bit scary, and not like Dad at all.

They went to live at 5 Vassal Street, Semaphore. The children loved being by the sea. It was an exciting place, and sometimes Dad would be the policeman who went out with the pilot to bring the ships into the port. There were tugboats with their huge ropes and their black smoke, and lots of men. Loud whistles and bangs and 'man noise' filled the air. The sailing clippers with their puffed-up sails bobbed on the water, getting bigger as they got closer. When they arrived into the port, there were ropes everywhere, and the docks would be swarming with people, and there were lots of exciting smells. It was all noise, cargo, men, dogs, carts and horses while the unloading happened, and you weren't allowed to go close.

Aub saw his first train on the day when Stan put him on the handle-bars of his bike and dinked him down Semaphore Road to watch the monster come in from the city. He had never heard noise like it! There were lots of people getting on and off, some others watched, and one man kept shooing them out of the way, so he could take some photos for something called 'history'.

Thora was his big sister and they were mates. She was a bit of a tomboy and, between them, they kept Clarrie right on her toes. She didn't have a sense of humour for their shenanigans, so when they painted each other with the shoe black from Stan's box, she gave them a rollicking, saying, 'Just wait till your father gets home.' Stan, however, didn't meet with expectations. He roared with laughter at their black hands and faces and clothes and raced for his camera. He was a keen photographer who captured images on glass slides that he used to dry in the sunlight. Something to do with 'bromide'.

They began their schooling at Le Fevre. At the end of the first day, Aub grabbed a cap off the hook in the porch and ran home to tell his mum all about it. Then, about three days later, he got his first lesson from her about nits! They were apparently DREADFUL! Both he and Thora had their hair scrubbed, their clothes scrubbed, their bedding scrubbed, and their ears smarted from both scrubbing and hard words. He just hoped they were all gone because they could obviously do awful things to him.

With Stan in a settled job, and a new baby expected, they moved to 113 Carlton Parade at Torrensville. The house was an imposing tall villa with an iron roof. A long passage ran the full length with rooms off each side. It was a big block of land with plenty of room for gardens, wood and water storage, and a few hens.

Here the new baby boy was born, looking very much in Stan's likeness. He was given the Christian names Ivor Hilton, and Aub and Thora were mightily impressed with him until their mother chose their favourite rocking chair for nursing him, and made it out of bounds for them.

Stan and Clarrie settled in to making a home. She was a good cook and could sew or make almost anything needed to make it comfortable. Aub loved the yummy smell of the warm bread each day, and he could always tell when it was nearly cooked by how strong the smell was. Stan was a keen gardener. He sank a bore in the side yard and planted roses around the inside of all the fences. Then he set out his fruit trees and vegetable gardens. Lasscocks Nursery asked him to grow trial plants for them and his garden was soon widely known. A watchful Aub would spot people leaning over the fence to have a look, and sometimes they would cut a little piece off one of Dad's plants, and he would shoot them with peas from his shanghai.

More houses were gradually being built, but the surrounding area was still mainly market gardens, mostly owned by the Chinese. They picked their produce and packed it in baskets to sell from their stalls in Hindley Street. Aubrey thought that perhaps they didn't go to bed, because they were always out there no matter what the time or weather. Each day to get to school at Underdale, the children wound their way through the patches, waving and calling out to the workers, before they ran across the single plank bridge over the Torrens River. Aub noticed that the smell of the gardens changed, sometimes stinky and sometimes nice, and he soon developed a very keen nose for soil, cow manure, pumpkin flowers, celery, over-ripe tomatoes and other 'good earth' stinks and aromas.

The two continued with their daredevil antics, and they climbed anything. One day, the lady next door nearly had a heart attack when she saw them sliding down the very steep gabled roof of their house, stopping when their feet hit the gutter. This was punishable by the strap and, of course, each blamed the other for starting it but, truth be known, they were both up for it. Clarrie kept them as busy as she could with lots of jobs to do – wood and kindling to collect, shoes to clean, plants to water and errands to run, in the hope that it might curtail their high spirits, but they still got into plenty of trouble.

Aub was jealous of Thora, though. Mrs Harvey was teaching her to play the piano, and he thought he should be able to learn too. He loved music and was entranced by musical instruments of any kind. He scrounged a tin whistle and played it all the time, loudly and happily, and was banished outside to the woodheap, where he spent hours playing tunes he'd heard, and making up ones he hadn't, but he still sulked about not being allowed to learn to play the piano.

3

His favourite place was his grandparents' farm, but trips were rare as it was a long day taking the horse and cart and Stan always had jobs to do when he was off duty. Henry and Susannah Jury were farming at Mallala, and young Aub loved the ponies Tossie and Dot and the constantly being outside that was not just allowed but was expected. The flies, dirt, and heat didn't worry him, but he was very scared of the bull that always turned to stare at him with a baleful look in its eye, so he always walked around that paddock and never through it. He learned to be careful too about not standing on the bull-ant holes!

There were lots of homing pigeons (as well as the usual farm animals) that Grandfather kept in a house called a cote, but it didn't look like one. He said the pigeons would always come back no matter where they were sent, but Aub couldn't see how they would find their way, because he always had to be really careful not to lose himself in the paddocks. There was a fig, a loquat, a quince and a mulberry tree, but he liked the pepper trees most. The horses often stood under them in the shade, and he would climb up and sit for hours with the gooey sticky gum from their pink berries all over his hands so the dirt stuck to them, and the taste was horrible.

On Fridays, Grandfather would harness the horses, load up the dray with eggs, marrows, melons and other goods and take them to the market in Gawler. Occasionally a 'good boy' was allowed to go. The old men laughed and greeted each other and transacted their business, and the dray would head home again loaded with all manner of things. It was Grandpa's job to unpack it, with a boy's help of course. The household items went in to Grandma Susannah, who sorted them out. Bags of sugar and flour went into the larder, and Grandfather stacked the ones for the farm in the lean-to shed by the stables. Aubrey learned that a workplace should always be kept neat and clean.

Grandmother made butter and bread. In the kitchen, a half barrel stood, full of biscuits for the large uncles, who would take a handful at a time. It was the biggest biscuit barrel Aub had ever seen. There was a little cool store too, dug into the ground and topped with sloping walls of stone that made a roof. There were three steps to go down, and then it opened into a treasure of ledges loaded with milk, butter and cream, meat, eggs, fruit, jams, preserves and vegetables. Grandmother was capable and busy, and she'd had lots of practice at cuffing a young man under the ear if it was needed, but always with a kind gleam in her eye.

The uncles were tall and fit. There were eight of them, and they all had a sister (she was Stan's sister too). They mostly worked on the farm and slept in a stone room outside that had nothing in it but beds. They always made sure that Grandma had lots of wood ready to cook their dinners. Often, they were out working on the farm and only came in if it was dark or pouring with rain, and there would be lots of noise and laughter. They said funny things too, like 'What day is it tomorrow? Tuesday if it doesn't rain,' so Aub thought they must only have Tuesdays on the farm if it was sunny.

Then there was the very old man. He was great-grandfather, and his name was William. He was a very tall man with whiskers, and plenty of them, so the children nicknamed him 'Whiskers' but not when anyone could hear them. He thought he was King Billie of South Australia, and his chair was placed at the end of the passage and he would demand of anyone going in or out of a room that they 'salute the King'. He used to be very sharp of wit, but they said that at around ninety or so he started to get a bit 'silly'. (Not too silly, though, because when another old man died, they found him peering under the blind to count the number of buggies going to the funeral, as that showed one's importance in the district). He had a collection of muzzle-loaders, and a gramophone that played tin discs with slots in them. He liked 'a drink' and sometimes he would sing a lot.

The Old Man had arrived on a boat from somewhere called England and had had his own gardens that he talked about, and everyone in the family thought he had been 'amazing' and was 'pretty good'. He was widely known and respected in the district, and in 1913 the Adelaide Observer featured a photograph showing the four generations of his family (William, Henry, Stanley and Aubrey). They all talked about how important it was to own a piece of land and to make it 'produce'.

Transport by horse and cart was slow, and so the grain from the farm was taken to the coast (by dray) to Port Parham or Port Gawler to be shipped. Perched on the load, Aub would smell the stinky seaweed on the breeze, feeling sick with excitement as he looked for the ship. There would be nets for crabbing, and fishing lines too, and while they were waiting for the tide to ebb, they would crab or fish or sit on the beach with their feet in the mud and Grandfather would tell stories by the bonfire.

The horses dragged the drays out at low tide to where a windjammer would be heeled over on the mud. Boys were allowed to sit on top of the load while it sloshed across the mud into shallow water, and then watch while the bags were stowed, and the birds swirled round, and the men talked about where the ship was going. When the tide came in, it would sail off away along the coast and Aub would strain his eyes watching the white speck until it was gone. Grandpa said that ships made voyages several months long, and told of fierce storms they had seen, and of ships that had 'gone down' last year.

Then back on the beach they'd have a cook-up of the crabs and fish before going back to Mallala. Even the horses seemed to love going to the coast and Aub would see them walking in the water and rolling in the sand and always imagined them with smiles on their faces. Never over the years did he forget the wonder of those special days.

4

The outbreak of World War I saw large uncles with moustaches and wearing uniforms and hats arrive to stay the night before embarking for overseas. There were many goodbyes, and a feeling of 'watch your step' for a few days as each one of them left. Stan's brothers Darcy, Allan, Vic and Stuart, and Clarrie's brother Ern, all went off to fight for King and Country somewhere 'in foreign lands'. Although it sounded exciting, it obviously wasn't a good thing, as everyone was so grave and upset, and for the first time, but not the last, Aub saw his mother cry.

Stan was needed to keep law and order at home and, with four brothers enrolled, was not allowed to go, so Aub and Thora felt safe.

The news from the war brought upsets, and Clarrie was always packing parcels to send – anything she could get or knit or make that she thought might be useful, mostly socks when she had wool. She was often quiet, and if an unexpected letter came, she wouldn't open it until Stan was home.

In late 1916, things were not happy in the house. There were conversations that stopped when Aub entered the room. Important people who called talked in the dining room in dull tones. Looks were dour, and children needed to be seen and not heard. Apart from his usual duties, Stan had been asked to take any crime photos needed for forensics at the police station. He was very well liked, but his doing the photography had caused some dissent and jealousy, as a couple of the others thought he was being favoured.

Flapping ears heard that a jealous man in the police force had arranged that a false charge be made against Stan. A lady had said 'it was him'. The big boss policeman didn't believe it and said that he knew Stan was 'innocent' and he was 'sorry' and 'of course there would be no charge, but you cannot still be a policeman'.

Children kept out of the way because Stan and Clarrie were very angry at the injustice, and tempers were short. No one could understand how such an unfair thing had happened, as they were sticklers for honesty and were devout Methodists, and Stan had worked hard and enjoyed his job. And he hadn't done it! Aub knew this, because he was always being told 'you must admit to what you've done if you're guilty' and, since Stan hadn't admitted it, he hadn't done it. Still, he had stopped being a policeman on 12 June 1917, when he was discharged, and they never saw his uniform again. Aub was scared and he was worried, and he spent a lot of time on the woodheap with his tin whistle. He'd learned something: not everyone could be trusted.

Athol Hilton Jury was born on the day before, 11 June. He was a larger baby than the others had been and despite the upsets in the house there was lots of excitement about his arrival. While it helped to calm the household a little as they all focused on the new boy, Stan was sad and pensive about how he would support the growing family. Aub followed his dad everywhere and asked question after question.

Stan was a known as a hard worker and was well liked and respected in the area, so he was rarely without a job. He grew plants for the market and helped set out new gardens and did labouring jobs. He took photographs for people and so there was always some money coming in. There was no real security for the family, though, without a permanent job. At the same time, there was wonderful news. All four of his brothers had amazingly survived the war in Europe and were returning home. The knowledge of this put everything else into perspective, and he knew what a fortunate family they were.

In the next year, many more people than usual began getting ill, and as winter set in there was talk of 'Spanish flu'. Lots of people were getting sick and some people even died. Aub was not allowed to go near the houses in the street that had large yellow crosses painted on the doors because they had something called 'quarantine', and none of the children were out in the street playing together any more. Everything that could be was boiled, and visitors were kept at the door.

Apparently, this flu was something called an 'epidemic', and you were going to get really told off if you got it!

People stopped visiting each other and when his uncles arrived home from the war, even they kept their distance. The town was in the grip of a natural disaster and no one was safe.

Years later, adult Aub learned that the epidemic had killed between fifty and one hundred million people around the world.

Learning the Rules

5

In 1919, Clarrie's father suggested Stan work with him in his carrying business in Renmark, and later perhaps become a partner, and it was a popular decision with everyone. Grandfather Alfred was a tall imposing figure, and the children were very excited because they knew he had once been a baker and a confectioner, and that meant he knew how to make lollies!

Aub was never quite sure why, but he was sent to live with Grandfather (Alf) and Nana (Martha) Hilton in their family home in Twelfth Street while things were sorted out, and until everyone else moved back from Adelaide. He knew that they were his mother's parents, and they had named her Catherine after her grandmother, and Clarendon after the town they came from where she had been born, and he thought that was quite clever. They said it wouldn't be for long, but he didn't want to go on his own. Had he done something wrong? Why was Thora allowed to stay behind? They said he would like it and would make some new friends, but he sulked about it and wouldn't talk to any of them. He hoped his sulking made them feel as bad as he did.

He went to Renmark with his dad, who said he should 'be a man' and 'be good' for Grandpa and Grandma. He sulked all the way, and to his chagrin it didn't seem to worry his dad at all.

Perhaps Stan knew what a wonderful experience his sulking son would find it to be.

There was plenty for Aub to explore. The stone house stood street-front in the middle of a triple block of land, and a lane ran past the back. There were bamboos, vegetables, a few fruit trees and a pet white cockatoo. Best of all there were horses, carts and drays, enclosed on one block by a post and rail fence and a large pair of iron gates.

Aub learned that Grandfather had gone to Renmark in 1892 to work as foreman in Henry John's bakery, and that then, with his brother-in-law Ted Chapman, had bought the business. Eventually he sold his half to Ted. In 1907, he bought the triple block at Twelfth Street and started the new carrying business. He built the depot and the thatched stables on the first block, the stone family home on the second, and the third one was kept for later use.

Besides running his business, Grandfather was a Justice of the Peace (whatever that was) and was on all sorts of committees for things like the town water supply and the institute, and he acted as the local coroner, which was something about dead people. Aub understood that he should be very impressed.

There was an instant bond between him and Nana. She was firm, but kind and gentle, and she seemed to be really happy that he was there. She had twinkling eyes and always saw if something was funny. She cooked good food and didn't mind handing out a biscuit. Nana had a kind and encouraging word for all and had lots and lots of friends. She worked hard on the Church Guild and was a Temperance woman, believing that intoxicating drink was the beginning of all evil. But the most exciting thing: she had flown 'the old golds' from Gawler to Renmark in a two-passenger open-cockpit aeroplane with Captain Harry Butler, and she really, really liked it. As far as Aub was concerned, this put Nana way up there as the bravest person that he knew.

Grandfather's horses and carts carried everything everywhere. The rubbish from the butcher's slaughterhouse was carried out across the river flats and dumped. The fence posts for the new soldier's settlement blocks were carted and delivered. The tools and food stores for the stations up the country were heaped high on the dray and dragged away with teams of four horses. They carted barrels and casks and bags and poles and boxes, anything that came off, or went on a paddle boat, and anything else that needed to be moved. There was always something interesting happening, and each night at around nine o'clock he and Alf would walk down past the bamboos to the stable to feed and water and say goodnight to the horses. They were part of the family.

Alf had a fiery temper and his bad leg gave him a bit of a limp. He would sit on his Morris chair by the fire, with his walking stick across the arms and his leg stretched out full length on a soft stool, while Ginger his cat sprawled by the fire alongside, leaving no room for a boy or a grandmother to sit too close. Sometimes he would play crib with his friends, and Aub learnt that it was apparently very annoying if you 'died in the hole', so he walked very carefully around holes when he saw any in the street.

Aub walked to school barefoot across the blue clay flats with some of his cousins. If you had shoes, they didn't go on until you got there. He found the 'river' boys quite different from the lads at Torrensville (who had always called him 'cockeye Jury' behind his back.) He soon made some good friends, but as he was slight of frame he practised hard and learned how to use his fists with the ones who wanted to push him around. He was going to do what he wanted to do.

Wally Wescombe, 'Puss' Riedel and several of the other boys introduced him to the river. It was the best backyard a boy could have.

He immersed himself in its colours and its moods, the living noises of the reeds (whispering or rattling, depending on the wind) and the haunting calls of the plovers, teal, quail, ducks, pelicans, shags and the like. The sunrises and sunsets that doused the days, ready for swimming, fishing, yabbying and mucking around in the reeds, told if it would be clear and hot, or frosty in the morning with a sunny cool day to follow. The boys went to school every day and to the river every

afternoon. They dived off the wharf and swam and clowned around and soon Aub was a strong swimmer.

He'd liked the boats when he'd lived by the sea, but the paddle boats plying up and down the river totally fascinated him. They were beautiful with their clouds of smoke and steam, their racked-up decks and their big powerful wheels spinning water out behind them.

Each steamer had its own distinctive whistle, and he soon knew which one was going to turn the bend before he saw it – *Ruby*, *Gem*, *Industry*, *Pyap*, *Decoy*, *Marion*, *Emerald*, or whatever. They burned wood, mostly red gum, to fire the boilers, and some towed barges carrying bags of wool or grain or sheep. Most other cargo was stacked on the decks. One steamer was a floating shop of fabrics, sewing threads, linen, books and all manner of things. One plied the river conducting marriages and baptisms, and others carried passengers to the upper reaches of the river in Victoria or New South Wales. Sometimes a boat wouldn't be seen again, and you would hear that it was stuck on a sandbar, or had burnt, or had 'blown its boiler'.

When it was busy, you had to keep watch from the bank away from the men and the drays that were loading and unloading, or you were in trouble. Aub would watch for Hilton's drays, and would feel a little warm glow of pride when he saw them.

Aub always looked forward to the *Alpha* being in town because his mate Norm Collins lived on it with his parents, two brothers and two sisters. Sometimes she was in town for a couple of weeks, or a few months in low water, or for just a few days. Upriver there was always a governess on board for the children, but if they were in town they always went to the Renmark Convent School. Aub's mates at the public school gleefully taunted the Catholic kids, chanting 'convent dogs jump like frogs' (and other things) and pelting them with pie-melons. The Catholic kids pelted stones on roofs in return, and it didn't worry Norm – he could stick up for himself.

Norm was a bit of a prankster and with his brothers was always in some sort of scrape. They would put a box under someone's waiting buggy in the street and jack it up, or unhitch the horse, and would laugh like mad when the expected result happened, and then race off down to the river on their bikes. He even rode straight off the wharf one day to avoid getting caught by the policeman. He could fish his bike out later!

One day on the *Alpha* they were all roller-skating, linked by hands, lined across the deck, spinning in a circle. Aub was flying because he was on the outside – and he *was* flying because they let him go, straight over the side into the river! He was a good strong swimmer, but with the heavy roller skates strapped to his feet and no preparation to hold his breath, he went down like a stone. He fought to rise up through the water, and his lungs were bursting. The others crowded on the side of the deck peering into the water. He struggled desperately, feeling like he would burst. It was quiet on the deck and no one was laughing when he finally did manage to surface. It was a pretty close call, and that prank was never repeated.

Late one night, there was loud banging on Grandfather's door and the men rushed off. Aub was not allowed to go. In the morning, he heard that a team of four of Grandfather's horses and a loaded dray had misjudged the punt across to Paringa in the dark, and had been lost in the river. The two drivers had managed to swim clear, but not the horses, and the rest had gone down. Ropes and pulleys and chains were set up and lots of people helped trying to retrieve what they could, but it was a dreadful loss. It was the talk of the town and of course everyone had a guess at why it had happened.

Grandfather was very cross and sad, and everyone was busy being careful what they said. Aub cried because he loved all the horses with their big feet and soft noses. They had been his friends, and it was horrible down at the stables. He kept out of the way, miserable, with his tin whistle in his hands. But in the evening at nine o'clock, he walked again with Grandfather down to the stables to feed the horses that were left.

6

Six months after Aubrey had arrived, the Jury family were all settled back in Renmark, and he realised how much he had missed them all as soon as he saw them. Thora was still a tomboy, and she teamed up with their cousins Lois and Carmen and some of the local girls. Ivor, who could run like a hare, was clever and made friends quickly. Athol, whom they always called Bill, was still only a toddler, but he was a happy-natured little chap, always smiling and gabbling away, and never in a hurry. It was real fun, and Aub was busy showing them 'his' Renmark.

Sundays were for Sunday school and Dad became the superintendent and he viewed a religious training for the children as essential. The family were Methodists and Temperance people, believing that drinking alcohol was the beginning of all evil. Clarrie was a staunch force in the church community and Stan was a lay preacher.

Aub liked the hymns and soon knew most of them by heart and happily learned the texts and psalms and the most common prayers, but he wasn't too keen on the sermons. He was a bit intrigued by the Catholic church too, because his friends the Lynn and the Lawton families went there. They had things like Mass, and Friday nights they went to talk to the priest for a few minutes 'in the box', and all that sounded very interesting to him. His mother, though, refused to answer his questions about it. Some evenings, the whole family went to evensong, and he enjoyed that a lot and he and Thora would sing as loudly as they could while giggling and digging each other in the ribs.

News came that Ern, Clarrie's brother, had been badly gassed in the war and was ill in England. He had been awarded the Military Medal for outstanding bravery in France, and this was very important. Dad said it was because he had crawled forward and accurately located three German machine guns and a *minenwerfer*, and that they had then been destroyed and the advance had been able to continue. He said that the lives of many men had been saved by Uncle Ern's action. He had been a postal clerk at home, and so he was to work in a London post office for at least eighteen months while being repatriated. It was clear that he would need much care when he eventually got home, and he might not be able to hold a job.

After much thought, Grandfather reluctantly decided that Ern should join him as a partner in the business instead of Stan. This was a blow for the family to suffer, and Aub wasn't happy because now A.E. Hilton and Son was to be the new name on the drays and his dad's name wouldn't be there.

Uncle Ern came home from England and married Dorothy Jose. Auntie Dot was a wee lady who always spoke nicely to everyone. She had been the first telephonist at the Renmark telephone exchange and had met Ern while he was working in the post office before the war. Everyone said they were a 'handsome couple' and they lived with Nana and Grandfather.

Aub never really got used to Uncle Ern. He was much fiercer than all their Jury uncles, exploding quickly with anger, and he didn't have a lot of time for 'kids in the way who were just a nuisance'. Clarrie explained that he was 'getting over the war' and that they should just be polite and careful when they were around him.

Aub's cute little kitten went missing, and he didn't find out for a long time that Uncle Ern had drowned it. He hated Ern for that, and never forgot it. Sometimes Ern could be kind, but Aub knew that you should never assume what mood he might be in. His ideas about 'toughening up boys' caused an angry boiling fire in Aub's heart.

Betty Clare Hilton was born to Ern and Dot on 4 October 1921. She was another little cousin for the Jury children and was a petite little baby (like her mother) and had quite bright deep blue eyes. Thora and

Lois took a great interest in her, but to the boys she was pretty much just another baby. She was 'family', however, so that made her a bit more special, although the men said it was a pity she 'wasn't going to carry on the Hilton name'. Auntie Dot was very proud of her, and she was always prettily 'dressed up' and Aub thought she was a bit like a doll.

Grandfather Hilton was feeling a bit off colour over the weekend. He fed the horses as usual, but on Sunday afternoon was quite ill with stomach cramps and diarrhoea and was taken to hospital.

On Monday, he didn't improve and at noon on Tuesday 23 February 1921 he quietly passed away due to heart failure. Alf had been a tall strong man who had never had any illness, and the suddenness of his death amazed the family and community. Aub couldn't believe it.

Everyone was very, very sad, except perhaps Bill, who was only four (and didn't understand) and kept asking where Grandfather was. There

AN OLD RENMARKIAN

Mr. Alfred Hilton Dies Suddenly

The death occurred suddenly at the Renmark Hospital on Tuesday of Mr. Alfred Hilton, an old and respected resident of the town. Mr. Hilton enjoyed good health until a few days ago, but became ill during the week end and did not recover. Last week he acted as coroner at an inquest and adjourned the inquiry until today.

Mr. Hilton came to Renmark about thirty years ago and established a bakery business with Mr. Chapman. Subsequently he began business as a carrier, in which he continued until the time of his illness.

Mr. Hilton took a keen interest in public affairs, had served as a councillor with the Town District Council and was at one time a member of the Hotel committee. He leaves a widow, three married daughters and a son. The family are Mesdames E. T. Ross, S. W. Jury and Hugh Gravestocks and Mr. Eric Hilton, all of Renmark.

Renmark Daily Feb. 24th 1921

were lots of tears and many hugs, but none of it helped the children much. Clarrie and Stan were quiet and stern and deeply, deeply upset. All the other aunts and uncles too felt the loss. In fact, the whole town was upset, as he had been a true pioneer of the district and had worked hard to help build a good life for everyone in Renmark.

His funeral was conducted at the Renmark Cemetery on Wednesday afternoon, and he was buried in the grave where his son Ernie had been laid twenty-six years before. Ted Chapman, Mr Piggott, Mr Brand, Mr Schirmer, George Jury and Harry Taylor carried the coffin.

Women didn't usually go to funerals but Auntie Ethel and Uncle Ted, Auntie Myrtle and her husband Hugh, Uncle Ern and Dorothy Jose, Aunt Belle and Nurse Reid, were with Clarrie, and Stan, and Nana. Aub didn't look up much because Nana's twinkly eyes were swollen, dull and red with tears behind her veil.

He couldn't imagine the bamboos and the stables and the horses and drays and the sheds and the house without Grandpa. In fact, he couldn't imagine not being around Grandpa.

7

Uncle Ern took charge of the carrying business with his Scottish friend Bill Davidson to help. Bill was a 'spiffy' dresser and a really good worker and he told lots of jokes, so Aub liked him. He was tall and good-looking, and he seemed to get himself into a bit of 'trouble' now and then. Dad said he was a 'ladies' man'.

There was a small Maltese man too, called Charlie Magro, who came to live in Renmark, and he did some lighter jobs. They said he had been Ern's batman in the war, but he didn't look like Batman to Aub. He was always cheerful and good to be around, though, so the two of them became friends.

Now there were a very few Model T Fords running around the town and Aub was totally in awe of these beautiful machines with their big round lights and their gurgly horns. Only a few people had them because they were very expensive, but Uncle Ern had seen them in London, and he decided to buy some trucks, as motor vehicles were now getting more reliable and his mate Bill had worked with engines in the war. They puttered down Twelfth Street to a gallery of excited onlookers and family, and photos of them were taken out in the street in front of the house. One was a furniture removal van while the other was a speed truck.

The children were allowed to climb around, try the horns, peer into the engines and have a ride. After the women had disappeared inside for cups of tea, the men stayed out around the depot until it was dark. It was Uncle Allen Jury from Monash who drove the first load to be carried and delivered on one of Hilton's trucks.

The smells in the depot changed from the leather of the tack, the fragrance of the hay and smell of the horses, to the less pleasant odour of oil and petrol, and there were lots of oily rags. Aub was fascinated by the trucks, but he really liked the horses too, so he wasn't sure if it was progress or not. The delivery trips up to the station country were quicker, though, so Ern and Bill were happy.

Later that year, there was a flood and it was a lesson for Aub in how quickly the river could rise and how far the water could go. The decks of the boats were up high at the wharf and the current was strong, and there were floating trees and debris up around the river bends. Lots of snakes had been washed out of hiding, and it wasn't safe to go swimming.

It was amazing to see just where the water ran, its little rivulets seeping through the banks until they let go with a rush of water that took all the dirt and rubbish with it, and then settled down to swelling around swallowing everything it could reach. The clay flats and the school were underwater. Everyone was filling sandbags and working day and night to save what they could from being ruined. Aub heard that in 1914 there had been a drought and the river had been low enough to walk across to Paringa. It was the first time he really took notice of the power of nature.

He was glad he lived in Renmark and he didn't think there could be a more interesting place anywhere. But Aub had learnt to go off on his own and sulk, or to play the tin whistle on the woodheap when something didn't suit him. He still missed Grandpa, and one day he was having a bit of a sulk down by the bamboos and suddenly found himself soaked. Uncle Ern had hurled a bucket of cold water over him, just to give him 'something to sulk about'.

Stan found plenty of work. He kept on doing occasional deliveries, took photographs for people and worked as a labourer. He and his brother Roy had had a piece of land on the flats just below Renmark where they grew vegetables, but they grew more than they could sell, and it wasn't a great money spinner. Now it was flooded, and Roy decided that he would go farming in Western Australia, and so he moved on.

Renmark was full of working men. The soldier settlement was being cleared and properties were being laid out at Block E as the men returned from the war. Two-room stone houses were being built on the blocks. Long channels were being dug to carry the water for the irrigation scheme, and locks were being built to make the flow of the river more even, so there was always water for the pumps.

A road and rail bridge was to be built across the river at Paringa to bring the new train into town, and it would lift in the middle to let the boats through. There was plenty of work for everyone and the paddle boats and barges were fully loaded and couldn't keep up with the trade.

The Jury children were happy. Aub was in the river every day, or bird-nesting, yabbying or fishing if he wasn't doing jobs. There were plenty of sword fights in the reeds and fist fights around the back of the school. Thora remained in high spirits together with her cousins Lois Ross and Carmen Chapman. She continued with her piano lessons at Nana's and she was becoming very accomplished, and Aub was still jealous. The older they all got, the darker their hair became, and the more the waves and crinkles and curls appeared. Aub didn't mind, because he had always liked Nana's crinkly hair. Thora's hair hung around her face in a bushy frame, and it was hard now to put it in plaits as it was so curly. Only Bill had straighter hair like his mother.

There were lots of other Jury relatives too, in Renmark and Gurra Gurra, as well as the uncles at Monash and the Jurys at Mallala, and they were all close. This meant the children were growing up with a great sense of family, and lots of naturally learned lessons about how different people could be, and where one fitted and to whom one should answer.

Sometimes Grandfather and Grandmother Jury would come up and stay with Great Aunt Mary Lewis at Gurra Gurra. She and her husband Thomas would come across the river to Berri and collect them in their small boat, and Aub always got very excited to see them, even though Grandmother and Great Aunt Mary wore flynets on their hats and they looked strange, and very funny.

Stan got a labouring job at the construction works at Lock 5, ensuring regular money for some time, and he and Clarrie began to think about perhaps being able to build a new house. The family were living in a small iron house that was boiling in the summer and was getting too small. It was on the clay flats outside the town and the thought of living in the street closer to shops was attractive for Clarrie as she wouldn't need to walk so far. Building their own home was their dream.

The boys were handy, capable country lads and learned things quickly. Aub was quick with figures and was a great reader. He read whatever he could find that he could learn something from, but he wasn't interested much in comics. Both Ivor and Athol were going to be tall like their father and the Jury uncles, but he was a much shorter and he felt this keenly, so he began to take interest in building fitness and body strength. He worked at exercises and acrobatics and lifting weights and was determined to build up his small frame. Whenever a circus came into town, the children would manage to get in and watch the show, and Aub had seen what the acrobatic performers could do, so he took to working hard on the bars and the Roman rings at the boxing hall. He was going to be strong, and he was going to be as fit as he could be.

But he and Ivor had one escapade that called for some strong discipline from Stan. All the dunnies were lined up along the back of Nana's lane so the night-cart man could open the flap at the back and drag out the cans. They had noticed that the lady across the lane was very slow in lumbering down the back, so they thought she needed a bit of a hurry up. They hid in the lane until she entered the dunny and gave her time to sit. Then very quietly they opened the door flap and gave her a tickle on the backside with a feather! She yelled and bolted out with her bloomers around her legs and headed for the house!

They would have gotten away with it except for the raucous uncontrollable shrieks of glee coming from the lane as they danced around in circles almost crying with laughter. The punishment for that was unforgiving.

8

Aub could see that Ivor, tall for his age, was quite the athlete without even trying. He always won the school and local races easily, could do anything with a ball and excelled with his studies. He was good-looking too, with straight eyes, which would have made Aub jealous if he hadn't been his brother, so he was just proud of him instead.

Bill was still just a boy, but he watched the others and often stirred them with a quiet but accurate observation. He kept out of Uncle Ern's way a bit, as he couldn't run too fast, but he had a quieter nature than the others, so probably got on better with him than they did. He always seemed to have plenty to keep him busy, as he liked prowling around the sheds finding bits and pieces to build things with.

The four of them had their dad as their hero. He made jokes and wasn't as stern as Clarrie. Everyone liked him. He could do everything, and he could grow anything. He would take the time to answer their questions and show them how to do things. He was always busy, seemed to understand them and always made everything interesting. He commanded respect, and you never gave him any lip.

You never gave Clarrie any lip either! She was a worker. There was always plenty to do between the family and the church and the town, and she often had to walk long distances for people who needed her. She was very superstitious – one never opened an umbrella in the house, and both opals and pearls were omens of bad luck and ill times. She was quite good at reading tea leaves too, and it was not unusual for one of the town women to come and ask what lay in the leaves. Clarrie was always very careful about saying what she saw, and Aub was very careful round his mum, because they said she could see into the future and he didn't know what he thought about that.

She liked the river, as he did. And when there was time, she and Mrs Taylor would sometimes row to see friends who lived just out of the town upstream. He was impressed by their rowing, because he knew you needed to be quite strong to move against the current, and he hadn't yet mastered it himself.

Clarrie had an adage for everything: 'Can't means won't'; 'A stitch in time saves nine'; 'All that glitters is not gold'; 'A fine appearance is a small substitute for inner worth'; 'A closed mouth gathers no feet' and so on. When Aub wanted to leave a job to race out to his mates, she'd say, 'Finish it now and you won't lose your label.' He could never get that one, until Thora explained, 'The word is labour, you silly clod.'

His nickname was 'Lobster', as he was always swimming (and an Aboriginal friend had taught him how to lie on the bottom of the river and look up to watch what was swimming above) so his mates thought this fitted pretty well. His mother was *horrified*. When Puss Riedel knocked on the door and asked was Lobster home, she drew herself up to her full height, sniffed and said, 'I presume you mean *Aubrey?*' The lads were instructed never to call him anything else, but Dad just laughed, and of course 'Lobster' stuck.

He still wasn't sure about Ern, but Aub liked his other uncles. Uncles Allen, Darcy and Stuart (Stan's brothers) had each taken up a soldier settlement block in the Monash Soldiers Settlement. This was a good horse and cart ride away but the family all managed to keep closely in touch. The men were all well over six feet tall, and very lean. They had come back from the war with various health problems and counted themselves lucky to have gotten home.

Uncle Darcy was a little quiet, Uncle Allen told lots of stories, and Uncle Stuart was really interesting. He had a crystal radio set! This was the first in Monash, and thin voices spattered out of it amongst the static. Broadcasting had just begun in Australia and when the Australian cricket team was playing, lots of men would crowd into the room to listen. Aub could never work out how they could hear anything for the noise they were making barracking, and the louder they got, the more the dogs would bark outside! Then they'd cook lots of sausages over the fire, on a cartwheel covered with fencing wire, and everyone would have a great time as long as the team was winning.

Mum had two sisters, Ethel and Myrtle. Ethel was jolly and laughed at everyone's jokes, but Myrtle was a bit sour and not much fun at all.

Auntie Dot (Ern's wife) had a very special job, because she was the first telephonist in Renmark. Phones were magic because you could talk with people who weren't there! The new telephones were slowly being installed around the district and the erection of the poles, slinging and tensioning of the wires and connecting everything was employing lots of men. The phones themselves were mounted on a wooden board in the hall of the house, and had a black mouthpiece fixed on the front and a black earpiece hanging on a hook next to a handle that turned in a circle.

Aub wanted to know how they worked and so Auntie Dot agreed to show him the exchange. He looked at everything and listened to everything she said. Lines were connected from outside and when you wanted to talk with someone, you took the earpiece off the hook, put it to your ear, and turned the handle to ring the bell in the exchange. When the bell rang, the line coming in from outside would be answered by Auntie Dot, who sat in front of a large board with plug-holes in it. You would tell her who you wanted to talk with and she would connect your line into their plughole and then you could talk to each other along the line. He still wasn't sure how you could talk along a piece of wire, though.

Being a telephonist was a much-respected job, unless of course the telephonist was one who listened in to people's calls and then told other people what they'd been saying! This caused lots of problems in a 'he said, she said' sort of way, not to mention certain private problems being aired, so the phone was usually saved for ordering things and arranging to meet. Auntie Dot explained that it was most important that she be careful never to listen.

These new things were fascinating, and he wanted to know more about everything. He was good at schoolwork but often used to get bored. His favourite lesson was poetry, and this sent him off to dizzying places all around the world. He would read any poetry he could get his hands on and learnt lots of it out loud. Some was happy, some was sad, some was thrilling or scary and some of it just silly ditties, but he loved it all. Mr Brocate, or 'old Brocate' as they all called him, used to occasionally take them outside to read poetry and it was Aub's favourite lesson.

The first Renmark Scout Group had been formed by Ernest (Fritz) Barber. Fritz had a passion to pass different interests on to the lads. They used to run behind his two-handed buggy out to the distillery, where they swam in the heated pool and learned new strokes and fancy dives and first aid. They went out to his block and they looked through his big telescope at the distant stars, learning their names, and hearing about constellations and black holes. Fritz encouraged them to approach everything with a spirit of inquiry, and Aub was in his element learning about new things.

He was not good at sport and it peeved him. Ivor and Bill and Thora were all good with balls and they could catch or hit anything. He was hopeless at cricket and tennis and anything else that involved a ball. His crooked eyes meant that he couldn't quite connect with the flying object. He kept working on his skills at acrobatics and boxing, diving and swimming, where his eyesight didn't matter so much, and his strength was improving all the time.

The river was still his first love, and the river boats his second, but the tin whistle was never far from his hand and he was more and more drawn to a deep liking of music. He used to sit for hours in the blue bushes outside Elsie Jury's home listening to her play the piano, and the classical music with its lilts and falls, its passion and its cadences drew something in him into a peaceful place, and this was one of his favourite pastimes. It was not the same listening in a room full of people as it was being quietly on your own amongst the bushes and letting the music seep into you.

In later years, he wrote,

> Elsie! Marion Victoria J — I remember Elsie as a late teenager a nice young woman well liked and a good mixer. About 1920 I would sit in the blue bushes that grew in the vacant block adjacent to the Jury home and listen to some very tuneful piano music. I think Missouri Waltz was one of my favourites. The strange thing is — I can't remember ever being in their house when Elsie was at the keyboard. I may / not have seen the action but I certainly heard it. Around that time at the age of 10 or 11 I was King of the Kids with mouth organ & tin whistle. That piano music had a profound effect on me. If we could turn back the years I'd love to sit again in the bushes and listen to the music. — Elsie's music —

He was learning all the time. His early years had taught him about being honest and taking responsibility. He had learned to value people, and to respect them and their property. He knew he had to work hard for he wanted, and that his actions always had consequences.

The Sting

9

The noise made by the huge steam-powered piledrivers forcing piles into the river bed dominated the town. Bang, bang, bang. The thudding and pinging and shuddering went on, and on, and on, never stopping.

The town was buzzing with all the work going on. There was building everywhere, plans and projects, land deals and shops, and houses, all being built. There were committees for the Irrigation Trust, the Community Hotel, Renmark School and Institute, the RSL and the DC power plant, and many others, with everything being developed as the town grew. It was an exciting time to be growing up.

Lock 5 and the Paringa bridge were being built at the same time and there were huge towering woodlots being stacked along the river banks as the massive amounts of timber needed for the works were cut. There were lots of working men, and makeshift camps had cropped up here and there on the river banks and flats.

Stan explained that the lock would be built with a weir to regulate the river flow in high or low water, and a lock chamber to allow the boats to go through. The water level would be raised or lowered in the chamber once the boat was in, so that it matched the level either upstream or downstream, allowing it to continue on its way. He drew it on paper and it looked simple. The river of course never stopped flowing, so masses of steel and wood and stone would be used to build a coffer dam to divert a small section of the river bed at a time, so the men worked inside it to make the foundations for the weir. The concrete piers had to be made, and barges with gantries had to be used to move them into position.

The noise from the piledrivers at the lock stopped on the morning of

23 April 1923, and the deafening silence sent an eerie message to the town. Everyone knew it meant trouble and there was a sense of foreboding. The doctor raced out of his surgery and headed for the works, with the policeman and some of the townsmen close behind him.

Stan was at work in the coffer dam with four others, placing a long heavy log called a dead man (to be used to support a wooden tower) in the bottom. They had excavated a thirteen-foot-deep pit, around twenty-five feet long, to sink it in, and were about to hoist it when a crack suddenly spread in the southern wall of the dam.

A warning was screamed out. The men rushed to get out of the way. Ten tons of clotted earth spewed and crashed into the pit. Crushing, smothering dust and muck blocked the sun. Chaos and noise, and then…silence.

Men rushed down, scratched, scrabbled and dug to free those buried, frantically aware that the state of the walls was now treacherous, hands and shovels trying not to cause more injuries, aware that ticking minutes might mean suffocation for their mates. No one just stood watching – they were all in and a chain gang of men and shovels made the only noise to be heard.

Stan was the first to be dug out. He was battered and bruised, crushed around the chest, and was ashen and cold. He had dirt down his throat and air was rasping painfully into his lungs. But he was alive.

The other two men were harder to reach, as the pit was so narrow. It was another quarter of an hour before they reached Mr Jeffrie. He was conscious, but unfortunately had been mutilated around the face and head. Dr Birch arrived and began to assess the injuries. They carried Mr Fitzpatrick up an hour later, on a makeshift stretcher, alive and in a state of great pain and exhaustion, with a broken leg and other more minor injuries. Thankfully and mercifully, none of the men had died at the scene and all three were sent off to hospital. The condition of Mr Jeffrie and Mr Fitzpatrick was grave, and both were operated on that afternoon.

The resident engineer, Mr Angwin, inspected the pit and it was clear that the men had been freakishly lucky, as the wall had given away in the middle. Had there been no warning shouted – had their workmates been less brave – none of them would have been alive.

Aub was afraid watching his dad over the next few days. He didn't look so tall any more. He was very quiet and sometimes he shook. He didn't say much, and he didn't go outside either. Aub didn't know what to do, so he took over chopping the wood and did what he could in the garden. He knew that his dad might have died, and it horrified him. The renewed thundering of the piledrivers banging out from the works seemed like a mocking reminder of how close his death had been.

Stan gradually got his strength back, but would easily get out of breath, and it was clear he would never be able to work as a labourer again. After a few light work jobs, he finally went back to work at the lock as the timekeeper, which was a very responsible job. There were in all one hundred and fifty men to keep times for and to pay. The bosses knew he worked hard and was liked by the men. He was good with figures and was scrupulously honest, so they had every confidence in him.

Now, with Stan back in good employment, it meant that he and Clarrie could start looking to buy a block of land, and they settled on a nice flat block in Eleventh Street, which was closer to the river, and in sight of Nana's home in the street behind them. Plans were being

drawn and Stan and Clarrie's dream was beginning to take shape. Aub was very excited. There would be building, a new house, a new garden and, as the oldest boy, even a room for himself. He couldn't wait.

In October, word came that Great-grandfather William had died in Mallala. Old 'Whiskers' had lived to the age of ninety-two. The children all remembered him fondly and sent him off in their own way with a salute to 'King Billie'.

That year, Stan received a bravery

award for pulling a lad out of the river and saving his life. When it was presented to him, he knew there would be trouble with his superstitious wife. He took it home and quietly put it away. Clarrie asked to see it because he hadn't shown it to her, and her face went from pleased to panic-stricken as she looked at it in its box. Tears ran, and she flew outside and dropped it down the long-drop toilet! It was an opal tiepin, and all of her senses told her that it was a bad omen. They didn't talk about it.

Uncle Ern and Auntie Dot had a new little baby boy, and Ern was delighted because he would carry on the family name. But in February 1924, little baby Alfred suddenly got very sick with enteritis and sadly died within a few days. There would be no more children for Dot and Ern – the loss was just too great. Betty was too little to understand, but she missed the baby and wanted to know if he would be happy in heaven.

Family life went on all around him, but now Aub was off on his own track, totally absorbed in his role as a King's Scout. He was chosen in the team to go to Queensland to contest for the Trenchard Miller Shield. They practised for hours, and enthusiasm was high that they could win against all the other competing teams. They were as keen as mustard, and no effort was being spared in getting ready. Every task was committed to memory, practised for speed and tested for perfection.

10

In July, Stan got a bout of influenza with the winter weather, but he carried on as usual. On Saturday morning, he was too sick to go to work, and by lunchtime he was in bed. He spent a fitful night and was running a temperature by Sunday morning. He looked dreadful, and his rasping breath was shallow and scary. Clarrie asked Aub to go down and get some medicine from Doc Holden (the chemist) and he jumped on his bike and took off. He said hello to a couple of people on the way there and on the way back but didn't stay to talk. But when he got home, his dad was much worse – too ill even to take the medicine. Aub was sure that it was his fault because he hadn't been quick enough. They called the doctor and at 11.30 Stan was transferred to the hospital, and at 1.30 that day (24/7/1924) he was gone.

Gone. Not there. Never to touch again, or laugh with again, or to hear again. His tall frame, his strong presence, his wit, his knowledge, his quiet encouragement, his smell, his feel, his voice, lost to them all at the age of forty.

The sudden horror of it held them in stunned disbelief. Their loss was profound. There were no words for each other. Their ashen, wooden faces saying the words they couldn't find. They were all welded together in an emotional knot of pain – totally bereft and unable even to comfort each other.

Clarrie had lost her husband and her friend, her future and her dreams, widowed at thirty-six with four children, in the year 1924.

At sixteen, Thora had lost the man she loved most, looked up to most. Her rock and her joy.

Eleven-year-old Ivor was in deep shock, numb and too stunned yet to absorb how consuming the loss would be.

Bill's noisy wail was a cry for help from a lost seven-year-old.

Aub knew he was to blame. He'd taken too long to get the medicine. Although the doctor told him it was pneumonia, and nothing would have saved his dad, he couldn't take it in. He was fourteen and his hero was gone. He was shattered. The ache was an abyss, and he couldn't look into it.

Uncles and aunts, friends and neighbours and people from work and the churches called. But there was nothing they could say or do to help. The house was quiet, and Aub couldn't bear being inside, half expecting to hear his dad's footsteps. He retreated outside, under the bushes with his tin whistle, but there was no being able to play it.

Somehow, they got through the first days, and the condolences, and the hours. They were grateful for the people who helped, by bringing cooked food, chopping wood and offering what they could, but there was no solace. Only Stan's enduring love sustained them. They knew he had loved them.

His black, flower-laden coffin lay on the bed in the room filled with flowers until Tuesday. The stultifying floral scent, seeping through the house, was dense and choking. Aub and Thora would hate the perfume and the look of stocks and flocks, for the rest of their lives. They couldn't talk to their mother. She was leaden, heavy, white, far off. It was only with Nana that they could share their grief, that they could get a hug, and that they could feel a little less alone.

The Murray Pioneer printed the following:

Obituary – *The Murray Pioneer*. Death of Mr Stan Jury.
A Well-Respected Citizen.

On Sunday last, after a very short illness, Mr Stanley Webster Jury, one of the best-known citizens of Renmark died in the local hospital about two hours after admission there. Mr Jury had been suffering from an attack of influenza but had still carried out his duties as time-keeper at No 5 Lock until Friday Evening. On Saturday, he was too ill to go to work, and pneumonia developing, was taken to the hospital where he passed away at 1.30 p.m. Mr

Jury was a quiet mannered courteous gentleman, and greatly respected throughout the district, especially by the children whom he taught in the Methodist Sunday School. He was a member of the school committee, and he took a keen interest in the temperance movement. For some years he was a foot constable in the South Australian Police Force and will be remembered kindly by members of that force. It is said that while he engaged in police duties he helped many and did his best to prevent crime. At the lock works his sudden death created a profound sensation, and it is safe to say that he was one of the best liked hands on the works. The department officers speak highly of him and found in him a man of high character. At these works in the serious accident over a year ago, Mr Jury received injuries from which he never quite recovered, and the suddenness of his end may be attributed to this accident. For some time, he engaged in fruit-growing, but sold his property and worked on block E. The returned men on that area offer their sincere sympathy to the family. The late Mr Jury was 40 years of age and married Miss Clarrie Hilton, second daughter of Mr Alfred Hilton of Renmark. There are four children of whom the eldest is sixteen years old. Mr Jury was born at Mallala, where his father and mother who are well known residents still reside. There are eight brothers living and one sister. The brothers Stuart, Allen and Darcy, returned men have blocks at Monash, William and Roy are in Western Australia, Victor is in Tasmania, Cleive, Henry, and Dollie, are in Mallala. Mrs Charles Hooper of Berri and Mrs W.R. Lewis of Gurra Gurra, are aunts of the deceased, and Alexander and George Jury of Renmark, cousins. The funeral took place on Tuesday afternoon, and was attended by the father of the deceased, and other relatives. The locks and weirs department was represented by the local officers, and a number of the lock employees. From the school, a number of girls and boys attended, and there were also many local townsmen present. A service was held in the Methodist Church conducted by the Reverend Darcy Dickson, and the Dead March in 'Saul' was rendered by Miss Plush.

A Memorial Service will be held in the Renmark Methodist Church on Sunday.

An obituary also appeared in *The Register Adelaide* on Saturday 13 September.

The Turn of the Game

11

He was called into the kitchen.

She sat in the chair at the head of the table, upright and stern. Her eyes fixed his in an unblinking stare, and she began. 'Aubrey, you are now the man of the house. Your father and I made decisions together and now you are going to help me as he did. You will be responsible for the boys, and for the general things around the house. You will have to bring in as much money as you can. Mr Matulich has agreed to carry on with building the new house, but we must finish paying for it now, without your father's wage. A lot of that will fall to you. Do you understand?'

He'd expected it, but he wasn't ready. Fourteen years old, Aub was overwhelmed. He didn't know how they could manage. He didn't know what he could do. And worst of all, he was scared by the great void he felt. He had no feeling that Stan was close, or still with him, or watching over him; just the complete feeling of nothing. Now it sounded like his mother expected him to fill his father's shoes. He couldn't!

He knew his mother was a strong woman, and she wanted to carry on as Stan would have wanted, but it was hard. They two had been a team, each with their own ideas and input, but always working together. He could see that her physical and emotional loss was pushing her to take charge, but he had walked in a fourteen-year-old boy, and now he was walking out knowing he had to be the man. It was expected, and it was expected now. He didn't know how she could seem so calm.

Then it was Thora's turn. It was explained that in the new house they would need to take in boarders to help with housekeeping money, and the two of them would need to share the double bed to 'free up a single'. She would also need to help with the housework and the cooking, and to find a few hours' paid work. Uncle Stuart and Uncle Allen had agreed to pay for her continuing piano lessons (she was up to her LLB) and to provide her with some nice clothes, as they were needed.

Ivor was to look after the vegetable gardens after they had planted them, and he was responsible for making sure there was always enough wood. Bill had to feed the chooks, collect the eggs and feed the dog. Aub and Thora would help the younger boys when they could.

Aub disappeared off over the river flats and for the first time since Stan had died he howled out loud, and screamed and yelled, but he came back after a few hours – he had new responsibilities.

12

Clarrie was fiercely independent and wasn't going to accept charity from anyone. She hid her sorrow under a pall of hard work and managed each day as best she could. She had another adage now – 'Live every day as if it's your last' – (and it stayed with her until she died in 1956). She hardened her approach to the children and became more of a disciplinarian than ever. There were no soft words even for little Bill.

Aub went to the scoutmaster to say he couldn't go with the group to compete in Queensland, and the scoutmaster said he could go with them to Adelaide to see the team off. He was there again to meet them when they came back victorious.

He did lots of jobs. Sometimes he and his mate Frankie Gaynes drove the horse-drawn ice cart delivering drinks around town from Sonneman's factory. That was more like fun than work because Frankie was a great prankster. Often, he weeded the garden for Mrs Taylor. She and her husband had come back from South America after being involved in the Utopia project, and he liked to get her talking about it when he could. They had brought back some new red table grapes that she called Isabellas, and she told him about the many plants they had tried to grow over there. Growing things interested him a lot and he could have listened to her all day, but most of all he wanted to be a pharmacist.

He got a job in Doc Holden's chemist shop and loved it. It didn't pay a lot, but it was regular money and it was a good job that made him feel important. He had to learn to identify all the different smells (iodine, ether sulphur, bromine and lots of others) until Doc could blindfold him and he could still name each bottle. He found it easy, because he'd developed a good sense of smell as a lad walking through the Chinese market gardens. He cut the pills, counted them into bottles, and prepared the fancy labels. Whenever he was needed, and sometimes when he wasn't, he would be in the shop.

One day while he was mixing a salve on the big ground-glass platen, it slipped, and there were smashed pieces all over the back-room floor. Doc Holden was furious and told him he would have to pay for it. It cost his whole week's wages, but he didn't get fired. He was terribly upset because he knew he had let the family down as there was less money to take home. He knew his dad wouldn't have done that. There was no room for mistakes and now Doc Holden was cross with him.

Aub was angry too because Uncle Ern seemed to think he could tell them all what to do now that Stan wasn't there. He would mutter under his breath, 'You're not our dad, so you can't tell us what to do.'

They moved into the new house but it wasn't a happy move for him. Although he was pleased for his mum and the others, he felt it was breaking all the old ties with his father. He planted vegetable gardens with the younger boys and they set up a chook yard and a woodheap. He missed Stan desperately and found that the more he kept himself busy, the less time he had to think. He could picture his dad in the old house, but he wasn't here in this new place.

Ivor and Bill felt the loss of their dad too but they didn't say too much. Aub kept an eye on them and was grateful that they both had some good mates. Thora did as much for them as she could, and she also worked for a few hours a week in the chemist shop. She was close to her girl cousins and they always seemed to be happily off doing things. He didn't know how she felt. They didn't talk about it.

Ivor was capable and clever and seemed to be able to do anything he wanted to. He liked looking after the vegie garden, and proudly brought in what was ready. He played sport and won any running races he went in. He found his schoolwork easy and often got into strife for playing around while the others caught up.

Bill was much quieter and by contrast moved slowly around the place in his own little world. He willingly did his jobs and everyone liked the amiable little chap. He was a thinker and was good at noticing that something someone had thrown away could be adapted for other uses just with a bit of his handiwork.

Clarrie showed immense determination and worked, worked, worked. She was not soft with any of them, and if she heard one of them had got the cane at school, they got a lash of the strap when they got home. If they said they were innocent, she would say, 'Well, that's one you should have got and didn't then.' She was exacting with them, but also with herself.

She took in boarders and looked after them well. Of course, she had chosen them carefully, as she was a temperance lady and wouldn't have a drinker in the house. She avoided working men and preferred teachers or bankers.

If she needed to spend her last shilling, no one would guess it by her actions. Aub would see her pay it up at the door, and then stiffen her shoulders as she walked away down the passage. She was a good and inventive cook. She could sew. She would always return a kindness to people in some way. She walked anywhere she needed to go and did whatever she could to help those that she knew needed it.

Aunt Belle and Uncle Ted Chapman (Clarrie's brother) still had the bakery they'd started with Grandfather. Each morning there would be bread (and sometimes some buns) on the Jury doormat. Clarrie insisted she wouldn't accept charity, and they insisted it was bread that was over from the day before, and that it couldn't be used, but Aub noted that it was always fresh and warm. It was a real help. He loved Aunt Belle for it, and always remembered her in later years as having been cheerful and happy, and very kind.

They struggled to get through the year, and gradually began to find their feet.

Aub still swam and fished and rowed. There were good-size cod and callop in the river and they were good eating. Sometimes he'd shoot a rabbit and Clarrie would cook it in her cast-iron pot with some vegetables. The favourite, though, was wood duck freshly shot and dressed, wrapped in pastry and slowly roasted with fennel and leek.

Nana was still his most-loved person, with her sense of humour and twinkling eyes that always suggested a secret. He could talk with her about anything, and she seemed to know how he was feeling without asking, and she would always seem to encourage him when he most needed it. Wonderful rich aromas wafted out across her bricked veranda, welcoming him into her kitchen, and her fingers were often stained from picking the berries off the mulberry tree to make tarts. She was very involved in everything that happened in Renmark, and always took an interest in whatever the children were doing. Usually she walked to church with them down the street past the fire station and would always jump when the siren was tested each Sunday, even though she knew it was going to blow. She had a lovely string of jet beads, that always seemed to make her eyes sparkle more when she wore them, and Aub thought she was beautiful.

The family shared the pleasure of getting a dog, and the boys used to joke, saying that Thora had more hair than it did. Gradually they were making a new life.

The new next-door neighbour Mr Douglas was the local undertaker, and he would call 'Aubrey' over the fence when he wanted a lift. Sometimes this would extend to going a bit further when a difficult situation required extra hands. Aub was always willing to help, but he wasn't overly comfortable with the dead, and when he was offered a job, he declined. Despite the respect the position was held in, the regular money and the offer of an ongoing career, this was where he drew the line. He didn't want to wind up dealing with the dead for a living.

Uncle Ern's trucks now competed with a few others around the town and there were more model T Fords about as well. Mr Angove bought one and he taught Aub to drive it so he could take him home after a 'heavy' night. Mr Angove's feeling bad made Aub feel really good. He felt pretty important to be driving around, and made up his mind that he'd have a car as soon as he could, and it would definitely be a Ford. Uncle Stuart had bought a Citroën, and although he thought it was the best, Aub thought it was a poor second.

Stan's cousin Ralph Jury worked in Lawton's cycle shop. There was nothing he couldn't do with a bike. Aub rode his bike everywhere and liked to talk to Ralph about his days as a successful racing cyclist, athlete and footballer, but now he had some shrapnel in his back from the war. He'd enjoyed his years racing, and he gave Aub the bug to practise, rather than just ride. He started racing around everywhere and got into a bit of bother for tearing around in a reckless manner. He worked out regularly in the gym and learned to box. Without the inherited Jury height and strong frame, he was successfully building his own.

In 1926, the piledrivers in the river fell silent once again. Lock 5 was finished. The new railway bridge at Paringa was opened and the first train bustled into town on the 31 January. Everything that could be was draped with streamers and colour and signs, and there was a huge air of excitement, as it was such a momentous day. It was a sight to see as the lift span raised to allow the streamer-clad steamers to pass underneath, but the little ferry that had served the town lay wasted like an extinct animal on the riverbank. Aub and his friend Sadie Flemming climbed to the

top of the lift span and had their photo taken to mark the history of the day, but he would never in his life have a photo taken at Lock 5.

1927 saw the death of Grandmother Susannah in Mallala. This was sad news for all of them indeed. He knew that going to the farm would never be the same, and all his young boyhood memories flooded back. He could see her kindly eyes looking at him from behind her glasses, always with the soft hint of a smile. He was just one of her twenty grandchildren, but she had always made him feel very special. Her kitchen had been the hub of the farmhouse, the meeting place of herself and grandfather with family and friends. He was sorry he hadn't seen her more often.

1927

Mrs. H. Jury, who died at her residence on Sunday, July 24, was an old and respected resident of Mallala. She was the second daughter of Mr. and Mrs. John Moody, and was born at Truro, South Australia, on April 25, 1857. With her parents she removed to North Kilkerran, Yorke Peninsula. t that place she was married to Mr. Henry Jury in 1883. They went to Mallala a few years later, and had resided there for about 37 years. Mrs. Jury was loved by those who knew her, and was always willing to give assistance in any good cause. She was a member of the local Red Cross committee for the full term of its existence, and also a member of the W.C.T.U. Four of her sons served in the late war. Her eldest son, Stanley Webster, died at Renmark three years ago. Her husband, one daughter, and eight sons survive her. They are Mrs. A. R. Rowe, Lower Light; Mr. W. C. Jury, Nanup, W.A.; Mr. R. M. Jury, Nyabing, W.A.; Mr. E. A. Jury, Mr. D. Jury, and Mr. J. S. Jury, Lone Gum, River Murray, S.A.; Mr. C. Jury and Mr. H. L. Jury, Mallala; and Mr. A. V. Jury, Tasmania. There are twenty grandchildren.

13

1928 brought about great changes.

Ivor had excelled at school and wanted to go to teacher training college in Adelaide and his application was immediately accepted. They were all very proud of him and Aub was committed to getting the best for his boys. They would manage the money as best they could and Ivor would receive a tiny training wage and would do what work he could find as well. It was agreed that he could board in Adelaide with Auntie Ethel and Uncle Ted Ross, and cousins Lois and Jethro in their new home at Fullarton Estate. They were all going to miss him, but he packed his bags with confidence and excitement, and off he went.

Doc Holden was particularly happy with Aub's work in the shop and offered him an apprenticeship. Aub was overjoyed to have what he wanted most of all. Doc couldn't offer an increased wage, though, and the additional work hours would limit the time Aub had to take other jobs to supplement his income. Nevertheless, to be a pharmacist was his dream. The family house still wasn't paid for and there was additional money needed now for Ivor. To encourage new chemists, the Faulding Company offered a scholarship each year to the dux of the Pharmacy Board's intake exam, so Aub knew that he just *had* to win that scholarship.

He devoted himself to studying, often sitting on the concrete outside the back of the shop or walking the river flats spouting out aloud from his books. Each evening, his efforts were feverish as he frantically tried to commit everything he could to memory. He knew that you had to work for the things you wanted, and he wanted this. On the day of the exam, he was tired and sick with nerves and, finding it hard to think and concentrate, he went in to do his best.

The days stretched out agonisingly and he was sure there were more than twenty-four hours in each one. When the letter came, he was afraid to open it and didn't tell the others he had it. When he found the courage to read it, he was devastated as his hopes and dreams were gone in a few written lines. He had come second and there was no scholarship for him.

Sadly, Doc needed an apprentice who could carry on, and Aub couldn't afford to continue and still keep contributing to the family. The die was cast, there was no fairy godmother, and it was the parting of the ways.

He didn't want to talk to anyone, because his direction was gone and he had to get his head around it. He went up the Ral Ral Creek for a couple of nights, took his tin whistle and his fishing rod and had a think about it. He couldn't even bring himself to fish. It wasn't anyone's fault, it was just the way it was. He thought about what it must have meant for his dad to leave the police force and to start out again, and he came back resolute, knowing that he must find another job that would help financially, but he had no personal incentive to look in any particular direction. He would search around for the best job he could find.

The Renmark Hotel was taking on some new stewards. The hotel provided uniforms, lodgings, and meals, as well as a wage, and he would still have some time for other work. This seemed like riches indeed, and as he had just turned eighteen he was eligible. So off he went and sat the required test, and did the required interview, and was mightily relieved and pleased when he heard he had the job.

Clarrie was having no son of hers going anywhere near any hotel.

Drink was the basis of evil. They had a huge argument and a major falling out. Aub was adamant, and announced that she needed the money, she wanted him to 'be a man' and she must respect his decision. She said his father would have been ashamed and he said that was rubbish. It was the very first time he had not deferred to her wishes and was a turning point in their relationship. He packed a few things and went off to his new digs feeling indignant and hurt, knowing he would not change his mind because he was going to do what he knew he must.

The first few days flew by in a haze of orientation and lists of dos and don'ts and the outlining of expectations. The manager Mr Halley was very clear in setting out his expectations for his stewards. They were a lively young bunch and they soon learned that handstands down the bar when it was closed were not appreciated, and cartwheels in the empty dining room were likely to get you fired. Sense of humour didn't exist, and Mr Halley had a considerable temper.

Aub was responsible for all the clocks throughout the hotel. This meant his quietly going around to put them forward by ten minutes before the six o'clock closing time because the licensing laws were very strict. This should be done carefully so that the patrons didn't notice or there would be arguments in the bar. It was essential that everyone was out by six before the police came to check or the hotel would lose its license. The irony of it wasn't lost on him as he thought how delighted that would make his mother. As well as other normal duties for the guests, he had the job of cleaning nearly a hundred brass plates on the big wooden doors.

One day he was suddenly fired! With his quick temper, Mr Halley was known for firing someone on a regular basis, but Aub was terribly upset. The old hands on the staff thought it very amusing and advised him to just front up in the morning as usual. What did he have to lose?

'Didn't I fire you?'

'Yes, sir. But if you don't know when you have a good employee, I know when I've got a really good boss.'

'Well, get back to work, you lazy little bugger. Don't just stand around!'

In the next few weeks and with more responsibility, the job was more interesting. Aub earnt more money, and although Clarrie was still very cross, she was pleased that he hadn't started drinking and still went to church. Gradually, she relented. She and Thora arrived one day to have a look at his room and he proudly showed it off, to be greeted with loud sniffs from his mother. A few days later, they both arrived loaded with a bedspread, curtains and cushions they had made for him. Aub knew that this had cost them time and he didn't know where they had got the material from, but he understood that it was a mark of acceptance by his mother. The new furnishings were a luxury, and he felt the love that is sometimes shown by actions and not by words. Never missing a good opportunity, Mr Halley began to always choose Aub's room to visit when he was showing people how well they looked after their staff.

Suddenly in 1929, headlines screamed about a huge stock market crash, and the terrible losses that had wiped out millions on a black, black day. Aub didn't know much about stocks and shares but he was quick enough to understand that this was on parallel with a natural disaster. He could never have known that it would herald in several years of economic depression that would change life for everyone. Suicides were reported and some families began packing up their houses. Very soon it was obvious that there was less cash around, and banks were tightening on creditors.

Clarrie's house still wasn't paid for and although they were in front on payments, Aub felt some pressure and desperation about getting the job done. He had been doing labouring jobs to supplement his wages and was fortunate that he was valued as a hard and reliable worker. There were fewer jobs available each week as people couldn't afford to pay wages, and lots of men began walking the roads looking for any odd jobs they could get and sleeping anywhere they could find a bit of shelter. Many of them had been in professional jobs like accounting and even solicitors and they were walking the roads. It was pitiful to see.

When Aub was not on early morning duty, he and his mate Frankie would go rowing. They kept a little boat under the willows just across from the hotel. One morning when they pushed off and dropped the oars into the water, Frankie's oar was heavy, and when he lifted it up an arm and shoulder were hooked over it and a body came up behind it. Sadly, an itinerant had died somewhere along the bank and the body had lodged under the willows. It was a terrible shock and after the police had been and the body had been taken away, they moved the boat onto dry land further up along the river bank. There was no breakfast that morning and Aub couldn't help but wonder what the poor man's story had been, and if he had a family he was trying to support.

Mr Halley was known for being able to identify any type of whisky as it was his tipple and there was usually one close to hand. One day a lad came up from the wharf with a message that while unloading the hotel's goods from the paddle-steamer they had found one of the kegs leaking. They weren't sure what it was and wanted him to come down and identify it.

He arrived at the wharf and his finger was duly dipped in, and the liquid tasted. 'Pure fox terrier,' Mr Halley announced.

They all had a good laugh and it was a favourite story in the bar that night.

That year, Clarrie took in a tall and striking young teacher, Arthur Adamson, who had arrived in town on a new posting. He was charming, witty and good-looking and soon kindled a twinkle in twenty-year-old Thora's eye. He was a real gentleman and as a good footballer was quickly accepted into the town, where you were usually never a local unless you'd been born there.

Ivor was doing very well at teachers college and was a valued cricket and football player. Tall now and good-looking, he was enjoying life in Adelaide. Aub wasn't jealous. He was just proud that Ivor was making the best of his opportunities and that when he qualified he would have a good job like Arthur, safe from the long-term effects of the Depression.

Young Bill had grown into a solid lad and didn't miss much of what was going on. He and his mates got up to a few pranks, but never into any real trouble. Although he had a somewhat easy-going manner, he was a very hard little worker. He missed Aub and Ivor being at home, but it did mean that he could do what he liked around the yard and in the shed, and he took full advantage of being in charge. He joined the Scouts and learned every activity he could with them, relishing the company of his mates.

Despite the misery of the Depression, Aub was feeling more comfortable that his life was more settled. He often played the tin whistle in his room and still loved music. He bought an old banjo (strung as a mandolin) and a book on chords, and filled his spare time learning how to play. He was still boxing, doing acrobatics and working in the gym and was a regular at the swimming club. He called in at home every couple of days and did what was needed around there.

Evensong on Friday nights was a must if he wasn't working, and he enjoyed it. He and Mavis Shaddock had become close, and he liked her a lot. She was a happy person, and he felt happy when he was with her, and she was always at evensong.

He had no problem filling his time and was often frustrated that there was never enough of it. He liked working in the hotel and was learning everything he could, moving on with his life, and never looking in at the pharmacy as he walked by.

The Twist

14

In 1930, Aub was boxing in a match against one of the local Renmark lads. They were fairly evenly matched and there was a good crowd watching. The barracking was spirited and plenty of advice was being given. Aub landed a strong punch and the lad fell. He was counted out and Aub's hand was raised. But the crowd was hushed as his opponent stayed down. The referee and the trainers tended him, and a stunned Aub heard the fearful words 'He's not coming round' as the ambulance was called.

He raced out and followed it to the hospital on his bike, in shock and numb with horror. When he got to the emergency section, they wouldn't let him in. He sat shaking and scared in the waiting room as people moved around him. Voices talked, and his head was buzzing, but no one was talking to him. He could hear the concern in their voices and he was mortified and terrified at the same time. Finally, they said the lad was in a coma, and tests would be done. He prayed and he cried. The last time he had been in hospital, his father had died, and the sounds, the scenes and the smell made his whole system revolt. But he couldn't leave until he knew the lad was all right. He slept on the hospital veranda and was grateful when Thora brought him a blanket and some food. His mother was angry with him again, and some of the people in the town were blaming him even though it had been a fair fight. All he was worried about was the lad himself.

For three days and nights he stayed, and no one could move him. Finally, on the third day the lad woke, and after another day in hospital was declared quite fit, with no lasting damage and was sent home.

The lasting damage, however, was Aub's. He was in shock, and he lay on his bed at the hotel in a state of misery. He couldn't focus on his jobs, and he didn't want to talk to anyone. He didn't want to go home because his mother was going to let him know again that she didn't agree with this 'boxing rubbish', and he could face neither her disapproval nor the lecture that would go with it. Stan had been a handy boxer and sparring had always been a bit of play with his boys, but she had never approved. Aub was lonely, and he missed his dad like he hadn't for years.

Clarrie came to see him and told him she had a message from Grandfather Henry at Mallala, that he wanted Aub to go down to the farm as he needed some help. Much as he loved Henry, he didn't want to leave his job, but she insisted that he couldn't let Grandfather down. He never let anyone down, it was one of his rules, so in the end he had to go. He'd not been to the farm since his grandmother had died, and he knew it would be very different. At least he would be able to ride his bike to Adelaide to see Ivor when he had time, and he did look forward to that. Uncle Stuart picked him up, and with his bike, his instruments and a couple of bags, off they went with no real goodbyes. He had no idea how long he'd be away.

The farm itself was as exciting as ever, but Grandfather had lost his spark. He missed Grandmother very much, and the farmhouse was clean and neat but felt drab and unhappy.

Grandfather grew wheat, barley and rye and kept the mandatory poultry, cows and a bull, some geese and of course the dogs. As a boy, Aub had learned to be cautious with the bull, and now he was a man it would be no different. They decided he should live with Auntie Dolly and Uncle Roy Rowe, at Lower Light, and ride up to the farm each day. Dolly and Uncle Stuart were twins, and she was the only aunt on his father's side. He settled in with them and four-year old Beth, and soon became very fond of them. He knew all the uncles who lived up the river well, but this was the first real chance he'd had to really get to know some of the others. Cleive, who was Darcy's twin, was a lovely gentle man and Aub liked him a lot. Young Henry, Stan's youngest brother, was only ten years older than Aub, and they forged a good strong friendship, finding that they thought very much on the same wavelength.

It was different getting to know Grandfather now he was an adult. The time they spent together was good, and he quickly saw how a farmer's sixth sense and an innate knowledge about all things farming often saved both time and money. Henry could look across a paddock and estimate how many bags it would yield, and he was always very close to right. He could measure the distance around a paddock easily, and it was a while before Aub realised that the 'old boy' counted the revolutions of the cartwheel to make his calculations. Henry knew days ahead when rain was coming, and by watching the horses, the cattle, and the ants he could almost say what time of day it would start. He would push his face into the breeze and know what the next couple of days were going to bring.

Most enjoyable for Aub was the old man's dry sense of humour and irony, powered by a satiric wit. He found himself enjoying the days and the work and listened for the many amusing sayings that old Henry had. You could never say, 'Well, well, well' without hearing the muttered 'Three holes in the ground,' and the kelpies were known as 'long-handled trotting dogs' while the terriers were 'Belgian mouse hounds'. He was a funny man and he had nicknames for everyone and everything.

Aub was confident with the horses although cautious with the high-spirited gelding, who liked to make his opinion known. He liked the paddock work, and much of it suited his long-standing habit of going off by himself to have a good think as the hours passed.

Mallala was a farming town, and as a Jury (one of its pioneering families), Aub was considered to be a local without the normal rite of passage of being in residence for some twenty years. The young Christian group were a friendly and happy bunch, and they welcomed him into the district. Soon he was out spotlighting with a couple of the young farmers and hunting for rabbits and foxes.

Now he met girls in his new group of friends and was never short of a partner at the local dances. He liked them, but there was no one he wanted to form a close bond with. A couple of the local farmers lined him up thinking he might make a good match for their daughters, but he was steering well clear of that.

Grandfather was paying him a part-wage as a farmhand, and each fortnight money was sent back to Clarrie with a letter. The letters were short (after, all how much did you tell your mother?), but he kept in touch.

Saving some money for himself became very important the longer he was there. He felt guilty about it, but he was beginning to form a secret dream that he wouldn't talk about with anyone but Grandfather and second cousin Linda Jury, who worked in the eye ward at the Royal Adelaide Hospital. If you have a problem, you should try to fix it. Right?

One season merged into another and when Grandfather didn't need him, he worked around the other farms. He was very strong and could lump bags of wheat all day with no trouble at all.

Neither the heat nor the cold ever worried him, whatever the job. It was just another day, but sometimes the nature of the work was governed by what could be done according to the weather conditions.

He harvested hay with the Wasley boys, and they let him take charge of building a stack at Korunye. They worked with great care as it slowly rose into the air. The bales had to be quite dry, because moisture caused mould and heat inside the stack, and the whole lot could go up in flames with spontaneous combustion in a few seconds and then burn for days. It was quite an art to build a safe haystack, as a toppling weight of hay could kill a man, and Aub glowed with pride

as they reached the top and took a photo. It symbolised for him that with hard work and care he could achieve anything, and he kept the photo until he died. By then, there were bales and stooks and baling machines, and the old free-form stacks were long since gone.

Henry had let slip that it had been his mother's idea to 'get him out of Renmark for a while', but as it turned out it had been a rich experience for them both. They had grown close while working, playing cards, crabbing and sometimes talking for hours. When they parted, Aub felt a great sense of missing Henry already, but it was time to move on and there was a special wedding to attend.

The older uncles and his two grandfathers had instilled in him ethics and morals that he would always live by, and ditties and sayings in his mind and his language that would be repeated for as long as he lived. They had become part of the man. For the rest of his life, he could never see a really tall man pass by without muttering, 'If he's not long, I'll wait.'

He listened to everything and learned what he could. He learned that good-naturedness didn't necessarily go with intellect, and that having money didn't automatically mean success. He learned that vindictiveness and nastiness cost a great deal, but kindness and tolerance cost little and buy a lot. He learned about the good boss who wouldn't ask you to do anything he wouldn't do himself, and the crook boss who treated you poorly and expected you to do all the dirty work that he wouldn't put his own hand to. (These were often known as 'Rundle Street farmers' – professional men living and working in the city who owned farms and needed farm workers, but thought that labourers were second-class citizens.) He learned that in the developing state of South Australia the key to everything was opening up and farming the land, and the production of the food and goods that were needed to support the population. He learned to respect women and to wonder at the amount of work they did every day, and that while you needed them and their support, it was men who should make the important decisions. He learned that you always paid your dues no matter the cost. If you owed, you owed, and that meant that someone else was giving you a free ride.

15

He was home in time for Thora's wedding to Arthur Adamson, the young good-looking teacher who had been boarding with them and who fitted easily into the family. This was the first wedding in the family and they were all excited. Young Bill was busting. Ivor had arrived, instantly distinguished and charming, and the local girls shyly giggled over him. Aub thought he'd never seen Thora look lovelier in her beautiful dress, and he caught a slight softness in the curve of his mother's face.

Clarrie was as hard-working and proud as ever, but he noticed that she was plagued with bad headaches. Aub could see that she hadn't been spending any money at all on herself and he was upset when he saw the state of some of her underclothing on the line. Clearly, she looked after everyone else before herself and he felt perhaps he hadn't sent enough money home, but underneath he knew that however much it might have been she would spend it on the others. She looked after her boarders and was still involved in the church and with her close friends, but he noticed that some of her feistiness was gone and there was a heaviness in her step. She was tired and was obviously going to miss Thora badly.

He was still fond of Mavis Shaddock and she was more than pleased to see him. She had written to him and waited patiently for him and they settled back into a pattern of seeing each other again, but he knew now that he had to tell her that he didn't want to take things any further than being good friends. He hated himself, but she deserved his honesty. Mavis was very upset and hurt, but accepted the situation with her usual good grace, at least on the surface. She maintained a soft spot for him and quietly put away the monogrammed gold cufflinks she'd planned to give him when he turned twenty-one. They stayed close friends.

The impact of the Depression lingered on, and the river was yet again in flood. Hardly anyone had any cash. People were still walking the roads, chopping firewood or doing any bits of jobs they could, in return for a cup of tea and something to eat. They slept in sheds, on ovals, in doorways or along the river and it was sad to see them trudging down the road with their few belongings in their swag. Labouring jobs were hard to come by and if you could get one, you had to be fit and prepared to receive little or nothing in the way of wages.

Mateship was more important than ever, and people supported each other as best they could. Families were split as fathers went away to find work, and the town had gone from a thriving town full of work gangs planting blocks and building locks and bridges, to a quiet moody place. Sometimes gambling and lack of money meant no food on a family table and fierce arguments could be heard as they floated through open windows into the streets. Everyone helped where they could with vegetables and eggs and fruit. Local businesses were struggling to keep afloat and many people wore the slumped shoulders of debt with no hope of help or recovery. Staff had been put off at the hotel and even the banks struggled to keep their doors open. There were few jobs around, and certainly no career opportunities.

Young Bill had finished school and needed to work. He found a few days at the co-op and then with the town gardener. He was a strong capable lad, but there was really nothing for him in Renmark, and unfortunately there was no work for him with the Monash uncles nor on the old farm at Mallala.

With a sinking heart and feeling of somehow having failed, Aub was going to have to send him away to manage as best he could. He was sick in the stomach and made himself ill thinking about it. He couldn't sleep and he couldn't eat, but there was no alternative that he could see. The decision had to be made and, in the end, he sent Bill off on his bike to find work wherever he could. He gave him what little money he had that he'd been saving for his dream, but his heart ached to think that young Bill was getting no start compared with what they'd done for Ivor.

Bill himself didn't mind. With his ever-present optimism and good nature, he saw it as an opportunity, so on the morning he set off for Adelaide he had no sense of his older brother's feelings of guilt and anguish. Soon they got the good news that he had a job on a farm in the Mallee with living quarters provided. This was followed a couple of weeks later by the news that he had left. He'd been working on a farm at Overland Corner cutting shoots for sixpence an acre, and the living quarters meant sleeping in the stripper. He hadn't minded that, but after ten days he woke one night with an eerie sense of weight on his side and found he was sharing his quarters with a large brown snake. He pulled his clothes out with a Mallee pole and asked the farmer if he could sleep in the shed. This met with a flat 'No', so he quit the job. His boss refused to pay him for the work he'd done because the job wasn't finished, and said he was a 'weak coward'.

Aub filed it for future reference, knowing the day would come when he would retaliate and call the farmer for what he was. Not paying a man for his work at times like these was as low as you could get, and this bloke reckoned he was a Christian. Bill worked around Mannum and Murray Bridge for a while and finally found a position at Richard's Motor Body Builders at Keswick in Adelaide, where he stayed for several years.

16

Later, Uncle Stuart had some work on his block at Monash but there'd not be too much money in it. Aub had worked for him before and rapidly staked his claim on the job. It meant he'd see more of Uncle Darcy and Uncle Allen too and he was pleased because he saw little bits of his dad in all of them.

Sam (Septimus) Durant, Phil Strachan and Aub set up camp together in the bush across the road from the blocks they were working on. They scrounged what they could and made a tent of wheat bags, canvas, hessian and bits of timber from a broken-down old shed. Aub was glowing – this was theirs, striking out on their own. They rounded up some kerosene tins for seats and had makeshift swags and an old hammock to sleep in. They built a fire pit with stones, covered an old cartwheel with chicken wire and put it across the top for a grill. There were a few billycans and forks and pannikins, and an old chest rested on cans standing in a tray of water to keep their food away from the ants. When they had a jar of jam given to them by Clarrie, and another from Darcy's wife Gladys, they felt rich indeed. Two sorts of jam in the Depression years was something. They shot rabbits and pigeons and ducks for meat, and cooked damper in the coals and argued about who was the best cook.

The three of them were great mates. Phil was the most brash (surprising since his dad was a minister) and he could swear like a trooper. Sam was the most gentlemanly, and the most sporting, and Aub was the most musical, and the most determined. They had a good time baching together and their friendship would prove to survive the tests of time, distance and adversity.

Stuart had always had an eye for new things, and he had taken up an agency selling implements and tractors. He showed the new implements on his property and did working demonstrations with them. Aub found it fascinating to watch them at work, to find out how they'd been designed and built, and he often helped in tooling up to get them ready.

Tractors were changing the whole way of working the land, and although horses were still being used every day pulling new improved ploughs and implements, sulkies and drays, it was clear that their usefulness was challenged by the tractors from a working perspective. Stuart was always working out the latest and most efficient methods in agriculture and he read up on all the news and often passed articles on to Aub, who devoured them with interest.

Wine grapes, drying grapes, stone fruit and citrus, all had different harvest and pruning times and Aub liked the change in the seasons and the differing work that each one brought. He watched and practised how to prune the different varieties and followed the best time and the best way to do things. He read about reticulation and the fall of the land for irrigation, and how much each fruit needed, and how deep and far apart the furrows needed to be to deliver that amount of water.

When there was time off, he'd ride to Renmark and see his mum, and then meet up with Wally Wescombe, Pus Riedel, Reg Ridgewell, Gordon Andrews and his other mates, and go fishing and shooting, or go dancing, or play music, or swim, or row on the river.

But he didn't look for time off because he needed to work. He had a dream.

The Gamble

17

He worked every hour of work that he could find. He scrounged and saved and kept everything he could that might otherwise cost him money. He was absolutely driven, because he had his dream. Ever since he was little, he had hated his eyes and hated how he looked in the mirror. He'd worn glasses since he was two, and he'd been known as 'swivel-eye Jury' and 'cockeye Jury' and a few other names as well, although not usually to his face. He still secretly felt a bit guilty because he had held some money back for himself, but he'd never put himself first before. Now, even worse, he was going to gamble the lot on a scary unknown.

In Mallala, he had talked often with Linda Jury. She was the head sister in the eye ward in the Royal Adelaide Hospital and she had been telling him about a new young doctor, Michael Schneider, who had some quite advanced ideas and was very skillful.

With her help, he managed to get an appointment with Dr Schneider, and the day couldn't come fast enough. Saying nothing to anyone, he rode his bike to Adelaide and, feeling very nervous, presented for the appointment. The doctor heard him out and examined him, and then explained that if an operation was done it would have an unknown outcome with regard to his sight, and that such surgery was purely experimental. Aub was adamant that he was prepared to take the risk, and they both decided to consider exactly what it meant before having another consultation. For his patient to be prepared to take such a risk clearly told the doctor how desperate he was.

At the next appointment, Dr Schneider carefully detailed what such an operation would entail. One eye would have to be removed from its socket, so the muscles could be tightened, altering the movement of the eye. Aub would have to be conscious, to say what he could see and to move his eyes on the surgeon's instructions. Even if the eye could be straightened, it was quite likely his sight would be damaged. He explained again that although every care would be taken, it was very early experimental surgery, and he could make no promises as to the result. There could be no guarantees, and Aub would have to sign a statement acknowledging that he fully understood and accepted all of this. Only under those conditions would he consider doing the surgery.

Aub desperately wanted this, and felt he had nothing to lose. He was scared by the operation itself, but the lure of not being cross-eyed was the most important thing to him. Linda told him that this doctor was absolutely 'the best', and she trusted him, and Aub trusted her. They discussed the fact that because his right eye had the worst sight it should be the one to be straightened to preserve the best of his sight. Everything was arranged, and the surgery was booked. He couldn't sleep, and Linda was sworn to secrecy.

After the operation was done, Aub put it in his 'never to be remembered' box. They gave him some sedation towards the end, but it wasn't very strong as they didn't want to risk him vomiting. It was imperative that the eye was not jolted or shaken for the first few hours. He didn't ever want to think about it again.

He woke to Linda talking to him. Both of his eyes were bandaged shut. Dr Schneider came in and told him that this would last for three weeks. He was in the eye ward and must call the nurse for anything he wanted, and he must definitely not move quickly or get out of bed. It was time for healing to take place.

The first couple of days passed quietly, while he felt miserable and scared. He was listening intently to the voices around him, and soon got to know the names of some of the men. Linda made sure he got enough to eat, and let the nurses know he was her VIP patient.

He had too much time to think now, and the implications of the huge decision he had made sank in. What had he done? He'd learned that every decision made, and action taken, brought its consequences, and now he wasn't so sure that he was ready for the ones that might come with this.

At last they let him up, but he had to have someone with him all the time. He badly wanted to go for a walk as he wasn't used to lazing around, and he felt cooped up in the stale air of the ward. In the end, it was agreed that a patient with vision in the left eye, and a patient with vision in the right, could take him into the Botanical Gardens next door, provided that he walk in the middle and they all take great care not to jolt their eyes.

As they set off, they'd tell him what everything looked like and give him instructions. 'OK, Aub, there's a ditch here and you're going to have to step over a couple of feet. Ready – away we go.' 'Big mud patch. We'll have to go around, and then when we tell you, there's about three feet you'll have to step over really carefully. Don't want to be covered in muck!' This was a brief escape and they all enjoyed it.

The night before the bandages were to come off, Aub got the runs and couldn't sleep. What if he couldn't see anything? What if his eyes were still crooked, or looked worse than before? What if he hadn't told them properly what he could see during the operation? His head ached, and he felt dizzy with sweeping waves of sickness. He had heard both good and bad reactions from other eye patients as bandages were removed, but he was the only one, of course, who had had the experimental eye-straightening surgery. He was supposed to be a man and he should not be so upset.

Linda came along and tried to calm him down before Dr Schneider arrived. The eye guards were untied. The bandages were slowly freed and removed. Aub looked straight in front of him and could see shadows and light! He was afraid to look left or right, but they coaxed him to slowly follow a finger each way. He couldn't see much at all, and Linda gave him something to make him sleep. When he woke, she came down and again got him to look to the left and to the right following her finger and quietly made the startling remark 'mm'.

He had to remain in the ward for the next few days as his blurry sight ever so gradually improved, and they told him nothing. Then Linda arrived with a mirror, and like a scared child he put it in front of his face. The eyes that looked back at him were swollen, puffy, bruised, – and straight! It had paid off. He didn't care that he still needed his glasses or that his right eye saw only shadows and nothing else. His eyes were straight, and he wasn't cockeyed Jury any more. He'd won the biggest gamble of his life.

He found out some other things when he could see, too. There was a nurse who used to come and read to him. She had a beautiful voice, and a good sense of humour, and he had pictured her a lot in his mind, only to find that fact and fiction didn't match. And his two one-eyed mates had obviously had a great time leading him astray in the gardens. The obstacles they had made him avoid weren't real, and he must have looked a clown trying to get around them. They'd been having a great laugh together at his expense.

Dr Schneider told him the sight in his right eye was not going to improve. He didn't care. The sight in his left eye was good, and nothing mattered now his eyes were straight. He left hospital completely broke,

but with a new confidence about himself, and set off walking the one hundred and fifty miles back to Renmark. He was lucky enough to get a couple of lifts on the way back, and arrived at Monash in the dark, wondering what his mates and Uncle Stuart would say in the morning. They thought he'd been down on the farm.

He could only do light work for a start, and had to wait before he could ride his bike again. But it didn't matter; he knew he looked good.

His mother was pleased for him but was astonished that he'd been so concerned that he had taken such a risk and was a bit brusque about him having done it. Thora gave him a big hug, and he got used to people looking at him carefully the first few times they saw him. None of them were surprised that he hadn't told them. Aub was like that.

It wasn't to be the last time that his eyes would affect his life.

The Trump Card

18

One day when he finished work early, he jumped on his bike and rode to Renmark. The sun was roasting, so he went straight to the swimming hole and dived in and swam across the river and back. There were two girls swimming and clowning around in the water, and as he dried himself on the bank, he watched them. It was unusual to find someone there that he didn't know, but he'd never seen these girls before.

There was this little one, petite with dark auburn hair, and he couldn't take his eyes off her. She had a beautiful smile and wasn't a bad swimmer either. He guessed she was about eighteen, and thought the two of them looked like sisters, but he didn't get a chance to talk to them as they swam down the river, further away. She was the prettiest girl he'd ever seen.

He asked around and found out that the family had only just arrived from Adelaide and their father was the new manager of the packing shed. Apparently, there were a couple of brothers too, and one in particular who rode his bike around, sported bright red hair and freckles, and the lads thought he was a bit of a bragger. They'd all noticed the girls of course.

He went to the river more often but didn't see them. His mate Wally Wescombe told him the little one was Valma Haynes, and the other was her sister Meryl, and said Val was a really good tennis player. He wandered past the courts when he heard she might be playing tennis, and she was as neat and quick in her movements as anyone he'd ever seen, and she fired a very mean ace down the court. She fascinated him, always smiling and laughing but not giggly. He just wanted to get to meet her without giving away how smitten he was.

In December, he agreed to act as Father Christmas in Saise department store, and there he was all dressed up in his red and white suit when Val came in. He asked one of the girls to introduce them, and she looked even prettier close up. He didn't appear to take much notice of her and let her walk away without more than a hello.

His trips up to Renmark became much more frequent, and he ran into her every time he could. She was a bit shy, and of course there was no way he could let her think that he might be interested. The more he saw her, the more he wanted to see her. Her sister Meryl was more outgoing and was into bike racing, and he got to know her very quickly and was able to suggest they go out on a group picnic. He was worried because the lads living in Renmark were on the spot, and he thought that put him at a disadvantage because he still lived down at Monash.

Val was working at the packing shed and she always seemed to be with a group of people. Meryl encouraged him, and finally he asked them to join him and some friends up the river for a fishing day. They had a lovely time and built a fire on the bank and cooked the yabbies and fish they'd caught. Aub felt he was glowing, but he kept a little distance from Val.

Finally (with Meryl's encouragement) he got the courage to ask her out, and she didn't hesitate to say yes. Soon they started 'keeping company' and very good company it was. Val was a happy person, not at all moody and always smiling. She didn't go to church like he did, but surprisingly he found that it didn't worry him.

Gradually, Val stopped playing tennis and he stopped going to church. Their pastimes became swimming, picnicking up the creek, fishing and dancing. Sometimes they would row up the river, and Aub would serenade Val accompanied by the old guitar he'd bought. He knew most of the professional fishermen upstream, so they would often call in at one of their reaches and have a cup of tea and a chat, and Val gradually got to know a lot of people that she might otherwise never have met.

Her mother, Mina, didn't like Aub at all, and he didn't like her. She was cross because she wanted Val to step out with Evan Tranter (whom she played bridge with each week) but Val couldn't stand him.

Mina would criticise Aub loudly so that he could hear, but then would ask him to stay for dinner. Aub, never one to be anything other than honest, would say, 'No thanks. You don't like me, and I don't like you, so I'll come back again afterwards.' It was difficult for Val but, for once, her father Bert disagreed with his wife and told Val that if she liked Aub he was happy about it.

Bert had Aub's great respect. He was well liked by the men at the shed and was known as a man of integrity and fairness. He never ran anyone down but could dress someone down if it was needed, and this would always be on a one-to-one basis. He was a very hard worker, thought before he spoke, and was very capable. If he thought the shed board were making decisions that would have a detrimental effect on production or workers, he didn't shirk from an argument with them, even though they were his employers. He would make sure his facts were correct and that his reasoning was sound, and he would always try to stay calm, even if he came home blazingly cross afterwards.

One night, tired and stressed after a very difficult day, he asked Aub to have a beer with him. Aub was now twenty-five and had never had an alcoholic drink in his life. He had been brought up in a strictly temperance home, and if he said yes it would be a major turning point. Bert didn't press him, but Aub thought about it and said, 'If it's good enough for you, Bert, it's good enough for me.' It was a measure of his respect, and they shared a quiet glass of beer in the kitchen. He didn't want to think about what his mother and father would have said, but the sky didn't fall in, and he didn't like it enough to think he'd ever get drunk.

There wasn't much money going around and Aub was still paying some money to Clarrie, so when Bert offered him a job at the packing shed during the harvest, he took it, going back to Monash to work for Stuart on the days when he was off. Val worked at the shed too, and she was a dab hand at packing oranges and knew most of the young people in the town through her work, her brother and sisters, and Aub's friends.

She was a good dressmaker and with her petite figure she was a snappy dresser. She had a good eye for colour and line and loved the new crêpe and taffeta materials, diagonal stripes, nicely cut jackets and softly flaring skirts that flattered her so well. Her auburn hair was wavy and cut in a bob, and her green eyes sparkled over well moulded cheekbones. Aub's cousin Lance said she was the prettiest girl on the river. Aub knew that, and he adored her, but couldn't admit that he might be in love. He was mighty glad he hadn't met her before his eye operation and that she'd never seen his crossed eyes.

His mother and Thora liked her instantly and Uncle Ern was a fan, saying he didn't know how Aub had found her but he'd better make sure he kept her. This was high praise indeed and was about the first thing they'd agreed on.

Val was the seventh of eight children, two of whom had died in infancy. Due to her mother's ill health, she had lived with her grandparents John and Eleanor McAlpine at Nyah, in Victoria, until she was nine. She went back to the family then, and it had been a big wrench for her. She missed her grandparents badly, and it was a big challenge for her to fit in and for her siblings to accept her. There had been quite a settling-in period to get used to each other. Since then, home had been in various places as Bert moved with the seasonal work managing the packing sheds, and each time the whole family packed up and moved with him. By the time she was fourteen, Val had attended fifteen different schools. This was amazing to Aub, who could only remember one school, in one town, and always thought of Renmark as home.

19

The third tier of the Renmark Hotel was being built and Aub got a job as a labourer. He had left the shed when Val's dad went to Irymple and she and her siblings, Meryl and Len, had all decided to stay living in Renmark. She had moved into a tiny two-roomed flat in the Stones' home in Seventeenth Street and worked at the newly relocated packing shed. She made curtains and trimmings and loved her cosy little rooms. Aub would visit her there and was always very gentlemanly. He had two rules: you never showed affection in public, and you never breeched your own moral code.

While labouring on the building, he didn't mind wheeling the heavy barrows or doing the fetching and carrying, and the view down the river from the top was spectacular. He learned a lot, but it wasn't a job to make a career of and he knew it was time he found a job that could lead to something permanent.

Ivor was settled now. In 1933, he had received his first teaching post at the one-teacher school of Devlin's Pound. He was doing well. He enjoyed his teaching but most of all enjoyed his football. He played for Barmera, and it took a little time for him to get there for training after school. He had even left the school inspector standing at the school one afternoon when the day finished, saying he had to get to football training in a hurry. He was the most athletic one of the family. He was an excellent runner and a top tennis player. In fact, he was good at anything he turned his hand too. His quick wit, daredevil attitude and natural charm meant he was good company, and he made mates easily.

Bill was still working in Adelaide and also picked up odd days of work in the Adelaide Hills cherry or apple orchards or vineyards. He was a man's man, who would have a go at anything.

When a position came up with the T&G Life Insurance Company for a job as a collector agent in the Riverland and Murray Mallee, Aub applied. After written testing and an interview, he won the job and began in mid-1933. He had a small car, a collector's book and a weekly wage for as long as he made the necessary figures. His job was to tour the district and collect the weekly premiums from existing customers,

and to sell life insurance. Having lost his dad so early, he not only understood but had experienced at first hand the crippling financial situation that families could be left to cope with, especially if death duty had to be paid. After all, whoever died at the right time? He was honest and had a good name and was trusted in the district. Being good with figures and able to think quickly on his feet, he was the right man for the job. He related easily to the various problems that people had and proved to be a very successful agent.

Sometimes on the rounds there were surprises. One lady left him a note saying, 'Dear Aub, the money's in the stuffed koala with the zipper.' There on the top step were lined up six stuffed toys – yes, including the stuffed koala with the zipper. He shook his head. Another day he was met on the veranda of a house by the family dog, with a large blue dummy in its mouth. When the lady answered the door, he explained that the dog had the baby's dummy, to be greeted with 'Oh no, that's his!'

He was going to visit one of three brothers who lived on a farm at Paita and had been told that the one he wanted to see was known as the strongest man around. When he got to the farm, there was a man working near the fence, so Aub stopped to ask if he was the one he was looking for. 'Oh no. You want my brother, who's working over the hill,' the man said, picking up the monstrous plough and pointing over the crest with it. Aub was amazed and wondered at the strength of the brother over the hill.

There were sandstorms as the Mallee was still being cleared, bogs in the drift sand, days of searing heat, and others with icy mornings. There were happy stories and sad stories, and families growing, and families falling apart. Following a death, Aub would go out to complete the insurance claims and although it would be sad he knew the money was always going to help. He never regretted selling a single policy, and he enjoyed his job.

In 1934, his much-loved grandmother, Nana, died. She was diabetic and had died from the infection of a gangrenous toe. She had been married to Alf on Christmas Day and she died on Christmas Day. Not a Christmas would pass without him thinking of the woman he had adored. She was a huge loss. She was only seventy-one and had always been his most staunch supporter and friend. He loved his mother but felt more respect for her than closeness. His grandparents and his father were gone now, and his sense of loneliness was profound. He was fed up with people dying.

Nana's son Alfred had been

RENMARK LOSES WOMAN PIONEER

Late Mrs. Hilton, Forty-Three Years Resident

By the death of Mrs. M. C. Hilton on Christmas Day, Renmark lost one of .ts pioneer women who in the early days of settlement p'ayed her part nobly and in the spirit of self sacrifice. She well knew the joys and sorrows of those early days, and one greeted her in the street as a sincere friend always. With her death, the chain of those who were first in Renmark grows shorter.

Mrs. Hilton was born at Clarenton in 1863, and came up river with her husband, the late Mr. Alfred Hilton, 43 years ago. The town, then a tiny hamlet, appealed to the husband and wife. They had to adopt themselves to circumstances and knew all about roughing it. But both were brave people and played their part in life.

During the Great War Mrs. Hilton was a prominent worker in the Methodist Ladies' Committee. What these good women did wi'l never be forgotten by soldiers. She was also a member of the ladies' guild of the church. Mr. Hilton died fourteen years ago. Mrs. Hilton was a sister of Mr. E. B. Chapman, also one of the first to settle in Renmark. What these early townspeop'e did for those sometimes in dire distress—there was no dole—will never be written. It is just to write of them that they had nobility of heart and had families a credit to Australia.

Mrs. Hilton died on the anniversary of her 54th wedding day. The family consists of Mesdames E. Ross (Fullarton), S. Jury. (Kendelsham), H. Gravestocks (Renmark), and Ern Hilton of Renmark, who is president of the R.S.A' and who during the War was specially decorated for service in the field.

Mrs. Fred Crabb of Wa'kerie was a life long friend of Mrs. Hilton's. Among the early sett!ers expressions of regret have been heard at the death of this highly respected pioneer woman. She was well known to many of the old time fruit growers, all of whose doors would always be open to her.

RETURN THANKS

THE FAMILY of the late MRS. M. C. HILTON sincerely THANK relatives and friends for floral tributes, telegrams, letters and personal expressions of sympathy in their bereavement. Especially thanking Dr. Harris and Sister Reid for their unremitting attention.

killed by a falling tree when he was twelve and there had been no time for her to say goodbye. Perhaps that was why she had loved Aub as she did.

Aunt Belle said that for years Nana had walked out to the cemetery every day, and of course Grandfather Alfred had been buried in the same plot. Now it was Nana's own turn.

Bereft as he was after Nana's death, Aub withdrew into himself and found his solace in work. Val was there to comfort him, but she found that it was not easy, and wondered at his need for his own space when he disappeared down along the creek with his guitar and tin whistle, rather than spending the evenings with her.

20

Thora and Arthur had moved to Rendelsham (in the south-east of South Australia), where he had been appointed as the head teacher. They had a little daughter Valma, and they had asked Clarrie to go and live with them. Aub knew she had missed them badly, but leaving Renmark was a big step for her because it was Stan's burial place and had been their home, and she would be leaving friends, family and memories behind. She felt too that she would be encroaching to a degree on the young couple, and it worried her, but although she was torn she made the decision to go, and with mixed feelings they packed up, cleared and sold her home.

Aub was grateful to Thora and Arthur but he was also concerned about the changes it would make for them. He knew that he couldn't live with his mother again for more than a couple of months at a time, and he admired them for making such a sacrifice of their privacy.

He was surprised by how much he missed her once she was gone. He hadn't expected to feel any real loss, as she was still alive. For the first time, he didn't have the worry about extra payments and he felt guilty at his relief now that the immense weight was no longer on his shoulders. Now he could organise himself and try to plan a future. Of course, he intended that future to include Val, but he wasn't in a financial position to think about that yet, so he wasn't about to express any long-term intentions, and was always careful what he said.

Sometimes he and Val worked as a team grape picking, one each side of the vine, picking a full row at a time. They could pace each other steadily and evenly and were a lot quicker than most of the other pickers and this meant they could always get extra work when they wanted it.

Val was saving for her glory box, trying to gather some linen, towels, cutlery and other items. She stored them in her little flat and couldn't wait for the day when she had a home of her own. She thought this would happen with Aub, but he was slow in asking and sometimes this made her pretty miserable. She was getting older and all the other girls seemed to be married.

Aub was oblivious. He had an account he kept separate from his wages as he was saving to buy a C.F. Martin acoustic guitar, and he earned extra money playing regularly on weekends in a five-member steel guitar group run by Dennis Hooking. They wore tuxedos, they were good, and they were very much in demand. His main interest, though, was classical finger-style guitar as played by people like Andrés Segovia. With his typical quest for the best, only a Martin guitar from America was going to do. He ordered the instrument and when it arrived he was almost afraid to open the case. The guitar was beautiful, undamaged, and the neck felt like it had been in his palm forever. He'd bought some fingerboard harmony, duet and finger-style books and began months of study and practice, totally absorbed.

Val would ask him round to practise at her place because otherwise she wouldn't see him for days. His job was going well. He was happy. For the first time, he was playing a winning hand.

Always interested in everything, he followed the news avidly. Overseas news was often reported here well after the events had happened, so he liked to make use of the new shortwave radio bands, particularly if there was a boxing match being broadcast. He'd listened to such interesting news during the thirties. Scientists had smashed the atom, and then he'd had to read all about that. The huge 'coat hanger' of Sydney Harbour Bridge had been opened and the wrong man had cut the ribbon. Don Bradman was the king, but cricket had seen the Bodyline scandal. Unbelievably the King of England had abdicated the throne! Men were flying around the world and the aviator Kingsford Smith had been lost over Asia in 1935. He could never get enough news of what was happening, whether it was sport or science or whatever.

1936 saw brother Ivor and Doris Bartel married at Cowell, on the Eyre Peninsula. She was a good tennis player, and an excellent dancer, and they were an attractive young couple around town. Dolly (as she preferred to be called) was a stylish young lady. They were happy when he got a posting and moved to New Residence (back up the river) and he and Aub saw as much of each other as they could. Ivor's first daughter, Maureen, was born at Loxton in 1938.

Aub had started competitive bike riding and was winning a lot of races. His eyesight wasn't a problem, and now he drove a car he missed the feeling of peak fitness he had enjoyed. His friends Frankie Gaynes and the Adams boys rode too, and they entered races all over the place. Their hero was Hubert Oppermann. 'Oppy' was blazing a trail for Australian cyclists, both at home and overseas. There was plenty of press about his exploits, and they read everything they could find about him.

When Aub went to live with Dave Schirmer in Twelfth Street, across the road from Ern and Dot in the Hilton home, he thought often of Nana's warm eyes welcoming him at the door of the old house. Dot kept everything like a new pin, and Aub thought she was a perfect lady, always pleasant, calm and serene. Betty was an only child and was now well into her teens. She was working as a dental nurse for Dr Cox. She was pleasant like her mother with customers, but Aub knew she had a fiery temper too, a bit like Ern, her dad.

The Hilton carrying business had been sold, and Ern was now an agent for the Shell oil company. Rail and trucking had taken over the paddle steamer and carriage freight, and now the big demand was for petroleum fuels.

The depot sheds, now unused, were ugly and bereft, and one old International truck stood neglected and spider-ridden, next to the battered loading dock. The third block of land stood vacant, with only the bamboos and the sentry mulberry tree remaining, to remind him of how it had been. In the evenings, he would look across and remember walking down to the stables with Grandfather to feed the horses at nine o'clock all those years ago. He remembered playing pranks in the yard with Ivor and Bill, and romping up the lane with Thora, and he was glad he had those memories.

Businesses were making a shaky recovery from the Depression, and morale in the town was improving. Plantings were bearing well and there looked to be a good future ahead for the growers. The silent movies had come to town, and everyone laughed at Charlie Chaplin and sighed in the romantic movies. There was a lot of grizzling if the old DC electricity plant next to the swimming pool spluttered and broke down and the films got interrupted. Boxing matches pitched locals against visitors and drew good crowds but Aub never felt he could go.

Dances were held in all of the halls around the district, with the locals from Lyrup, Monash and Moorook all joining in to kick up their heels. When there was a ball, everyone decked out in their finest and danced the night away. Thin-voiced songs and scratchy music wafted through windows, as His Masters Voice gramophones played in the evenings, and tall standing radios announced the news, together with static and whistling noises, interspersed among the worrying words about the unsettled times in Europe.

The Salvation Army band would march around the town and play on the street corners, and everyone would come out into the street and listen, and those who could would drop a donation in the box. Aub loved the sounds of the brass, the tambourines and the drums but he didn't think they were the best of musicians.

When the town band met in the evenings at the rotunda on the reserve, he went as often as he could. There was plenty of brass and plenty of volume, and a lot of talented players. There were just a few, too, who probably should have stayed at home. He'd listen to the instruments, carefully following the French horns, or the trumpets, or the trombone, or the base-voiced tuba, and he followed the music sheet as they played. There was no doubt in his mind that he was going to be part of this music business. He didn't make a conscious decision but just knew it as fact.

It wasn't going to be strings, other than his acoustic guitar. Nor drums. It wasn't going to be brass either. He decided it was going to be woodwind. After all, he'd always loved reeds – they reminded him of the river. Saxophone. Bass? Alto? Soprano? He listened to them all, and it was the alto sax that stole his heart.

The Joker

21

The news came in September 1939: war had broken out in Europe. There was a cold sense of horror and disbelief that this could happen again. Families remembered their dead, and their injured, the grief, and the wastefulness, and the mental wounds and hopelessness, after the war that had ended just twenty-one years ago. The pain steeped their minds and they waited anxiously for every word of every news broadcast.

Aub could still remember his uncles going off to fight. The uniforms, the boots and big moustaches and the sad goodbyes, and a little boy watching his mother pack and send off parcels. He was older when they came home, those who did, and from what he knew there was not one good thing about war. He didn't see how there could be any winners, but he knew there would be losers.

At twenty-nine, he already felt a sense of loss, foreboding and uncertainty. The stories from the First World War, and the images, and the people who couldn't talk about it, made him fear for the future. Could it happen so badly, and for so long, again? How could this Hitler do such inhumane things to people? The older people in the district, and his uncles and aunts, had all lived through it before, and they each carried the scars in their own ways, none of them untouched. How could it all happen again at all, let alone so soon? What would it mean? South Australia was only 109 years old, not grown, not developed, but with strong ties still to Britain. How would this change the world? How would it change the country? How would it change their lives?

All questions, but no answers.

The talk in the town was less of what it was about, but more of who would go off to fight and how soon. There was recruitment on a massive scale, and young men flocked to enlist. There was a mood of optimism. 'Get over there, help the Brits clean it up, and home in no time.' Some saw it as an adventure, others as a duty, and a few intrepid boys lied about their age in order to enlist early.

Some occupations, most in the area of skilled jobs, were exempt from enrolment (to prevent a labour crisis). Teachers were exempt, so Arthur and Ivor didn't need to go.

Val had brothers and brothers in law who went, and she couldn't shake the worry that filled days and nights. How could anything good come out of this? But how could you let such awful things happen to others and not lift a finger to help? How much of the news she was hearing was right? She heard Mr Chamberlain, Mr Menzies, and the King himself, all speaking grim words. How long would it be before Aub wanted to go? Her brothers had enlisted, and they suddenly seemed older, and yet painfully young, as they wore the military garb.

Uncle Ern enrolled straight away. He felt a strong sense of duty to

fight for King and Country. He had won a Military Medal in the First World War and had achieved the rank of major, but due to his former injuries he was not allowed this time to fight at the front. He was to travel on the troop ships (taking the lads overseas) and was tasked with helping to prepare the boys for battle.

Much to Val's concern, and not with her agreement, Aub enlisted in the air force. He considered it his debt to pay, his duty, that he must fight against what he saw as unacceptable and immoral treatment of others. There was no excitement about it, just a resignation that good men must stand up against bad.

Many of his mates had gone, and women were signing up as well. But when the letter came he was terribly upset. Fit as he was, they wouldn't accept his sight test and had knocked him back. He was yet to find that his sight would be a major impediment with both the army and the navy as well, and that all three would decline his enrolment.

The Germans living in the area were experiencing a coldness towards them in the district, as some people suddenly considered them to be a threat here at home. They were rounded up and sent to the new internment camp at Loveday. This was a very divisive issue, because they had generally been well liked, hard-working members of the community. Some of them had been friends, and now they were distrusted and treated like spies.

Aub was living with Dave Schirmer's family, and Dave had taught him quite a bit of the German language, as well as several songs. Aub refused to think of Dave as no longer his friend. There were people, though, who said he was obviously a German sympathiser because 'he hasn't joined up, and you only need to look at where he lives'. Aub couldn't understand how people could turn so quickly and so nastily against each other.

The local butcher, who was German, was known for his wonderful smallgoods. The women in the town campaigned to get him back, and after a lot of heated and emotive argument, he was able to return from the camp (with restrictions) on the grounds that he was needed to produce food. It wasn't a happy situation for him, though, as prejudice often reared its ugly head and he had to ignore the rudeness.

Some of those whose sons had gone off to fight were vocal and insulting about men who were still at home, and a fair share of this was directed at Aub. After all, he looked strong and healthy and he wasn't in an exempt occupation. Fortunately, those who knew him were supportive, but he felt the snubs and the rudeness. Even from a distance, war changes people.

One day when he walked into the grocery shop, it started, and he'd had enough.

'Hmpff! I don't see how it is that certain people think they're too good to fight! Scum they are, who leave it to everyone else. Should be ashamed to show their face! We don't need them in our town.'

Aub walked right up to her, his eyes boring into hers with blazing anger. 'You think that, do you? You have been put on this earth to judge?' He stared at her, inches from her face, his anger palpable, and the silence in the shop was deafening.

Gradually, her eyes wavered and then fell. She stood uncertainly for a few moments before she edged around him and went.

He made his purchase and left, but he was seethingly angry, explosively furious and hurt by the injustice of it. He already felt ashamed that he couldn't 'do his bit', and her calling him out in public hadn't helped.

He continued to work around the district in his job as an agent, and also filled in here and there where hands were needed. Apart from the main jobs of work, he found others. More than once, a young mother found her vegetable patch weeded, or a load of wood chopped and stacked at the wood heap, and she would be grateful for whoever it was that had done the deed. He kept his eye on some of the older folk whose family were now away and did what he could. He had the utmost respect for the women who were working in the Land Army, and those who had taken on demanding skills that would have been considered beyond them before the war.

Things were getting harder. Ration books appeared. Money in the district was scarce. The air of optimism had gone, and people began to settle in to what was beginning to look like a protracted and long campaign in Europe.

22

Val had become a bit distant and was spending more time at home and with Meryl. She seemed to be avoiding him and Aub didn't know why. Perhaps it was just the general mood of things, but she had always been so cheerful. She wasn't smiling so much, and then she told him she wasn't sure she wanted to keep company with him any more.

He was shocked to the core, sick and not able to think. He hadn't felt so lost since his dad had died. He knew there was no one else for him. He didn't know what to do and all thoughts of the war just didn't seem to matter. He went to Irymple to see Bert, as Val was close to her father and he got on well with him, and he didn't know what else to do.

He didn't get the reception he'd expected. He was met at the door by an angry and not sympathetic Bert.

'If you don't know what's wrong, you're a fool! Haven't you seen how miserable she is? Six years you've been going out together. She's twenty-five. If you want her in your life, you better do something permanent about it, otherwise get out and let her go. How many years is she supposed to wait? You're thirty and you shouldn't need to have the problem spelt out to you.'

Aub was absolutely taken back by the outburst and the anger directed at him, so there was plenty to think about on the way home. He'd always held his emotions in check and to himself. He didn't go much for expressing how he felt, and he would certainly never give Val a kiss or make any show of affection in public. He had learned to keep things in reserve ever since he was a boy. Some things were for a private place. But he knew how he felt. Didn't she know how he felt? After all, she knew there was no one else. Bert had told him that if he wanted Val in his life he had better 'let her in'.

There was no security with a war on, and even apart from that, he felt he didn't have enough to offer her and he didn't think he had enough money together to marry her. He knew what scraping to make do was all about as he'd seen his mother do it for years and he wanted better for Val.

What could he do? He had to have her in his life. She was his beautiful petite pride and joy, his 'sandy cat', tiny enough for him to put his hands around her waist. He knew he couldn't manage without her and was beginning to realise that he stood a real chance of losing her. Plenty of other blokes had their eye on her too. Underneath, he knew it was fair enough. He didn't feel trapped but he did feel a bit afraid of being responsible for her the way he would like to be. But he couldn't lose her either.

Finally, he went to see her and told her he had been to see Bert. He said he was sorry, and that he loved her, but he wasn't good at showing what he felt. He asked her to marry him and she instantly said 'Yes' all mixed up with lots of tears. He couldn't understand how she would want someone like him but he was ecstatic that she did.

Of course, ecstatic for him still meant keeping everything quiet. Bert wanted to give them a lovely wedding like he had for his daughters Win and Meryl, and he wanted his Val to have the joy of sharing her very special day with family and friends. But Aub was having none of that. He was insistent there would be no fuss at his wedding, and he'd prefer that no one knew about it until afterwards. It was unarguable.

A disappointed Val accepted his ultimatum knowing that there was no choice. It was how he was. Despite his engaging outward and sociable appearance to other people he was a very private person. She would still be Mrs Jury and that was the most important thing to her.

On 16 March 1940, they picked grapes for Don and Glad Bruce at Block E. When they'd finished, they both went home and cleaned up and changed. Then they drove to New Residence to get married, with friend Lou Nuske and Ivor as witnesses. When they got there, Ivor had forgotten and was playing tennis. They got him off the court and went

down to the little church at the top of the river bank to be married by Reverend Kloeden. That was it. There was no photo, just a quiet drink and they were back in Renmark.

They could not have foreseen the life ahead of them, nor known how long their partnership was to last, but they both felt complete, being with the other.

The next day, while they were picking, Don's wife Gladys noticed Val's shiny new wedding ring, and of course made a big fuss, with congratulations all around. Val was very happy to be Aub's wife, but perhaps a little crestfallen about the way it had taken place.

She was very excited that Aub had arranged the rental of a house in Berri and they quickly moved in to begin their life together. The vegetable garden was set up and a couple of fruit trees were planted in the yard. She moved their small amount of furniture around the house to where she wanted it and set out some of her pretty bits and pieces. Aub didn't care where she put things, saying the organisation of the house was 'Sheila's work'. That suited her. She relished the role of new housewife, baking and sewing and keeping things spotless. She had left her job in Renmark and had plenty of time now to enjoy the house and garden chores.

Aub got a black cocker spaniel pup to train as a gun dog (duck shooting still being a favourite pastime) and named him Mack. With his black curly coat and deep brown eyes, Mack was smart, intelligent and adoring. He hung on Aub's every word and was easy to train. Aub's heart swelled every time he got home to a warm, loving welcome, and somehow Mack seemed to know not to charge in for a pat until he was invited. There he'd sit, just bursting to wriggle and rub, brown eyes firmly fixed, just waiting for the word.

He was a quick learner, wasn't gun-shy and of course loved the water. Such trust was built between them that Aub put pins in the duck wings for training on the back lawn, and Mack would pick them up very gently and carry them back on the word 'Bring'. When he started retrieving ducks, he would pick them up very gently and never ever bit or injured them. He would walk slightly behind and then sit until given the word to move. He learned that if there was an injured duck it must be brought out first and not left to suffer. Aub had seen gun dogs that mauled the ducks bringing them out, or decided they'd had enough and would go for a swim or a sleep, but Mack was right there waiting for every task and command. They were great mates.

Aub's insurance inspector arrived from Adelaide to look at the business and let it be known that he'd like to go shooting while he was there. Aub, of course, totally ignored this and took him out around his clients on his normal run.

On the second last day, they were making calls in the Mallee when the inspector announced, 'Righto, Aub, I've had enough of this. Everyone's been telling me about your dog and I want to go shooting and see him at work. Bugger the clients.'

'Well, they're more important than you are, so we'll finish seeing them first, and you can put that in your report. I'll pick you up at daylight tomorrow, and we'll go out then.'

They headed out in the dawn light, with Mack in the back of the ute. It was quiet on the bank, except for the rustling of the reeds. Mack sat stock-still, every muscle tuned, shivering slightly in excitement, but not making a sound. When the inspector stepped on a stick that made a loud crack, two pairs of eyes turned on him with a look that made him more careful.

Quack, quack, quack... Bang! Bang! Two ducks dropped. Aub signalled and Mack took off – found them, sniffed them both, delivered one back to Aub and then went back for the other. All done quickly and with no fuss, just the adoring eyes staring up at Aub.

'Why did he sniff them both first?'

'Because if there's one injured, he's been trained to bring it out first.'

They shot five ducks and the inspector was just getting into it when Aub started to head back to the ute.

'Get a couple more, eh? Best time I've had for ages.'

'No. You only ever shoot what you need to eat. That's two for me and three for you to take back to Adelaide, after we've cleaned them.'

The inspector credited Aub with a bit more respect. He had learned a couple of things today, and he knew he wanted the dog. Despite several generous offers, he went back to Adelaide without him.

23

When Bill enlisted in the army, the family had gathered together in farewell at Thora's home at Rendelsham before he left for embarkation from Adelaide. Clarrie was very stern and sad. She had hoped never to see another world war and had certainly never foreseen that she would be sending her own boys off to fight. She feared for them, but fortunately couldn't know then that they would not all make it home.

For Bill, it was an escape from the uncertainties of life but he was motivated mostly by patriotism. He was posted to the 6th Australian Division of the Cavalry Regiment AIF and was sent off to fight in the Middle East.

Ivor received notice that his school was to close in 1941 and that he would then be posted to Nildottie. He applied to go in the air force, and they had already moved to his new school when the letter of acceptance came. He had three children now – Maureen, Lindsay and Wendy – and Dolly was very upset that he was going to fight overseas.

Cousin Betty enrolled in the WAAF (Women's Air Force) and was posted to Melbourne (Embarkation Depot 3) in 1941. It was clear now that the war was going to be long and drawn out, and a lot of women were joining the Land Army to work for the war effort on the home front. They learned to be mechanics, farmers and land managers, and to fill in the many jobs left vacant by the departure of the men.

Mack was a happy black cocker spaniel because he had Val around all the time, instead of being on his own all day. He had learned that because he had a garden it wasn't an invitation to dig, that it wasn't a good idea to chew holes in the hoses, and that good dogs didn't swing on the washing. Val was soft, though, so he knew he could get away with more when Aub wasn't home.

He'd been trained to collect the paper from the garden in the mornings and get a biscuit in return. It was his favourite chore. One Sunday morning, Val went out and there was a pile of papers on the back mat. He'd been collecting along the street and was duly sitting wagging his tail waiting for his rewards, only to learn he still only got one biscuit. Then he had to walk around with Aub returning his spoils, but he did get full marks for trying.

At night, Aub went out playing his saxophone to earn extra money. He was still trying to enlist, and it was still a 'No' because of his sight.

Val would stay home sewing and listening to the radio. She was pregnant and would often let Mack inside with her for company. When they heard the car come, she'd say, 'Quick, here comes your father,' and he'd rush outside. As her pregnancy lengthened, she couldn't bend, and ever-smart Mack started to decide he might stay in, knowing she couldn't lift him out.

Of course, Aub got home one night to find them both asleep in the lounge. 'What the hell is this?' he yelled, and Mack took off as fast as his legs would go.

Val received the rest of the tirade and that was the end of Mack's brief life as an indoor dog.

In April, Jennifer was born. She was beautiful and very tiny, with a

head like a small orange. There was some drama at her birth, as the doctor had arrived at the hospital drunk, and the sister, fortunately, had capably taken over. Although tiny, Jenny was perfectly formed, and slept and fed well. She had rosy little cheeks and the very beginning of some blonde hair. Aub was in awe, and very awkward with her, and was glad that Val was such a good natural mother. He reckoned he didn't know much about girls, but he was immensely proud. Over the first few months, her hair grew into little blonde ringlets, and she proved to be a very happy little baby.

Aub was less happy, though. He still enjoyed his job but anger and frustration were getting to him, as he hated that his brothers and his mates were putting their lives on the line and he felt that he wasn't contributing. The war was dragging on, and through a friend in Adelaide Aub heard that there was a desperate need for men who were good with figures. He had always been quick and accurate in this department, so he applied again adding additional information to the standard application form.

This time, the army gave him limited conditional acceptance. The applied conditions were that he was not able to leave Australian soil due to his poor sight. They would take him now as they needed both his excellent figure skills and his expertise with physical fitness and strength building, so it was to be a special posting. The T&G Company were sorry to lose him and guaranteed that his job would be there for him when he got back.

Mack was a trained gun dog, and a loving loyal mate, and Aub didn't want to leave him. With aching sadness, he gave him to his mate Don Bruce to look after. Don knew the dog well, as they had often been shooting together and Aub had no doubt he'd care for him well, but he couldn't think about how Mack would feel. How do you explain to a dog why you're leaving him?

Val decided to go to Nyah to live with her sister Win, whose husband Fred was in the air force. They packed up their house and stored the furniture, expecting to come back again.

With his kitbag and his saxophone (its case adorned with his army number SX25545 scrawled in white paint), Aub saw a tearful Val, and little Jenny, off on the Murray Valley bus. There was no fuss of course, because that was who he was, and he was setting off to do what he had to do.

The noise was relentless as the Ghan train hauled them all, stinking and packed like sardines gone off in a tin, up to the base in Alice Springs. The hours were interminably long as the train ran at times at walking pace. Sweat ran down their backs and into every crevice as the wooden cattle truck rattled along the rails. Aub thought of stories he'd heard told by the camel drivers who had passed through Renmark and knew now that they had all been true.

Alice Springs was home for their basic training before they went off to their postings. It was hot through the day, and freezing at night, so they went from shorts to trench coats in the space of a few hours.

To his surprise, Aub was chosen to help in improving the men's physical endurance and fitness before the men's jungle training, as it was soon apparent that he was stronger and fitter than most of the others. His years of training, exercise and body building had paid off. The training itself was physical, and mostly boring, but occasionally it took them out to the Olgas or the McDonnell ranges, and it gave him a brief introduction to the startling outback scenery. The dirt, sweat, flies and exhaustion were an endurance lesson for lots of the young lads. They were not to know that it couldn't begin to compare with the physical discomfort and mental challenges that were yet to come.

When their postings arrived, Aub found he was going to be near Mt Isa in Queensland, at the site of the Australian fuel depot. His expertise in figures was needed here because fuel estimations and calculations of storage in the dumps had to be absolutely accurate. The American base was close by. Fuel was transferred as necessary and there was a regular amount of transport coming and going out every day. It was considered too high a risk to keep the fuel depots in Darwin in case there was an attack on the city and the airbases.

The land was unforgiving, with the camp perched like some unsightly growth on its surface. The dingos owned the hills at dusk, prowling around the perimeter, and at night they owned the air with their howling. It was a desolate sound in a desolate landscape, and Aub thought about his river often. He missed it, and Val and Jenny, and his true mate Mack. The men were all united in their missing of loved ones, except for those very few who felt pleased to have escaped from home, but none of them really escaped. They still took their troubles with them.

The Australian camp had the mere basics, but the Americans had everything. They were still prone, though, to arrive and take anything they thought they wanted from the Aussies. Their arrogance annoyed everyone, and they soon worked out that the only way to get some of the more special things themselves was to reciprocate and steal them, or to do a deal. Aub had put his name down to play saxophone in the Entertainment Corps and they played often. When he played at the American camp, he always made a deal to take something back for the boys, most often in the way of food.

There were fierce electrical storms, and it was eerie being surrounded by hundreds of lightning strikes on the gibber, with fuel so close around them. One night, Aub was in a galvanised-iron hut when it was struck. His mates feared the worst, but they found him dizzy and numb, disorientated and mostly deaf. The mirror propped on the wall was completely black. Luckily, he had been standing in the middle of the floor touching nothing at that moment and was just completely stunned. They reckoned it was his lucky day.

In 1942, Japanese bombs devastated the airfields and caused death and injury in Darwin. The wisdom of having kept the fuel storages well away was proven. (Luckily the Japanese never located the depots, but they bombed Darwin, in all sixty-four times, ending in 1943.)

News came that Ivor had been sent off to England for training with the RAAF. Arthur had enlisted and was posted to the 10th Battalion Volunteer Defence Corps, as a lance corporal. Bill was still somewhere in the Middle East. Now both the boys were overseas, and Aub wished he could be with them. There was no envy in it, just fear of what they might face. He had promised Clarrie that he'd look after them, and now it was all out of his control, and the dice would fall according to chance. It was just as well he couldn't know then what was in store for both his loved brothers.

The war seemed to be escalating. The news was both mixed and limited. Occasionally in the Entertainment Corps when he was playing at the American base, he would hear things that weren't in the news broadcasts, and pilots would arrive back from other places with their first-hand stories to tell, and often none of it matched the official reports.

Playing in the Entertainment Corps was a welcome escape. There were some very talented musicians amongst the band, and one of the Americans was able to order music direct from America (at a price), so they were right up with the latest swing and big band tunes.

There was a mad piano player who was quite a talking point. He would sit out under the fig tree and while away the hours on the old piano he'd scrounged from somewhere, saying, 'What do you want?' and then he'd rattle out the request. It was rattle, though, because the piano had no strings. Sometimes he'd organise a sing-song, and they'd sit in the dust under the tree and sing to the clacking of the keys accompanied by the evening howling of the dingoes. The real joke was that when they went out to play in the corps, and he had a real piano to play, he would, and could, play anything from popular music to jazz and classics on request, and he was a very talented musician. His nickname was 'Clacker' of course.

For one occasion, they were flown to Darwin to play, and one of the other sax players there couldn't believe that Aub had a case of all the latest music from the States. He was very matey and offered to give him a quick tour before he had to return to Mt Isa, and of course the music case 'somehow' got lost. 'No worries, mate, I'll send it back to you.' He never did, and Aub realised he'd never intended to, and it was another expensive lesson learned.

He felt like he was standing still, as if while all this unimaginable awfulness was happening overseas on a huge scale, he was in a giant void, waiting for life to resume. But of course, it would never be the same. Whatever happened, there would be no winners – not now. It had gone too far. History would be littered with peoples and countries changed forever, and with hatred. None of it fitted with his early training about the justice of treating others like you wanted them to treat you.

The Hidden Hand

24

Val wrote saying that she and her sister Win were getting on well. While Win worked in the local chemist shop, she did all the cooking and housework. She always felt at home at Nyah, after living there with her grandparents as a child, and had settled in easily, although of course, she missed their life in Berri. The photo of her taken with Jenny stood on the box alongside his camp stretcher.

There was sad news too about Val's dad Bert, who was living in Bendigo with Mina. He had been unwell, and they found he had cancer of the glands in the throat, and epithelioma of the lip. Val was able to get down to see him, but it was very sad, as he was so debilitated and was suffering in dreadful pain. This wonderful courageous man asked her to 'just put the pillow over my head, love' and it broke her heart. He didn't want them to see him so sick.

Aub felt the disappointment of being in Queensland and not being able to help. He and Bert had spent many evenings in Renmark playing duets on their tin whistles while working their way through Mina's large and wonderful old *Globe Scottish Song Book*. No one else had ever shared this interest with him. He had found Bert to be a man of his word, considerate, hard-working and appreciative of those around him. He held him in the highest regard and was grateful to know him. He wrote letters to him, knowing it was all he could do, but he felt useless.

Bert passed away in February 1942 and was buried in Bendigo, a merciful passing for him in the end. Aub would always remember him for his kindness, his quietly spoken manner, and his absolute integrity in his dealings with everyone. He was glad that Win and Val were together to comfort each other. Another of his much-loved old men was gone.

The next letter from Val shattered him to the core. He wasn't ready for it. Could you ever be ready for it? He couldn't think, and the bile rushed into his mouth, and his eyes were on fire.

'Jenny is very happy. But she never crawled, just pushed herself around, and I noticed she made no attempt to stand, and I was getting worried. So I got a referral and took her to a specialist in Melbourne, and he says that she's crippled.'

He tore outside and retched, doubled over, unable to take in the words that had ripped through his mind.

'He says that it might be cerebral palsy suffered at birth, and at this stage the amount of mental and physical impairment can't be assessed. I'm sorry I didn't tell you, but I didn't want to say anything and worry you, in case everything turned out to be all right in the end.'

The tatters of his emotions lay around him like broken shards of glass, and he walked and walked and walked, with a void for a mind. He could only think of poor little Jenny, and of Val, who hadn't warned him, and that he wasn't there. The rest was a blank.

In his typical fashion, he didn't share his news with the others, but he did manage to arrange some leave to get to Swan Hill.

There was Jenny, pretty as ever, smiling and happy and now talking, big words and all, and not looking like there was anything wrong, except that she was shy with him and she had a mind of her own. The implications at this stage were not clear; there was weakness in her left arm and leg, and spasticity in her left hand. Therapists were going to put irons on her left leg and would encourage her to walk on a sloping surface. Val was to take her by train to Melbourne each month for treatment, and she would have exercises for strengthening and balance, to do between visits.

When he asked questions, Val got defensive (feeling that he was criticising her) and they both got upset, and Val got teary, and in the end he didn't know if he felt better or worse, or just inadequate and sad. He thought Val was coping better than him, and that perhaps women were just stronger with this stuff.

Soon his leave was over, and he was back at the camp. They were very

busy, and the movement of fuel through the depot was relentless. Sometimes he found himself waking at night adding drums and calculating loads, and he'd wake up in a sweat because it didn't add up, and that meant planes might come down. He thought of what would happen to Ivor if there was no fuel, and he'd go into the office hut stressed and anxious in the mornings.

Photos came of Jenny wearing her irons, and Val explained what was happening at the appointments. 'She stands there at the top of the little sloping platform, and they give her a little push, hoping that she'll throw her leg out and save herself from falling. It's just awful. She falls and falls, and its soft and they make it a game, but it's hard to watch.'

Finally, Jenny did throw her leg out, and the hard work really began. There was less success with the use of her left hand, but they were still hopeful that there would be steady improvement.

'The train trips are long, and the troops on board are so good and very willing to help with the luggage, etc.'

This both pleased and displeased Aub. He was glad they were helping but was quite sure they'd be eyeing off his strikingly lovely Val as well.

When he was next able to get back to Melbourne on leave, he found Val and Jenny better than he had expected. Jenny was walking, although somewhat unsteadily, as her balance was poor due to weakness on the left side. She had little strength or control in her left hand, and it was still too early to know what the loss of mental capacity might be.

She was happy, though, as long as no one moved her toys or anything else from where she put them. She didn't actually play with them but would set them up and tell them what to do, talking all the time. They were her subjects. She spoke beautifully and took everything you said to her very seriously, and Aub soon learned that his jokes were not funny. She was gorgeous, and he loved her to bits. It scared him to think what might be in front of her, and he began to question just how he felt about having more children. But then, he did really want a son.

25

Sometimes on a free day, a few of them would go out to one of the waterholes to swim. He enjoyed the beautiful water, warmer than the river, the scenery, and the exercise. After one trip, he didn't feel too good for a couple of days, and then he got diarrhoea, and it just didn't stop. After a couple of weeks, the army medic said he thought Aub had ingested some sort of bug and he was sent off to the army hospital in Charters Towers in a very poor state.

The diagnosis proved to be correct, and they confirmed he had a parasite in his bowel. They were not easy to treat (with none of the modern drugs now available) and the treatment was unpleasant. There were daily bowel washes, and they became a spectacle in the open ward, with a few blokes always lining up to watch, and a fair bit of chiacking going on. Aub hated it. He'd always been a private person and he was totally humiliated by the whole circus, but you just had to go with it. He was too weak to fight, and he was losing weight rapidly.

There was a tropical cyclone coming in, and things were tied and battened down as much as possible. It was a tent hospital and it was complete chaos and mayhem. The shrieking winds took everything in their path, leaving a soaked mass of useless waste. The recovery effort would be huge, and the men had to be transferred to a field hospital in Townsville.

After many long weeks, he gradually improved and was allowed to go outside and walk to try to regain his strength. He found the lush growth, the spectacle of Castle Hill and the feel of the sultry air very different. It was his first and only real experience of the tropics. He thought he might like to come back one day under better circumstances. Unfortunately, the parasite had done its damage, and for the rest of his life he would continue to live on medication to control his diarrhoea, and just like his poor eyesight this would come to limit and dictate some of the things he would and would not be able to do.

When he was back, he learned in the mail that Bill had returned from the Middle East on leave and had gone to Tasmania with his mate. He had been corresponding with Doreen Cowburn there for a long time, and when they met, they fell in love. They had been married in 1943 in a place called Possum Bay. Bill was in jungle training now and was expecting to go to New Guinea. He yearned to have a yarn with him, just a good sit-down yarn, there was so much they could talk about, and from what he'd heard things were very bad in New Guinea.

Ivor's third son Michael and Bill's son John were born in 1944. Aub was now the fully fledged uncle of eight. He looked forward to them all being together again, so he could be a caring uncle. He wanted to fill the role that his own uncles had filled for him.

Arthur and Thora and family (three girls, Valma, Erica, and Kay) had moved several times with Clarrie. Arthur had taught at Rendelsham and Myponga, and now he was at Keyneton near the Barossa Valley, and Ivor's wife Dolly had moved to Angaston with the children to be nearer them. She had a very young family of four and with Ivor away was grateful for the support. Clarrie enjoyed the grandchildren immensely. She felt useful, kept busy, and had made a few friends of her own.

Ivor was the best of her boys at writing letters, and in January 1945

Arthur received a letter from him saying he was enjoying his posting in Scotland, how beautiful it was, and how good it was when navigating back home from missions over Europe to sight the fishing villages on the English coast. He said he even gave himself a chance of pulling through the war now. Aub, though, received a letter from him saying that he liked navigating and found it interesting, but he didn't like it at all when they were the tailplane on a mission, as it was the most dangerous place to be. It was a prophetic statement.

On 8 March 1945, four squadrons of Beaufighters left Dallachy for a wing strike at the Midtgulen fjord in Norway. Warrant Officer Bill Mitchell was flying, with Ivor as his navigator. Red tracer was seen off the coast, arcing down into the sea, and when their plane did not return to Dallachy, it was presumed that they had been shot down.

Clarrie received the telegram informing them that Ivor was missing in action, and they knew he was not going to be found alive. Aub was completely devastated. Tall, happy, bright, intelligent Ivor. His talent and promising career, and his chance to be a loving, caring father, all shot down with him. Ivor, his happy, capable, devil-may-care brother, who had seemed the most indestructible and the most promising of them all. What a waste and what a terrible loss.

In typical Aub fashion, he didn't share his anguish. His mother and Thora and Arthur were devastated too, but Aub had learned from Stan's death that he had to be the strong man who didn't show weakness. He couldn't have talked about how he felt if he'd tried. He didn't believe in life after death, but he wished and wished that he could, because then he'd think Stan, and Ivor, and Nana, and all the others were together again.

He was acutely aware that, in a repetition of history, Dolly was now widowed with four children as his mother had been. She was totally bereft, and little Maureen shared the tears and the loss with her most, as the other children were younger. Michael was never going to meet his dad, and for Maureen, Lindsay and Wendy there would be little memory of the man himself. Like so many other families, a loved son and father was lost somewhere in a faraway sea.

There'd been too much sadness and he knew that he'd changed. He felt that the sum of his experiences had changed him, right from when his father had died. A bloke had to dust himself off, stand up and keep on, because he owed it to those who no longer could.

He had always had a more melancholy side to his character than any of his siblings. Ivor's death ran deep, and it came to the fore in the form of his quiet brooding, and the solitary playing of his saxophone, which had largely replaced his tin whistle. The next few months found him more subdued.

He was very pleased when a short leave home meant he could see most of the family and, although he found them all in saddened circumstances, it was wonderful to be able to talk to them face to face. He could still be his witty engaging self and they managed a few laughs together as well.

He couldn't believe how beautiful Val was, and how well she managed Jenny. Now she was getting a little older, it was clear that Jenny had some significant areas of mental loss. She was quite obsessive, and it was very difficult to teach her the easiest way to do things as she would scream, 'No! No! No! I do this way!' She was quite used to being the centre of attention, and was not beyond telling Aub, 'I'm the boss!'

26

In November 1945, the war ended. The long awaited, wonderful, wonderful news. There were ecstatic and feverish celebrations everywhere, but they were both tempered and sweetened by the sadness of the loss of loved ones, and there was as much sadness as there was joy. There was hope, and there was relief. There were tears of joy and reunions everywhere. There was a lifting of spirits and the beginning of new challenges, as families began to find that the men had come home changed, and women had to return to their old, more traditional roles.

Order had to be maintained until the effective shutdown and disbanding of the camp could be effected. Aub received news that he was to report immediately for duty to Springbank in Adelaide. He was posted to the Pay Corps at Wayville, and he would not yet be discharged. His talent with figures was to be used on the mammoth task of working out post-war entitlements and payments. While he would not be out of the army, it did mean he would be back in Adelaide and, as he didn't expect the deployment would be for too long, he hoped to be back in Renmark sooner rather than later.

There was no news of when brother Bill might get back from New  Guinea, and it seemed there was ongoing conflict in the jungle. He was the brother with the most contented and loveable disposition, and they worried that there was no recent news of him. It was known the war there had been very hard-fought, in tough and rough terrain. As the war was officially over, there should have been news, and they worried about him every day.

Aub rented rooms, and they shared a house with the owner Blanche Phillips, who also worked in the Pay Corps. She was supporting her little son Geoffrey and was happy to have some extra money coming in, and some friends to keep her company. When Val and Jenny arrived at 16 Glenavon Street in Woodville, it was a very, very, happy reunion. Jenny was not too happy about Geoffrey, though, because he was living in 'her' house, and she wasn't sure about sharing her mother either.

Aub rode an army motorbike to Wayville each day, sometimes with Blanche on the back, and his sax strapped on the side. He was now playing in an orchestra that was well organised and had a very good conductor. They were a terrific bunch of people, and he became particularly friendly with Wally Jose who (small world) was Uncle Ern's brother-in-law.

Now there was the opportunity, too, to reunite with friends who were back home, and there were many happy yarns with old mates over the bars of hotels all around town. Apart from the fact that he wasn't discharged, Aub enjoyed it all, and best of all was coming back to Val and Jenny every night.

When he learned that Val was pregnant again, he couldn't help hoping for a son. Taking no chances after their first experience, he wanted the best doctor they could get. This was Dr Verco, who attended both the Queen Victoria Hospital and McBrides at North Adelaide. Bookings at the Queen Victoria were full. And so Val was duly booked in at McBrides. This was a home for unmarried mothers (with a small complement of paying patients) run by the Salvation Army.

In the morning on 20 December 1945, Val ordered the maternity taxi and phoned a message to Aub. (Jenny, who was nearly five, was to stay with Thora while the baby was born and was quite excited to be having a holiday.) It was a rush, with both Val and the driver thinking they wouldn't get there in time, and the little girl was born at the hospital steps.

Aub phoned as soon as the whistle went at lunchtime. 'Has my wife Val arrived?'

'Yes, and so has your daughter!'

Despite his relief that the baby was born and all seemed well, he was bitterly disappointed that it was another girl. He wanted a boy. He knew he'd love her, but a girl couldn't do boy things, and she wouldn't carry on the family name. He had grown up mostly with men – father, grandfathers, uncles and brothers – and had always felt that girls were necessary, but not like boys. Ivor and Bill had both had sons. He was crushed. He loved Val and Jenny, Grandma Jury, Nana and Thora, and respected his mum, but women had a different place in the world, as all men knew.

Nevertheless, he did love the little scrap right from when he first saw her. Finding a name, though, was a problem. He said he didn't care what she was called, but everything Val suggested he didn't like, so she became Bub. After some time, she was named Marilyn, but Bub was to stick with everyone until she was sixteen and left home.

The first night home, Bub cried and was very fretful.

Jenny screamed, 'You can just take her right back where you got her! I don't like her!' She didn't like the change, or the sharing, or any of what had happened in the last few months.

Although they'd not discussed it and Aub certainly didn't say anything, Val felt his disappointment, as she was aware how desperately he wanted a son. She even felt a bit guilty that the baby was a girl. The first few days were very tense and stressful.

Three months later, on 29 March 1946, Aub was discharged. The family was going back to Renmark, and he would be returning to his job with T&G.

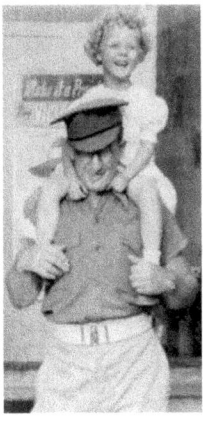 

Setting Up the Strategy

27

They were going to board with Uncle Ern and Auntie Dot, and Val would help Dot with the housework. Betty was home again too. Now aged twenty-five, she worked as a dental nurse, so they were a big household. Jenny began kindergarten at the Church of England School at the end of the street, and a new routine was established for them all.

Aub settled quickly. Now that he was older, he had a different view of Ern. He could see that he had always cared but just had not shown it in the ways someone else might. Now he and Dot treated the girls as if they were grandchildren, and Betty was like an aunt. In the years ahead, the love they shared with the girls proved to last through both child and adult experiences. Jenny was Betty's bridesmaid when she married, and Marilyn was her enduring power of attorney and guardian for the last of her years.

Aub was trying to make long- term decisions about the future, and he worried about financial security for them all. He knew what it meant to be poor, and even though they weren't boys he wanted to be able to educate the girls. Education was the thing – the thing that could open the doors to opportunity. He'd missed his chance, and he didn't want them to miss theirs.

He enjoyed working with the T&G company and especially the contact with his clients, but he couldn't see himself doing that forever. His music could earn them a living but it would also mean travel away with the touring orchestra. He knew that he would prefer to work for himself and that the heavy demands falling on Val with the ongoing care of Jenny would continue and even increase over the years.

He had grown up with men who believed that you must own land.

The Jury forebears had been pioneers. They'd cleared, built, worked and lived the land, and as a young man he'd learned that his grandfather and uncles had all considered that a man who owned land was to be more respected than one who didn't. He wasn't of the original pioneering generations, so he didn't hold that particular view, but he did see the eventual owning of land as providing some solid security.

While he continued his rounds, he really looked at and considered what was happening in the district, and it took him about a year to make a decision. He talked with Val and, thinking they would like to work together, they decided they would like to buy a block.

Aub didn't qualify as a soldier's settler. Because he hadn't been overseas in the war, his years of service didn't count for anything. It was impossible for him to get a bank loan, or to get one of the new blocks as he was not a returned man. He was excluded from all the government programmes and all assistance packages.

He couldn't join the RSL either. He had no problem with that. He felt for his friends and his relatives, many of whom had come home with traumatic memories and debilitating physical problems, and he was very glad that he had not had to see or experience what many of them had.

But the problem was once again money. He tried all the avenues there were, but for him and for Val there was to be no block.

The solution came after months of turmoil. Clarrie's sister Myrtle changed their lives. Auntie Myrtle had some money from a business she and her husband had sold when they parted, and she guarded it very carefully. She wasn't one to share and had earned herself a reputation in the family for being a skinflint. She had never shown any generosity to them

at all after Stan's death, and was not particularly close to Clarrie, so this was completely unexpected. In fact, her family considered her to be not just miserly, but mean.

Nevertheless, it was indeed Myrtle who came to him and offered the loan he needed. It would be at the standard bank lending rate and term, and he was not to tell the family where he'd got the money. Furthermore, she said she had always liked him and didn't doubt his honesty, integrity or ability to succeed one bit, and considered it a very good investment. She was not trusting of the banks following the crash of the New South Wales Bank a few years prior. She would invest in the fruit block.

Aub went up the river with his mate Reg Ridgewell and had a good think while they were fishing. The golden rule was that you never borrowed money from family, and the only experience he'd with debt involved the borrowing undertaken when they had built his mother's house in Eleventh Street, and that had been a millstone round his neck. He talked with Reg because he worked in the bank, and his advice was that Aub should thank his lucky stars and grab the loan with both hands, because where else was he going to get it?

Returned settler soldiers had concessional loans from their war service, and the rate of interest and payment was much lower than Aub would have to pay. He'd seen many of them struggle after the First World War and was worried about finding a property they could earn enough from to pay the top commercial rate of interest and still make a living for them as well. But he wanted it.

He didn't doubt his ability to work, nor Val's commitment to helping him, but it would be tough for her for many years. Jenny needed lots of help, and although he could earn more regular money (in the short term) as a professional musician, he still knew that that lifestyle really wasn't best for the family. As it was, he still went to Adelaide for some orchestral jobs, and although it provided extra cash flow, it always meant that Val was on her own. They wanted to buy a block, and he couldn't see any other way to get the money.

Val was overjoyed. She had some reservations about Auntie Myrtle but was very grateful for her generosity. They would just have to make it work. Apart from that, she couldn't wait.

Aub had seen a block down at Glossop that was for sale when he'd been on his rounds, and in fact his mate Wally Wescombe had one on the same road. The house was very basic, but most of the houses around the settlement were, and the property was within what they could borrow, so they decided to go down and have a look. They walked together all around the twenty-three acres, which were slightly sloping down to a drainage soak with reeds filtering into the huge Puddletown sump. The small stone channel that ran through the property for irrigation also carried water to fill the concrete underground tank providing water for the house.

The soil was a deep red sand and loam. The mixed plantings included stone fruits, orange and mandarin trees, wine and drying grapes and some pear and walnut trees. It seemed there would always be something to harvest, with one crop to support another that might not be bearing well. It was very run-down, and nothing was in good condition, so there was plenty of room for improvement. There were old stables, two Clydesdale horses, and a long dray over on the dry block. A large earthen floored shed housed what plant there was on the home block.

Vince Bahlog, who owned the place, wanted to live there for six months after it was sold, but luckily there was the opportunity for them to rent Massey Harris's house on the block next door for a short period.

For Aub, it was a mix of excitement and feeling sick with anxiety while they tried to make the decision. At last, he went and talked to Myrtle, and they set about getting the papers drawn up, and the die was cast. There would be consequences, but it was up to him, and to Val, to see that they were all good. It was time to stand up and back himself.

They sat down to a celebratory dinner with Dot and Ern, who had been so good to them while they were there. Aub and Ern would always continue to have their egotistical battles, but Ern was quite supportive these days, and Aub now supported him as a son would when it was necessary. A closeness had been forged between them that had never been there before.

Val and Aub read carefully through the following:

Memorandum of Agreement Papers
For the sum of Four Thousand Six Hundred and Seventy-eight Pounds.
443/6 acres being Blocks No 388 and 775 in the Berri Irrigation Area of Hamley
Together with
1. all buildings, sheds, racks trellises and fences, erections, fixtures, fittings, trees, vines, and other improvements thereon
2. the items of loose plant set out in the schedule hereto

The schedule of Loose Plant as Follows:

Item	Price in pounds	shillings	pence
Reversible 2-disc plough	10		
Horse 8-plate disc	8		
Bursting out unit 4-furrow	5		
Horse cultivator	6		
2 Single-furrow ploughs	10		
French plough	5		
Double-furrow harvest plough	8		
Horse hoe	2		
Manure seed drill	20		
2 Horse mower	10		
Hay rake	10		
2 Leaf harrow and beam	3		
1 Dray	3		
2 Horse trolley	10		
Cutting rake	1		
Spraying outfit complete with nozzle	15		
Riga dusting gun	5		
Fordson tractor complete, cultivator lift & drawbar and offset disc	240		
2 Block horses	15		
340 Dip buckets	59	10	
200 Picking buckets	5		

140 Picking bags	3	10	
Hessian and sisal craft	20		
250 2x3 Apricot trays	25		
200 Bricks	1		
4 Concrete six-ft. pipes	1	10	
3 Hammers, 10 washers. 60ft ¾ piping/sundries and cultivator tyres	1	10	
Crowbar, 3 shovels, 2 picks, 1 fork hoe	1	13	
2 Hoes, 1 scythe, 3 hay forks, 1 manure fork	2		
3 Tons lucerne	15		
Horse stable and trough	5		
1 Stiltson 24-inch, 1 stiltson 12-inch	1	9	6
1 4-inch Vice,	1	10	
3 pr Rollcut snips		7	6
2 pr Rollcut double hand new blades	15	6	
2 Grubbing axes		10	6
5 Prs picking sec		10	
2 Prs Riza sec		18	
2 Pruning saws		7	6
1 Hand saw 2' long		7	6
2 Chisels, 2 trowels		11	
30 Dozen outlet pipes	1	10	
3 Dozen W.W. strainers		9	
1 Scythe		2	
1 Sulpher box		10	
Cow chain peg and hammer		10	
2 Sumps	4		
2 Tons dipwood	1		
50 Mixed posts	2	10	
1 Garden hoe		3	
1 Pair orange secs		7	6
1 Ton mixed manure	3		
2-wheel Fruit handcart	2		
14' Steel pipe		10	
1 Green feed cutter	2	10	
120' Clothesline		3	
Total	553 pounds	6 shillings	6 pence

On 7 June 1948, the agreement was signed, and 250 pounds were paid by way of deposit, with the remainder to be paid on receipt of transfer papers.

Now he had his piece of land!

Aub gave notice at work and he and Val packed up with great excitement. He sold his car to get some money and they moved into the house next door to their block. He was full of ideas and energy and couldn't wait to get into it and make things happen the way he wanted. Everything he wanted to do was a priority and he wanted it all done yesterday.

Jenny began school at Glossop Primary School, with her little case, and her special lunch in her tin, and new pencil case with two pencils in it. Marilyn took it all in her three-year-old stride, singing to herself and playing in her own little world.

When they moved across to their own house, Vince (the previous owner) was to live there for another three months. He was dour and brooding, and when he did say something it was mostly unpleasant and he expressed disagreement with what they were doing with the property. Aub had a few things of his own he'd like to say, but prudence suggested it should wait until the living situation was different.

He had found the horses unwilling and untrustworthy, and it was clear they had been badly treated. It was too late to improve their temperament as working horses. He felt sorry for them, but they were a liability, particularly with two young girls around, and there was no room for sentiment. He had to let them go, which meant he had paid for them for nothing.

Things came to a head the day Aub went into Vince's room to check if water had leaked through the ceiling from a pipe in the roof. Vince was out. Aub knew there was a communist flag in the bottom of the window, but he wasn't prepared for the hand grenade hanging underneath the windowsill. He didn't bother to check if the pin was in it or not, and reported it as required, angry as anything that it was even there. (Quite a lot of men had kept war souvenirs and it was mandatory that if any were found they must be reported and the site must be inspected and checked for safety.) The powers that be came to inspect the room and although they made no comment on what they found and removed, they moved Vince on. Val and Aub finally had the property to themselves.

28

That the house was old and not in good repair wasn't unusual, as living quarters weren't factored into the cost of the land and plant for sale. The stone building had two main rooms (lounge and bedroom) each twenty feet by twelve, a long thin pantry, four feet wide, and a store room eight feet by ten. On the side was a lean-to kitchen and bathroom. A veranda ran along the side, and a half-height wall at the front had the top filled in on one end to make a lean-to sleepout. A huge old fireplace served both the lounge and the main bedroom, and it wasn't unusual for a cloud of soot and a black clod or two to fall into the room. When a bat was found flying around in the bedroom, Aub rapidly sealed that side up.

The ceilings had been painted with kalsomine and were decorated with strings of peeling paint that hung down in ribbons and curls and ultimately dropped on the floor. Val was continually getting up on a chair to brush them down with her broom, and it was quite a stretch being only five foot two and trying to reach a twelve-foot ceiling.

A tiny slab of concrete closed on two sides with a couple of sheets of galvanised iron housed both the copper and Val's old dolly tub, with two concrete washtubs (nearly as high as her) standing at the edge of the laundry, with a fierce-looking mangle mounted sentinel on the middle of them. The open drains from the old bathroom and laundry were a filthy, mucky, smelly mess that needed immediate attention.

The pan toilet under the apricot tree was shared with spiders and other creatures and featured a pretty pattern of light shining through the small holes in the galvanised-iron walls, with a thatch of square newspaper pieces dangling on a nail for decoration.

In the kitchen, there was a burnt-out wood stove, but Aub found a second-hand Metters stove in good condition and fitted that into the fireplace instead. Perched on top of this green and cream wonder was the fountain (with its little brass tap) that Val kept full for hot water. It was a wonderful feeling to have a home of their own and to look out towards the west and see their piece of land stretching away down to the Loveday hill in the distance.

Over the next few years, Aub spent every possible hour between morning and night working somewhere on the block. There was plenty to do. He was always a perfectionist, and everything was always done in the most time-consuming of ways. The improvements gradually began to take shape.

Rainwater tanks were put in to provide good drinking water, and a better chip heater went into the primitive bathroom. The girls were bathed in a large iron tub in the bathroom. Val cleaned the whole house up and painted what she could and made curtains for all the windows.

A tall, large old tabby cat, came with the property, and although she would disappear for days at a time and didn't like to be patted, she would otherwise sit outside near the back door and listen, and watch what was going on. She was seen now and then with a kitten or two, but Aub never found where she hid them, and they never seemed to appear grown. He named her 'Mumpuss'. She was an experienced and talented snake catcher and would often leave one, small or large, at the back door as much to say, 'There, see what I've done.' This was important, because there were plenty of snakes around, encouraged by the reed beds at the bottom of the block and the myriad of hiding and breeding places in general. Mostly they were brown or tiger snakes and everyone had to keep their eyes open, particularly if Aub was irrigating.

When the odd snake was found in the sitting room, it would disappear up into the webbing under the cut-moquette lounge suite. Everyone had to get out while Aub came in with his wide-mouthed shovel and upended the chairs and the lounge. The whole performance would be punctuated with banging and swearing until he could frighten out and kill the offender. He made up five-foot lengths of plaited twelve-gauge wire and placed one in the corner of each room so Val had a long flexible weapon if she needed it.

There were scorpions and centipedes too (but mostly they were outside) and when Val got a centipede bite on her big toe one night, it took ages to heal. None of these things worried Aub too much; they were just things you were used to when you grew up on the river. What did worry him was money. There was never any cash.

He bought an old 1927 Chevrolet cut down as a buckboard for a family car, and this served the job of a trailer as well. It was an awful squeeze to fit the whole family together on the front seat, with Marilyn sitting on Val's knee, under the canvas and perspex cover. It was a challenge to drive, but it did the job. It was a rattletrap and was generally viewed as such by the neighbours.

These were the beginning years in the area, and in order to develop the fruit industry, the earlier growers had agreed collectively to set up a cooperative system of processing and marketing. This operated through the cooperative packing sheds and the cooperative wineries.

The fruit was delivered and a door payment was made at a price per ton. Remaining payments were deferred to be paid to the grower in future years, at a price unknown, depending on the market at the time. Development and storage, marketing and delivery costs would all come out before the final payment to the grower could be calculated. While the door payment was cash, it didn't cover the grower's own development costs, irrigation fees, land tax and so on. And there was no guarantee of course on how much the future payments would be or when they might be made.

Purchases could be made from the cooperatives for plant and equipment, fertiliser and working materials, with any debt to be taken (under an overdraft system) from future payments as they came due. This allowed the packing sheds and the wineries the necessary capital for establishment, expansion and the development and supply of markets.

Money was the biggest problem on a daily basis. With no ongoing previous year's payments and needing to repay Myrtle at a higher rate than the soldier settlers were paying, there was no cash for daily living. Aub would go down to the creek and shoot a couple of rabbits, wood ducks or pigeons, and they would come home for the pot. The chooks laid eggs, and there was plenty of fruit. Val sewed and mended and was very resourceful with cooking and preserving. She cut the family's hair, including her own, and went without make-up or face creams, and there were no treats or outings. She washed up in the large dish on the table and coped with the most basic of cooking utensils. But there was still always a shortfall.

Inevitably, to earn cash, the sax came out of its case, and at night after a long day's work on the block, Aub went out playing dance music till the wee hours of the morning. Val would wash and iron and cook while he was out, always with the radio on, and sometimes till one in the morning. She worked a full day on the block as the 'permanent man', so all of her household jobs had to happen at night.

Aub was always tired, but he wouldn't give in. He was determined to get the block the way he wanted it. The first few years disappeared in a haze of the seasonal work each variety of fruit demanded. Soon they realised that having such a variety of crops wasn't such a good thing from a work perspective. There was never ever a break, even for a couple of days. The working of each small area, constant pruning and harvesting, and the general upkeep of all the trees and vines were gradually taking their toll and weren't cost-efficient.

Aub developed nasty boils around his neck and needed to go into Berri each evening to the hospital so that they could be lanced and dressed, and he was given penicillin.

'You're run down, and if you don't change things, you can expect your body to come up with more drastic measures to make you do it.' The warning was delivered with a glare, and Aub decided that since the doctor had no money worries, he wasn't in a position to tell him what to do, and besides he had no sense of humour.

Of course, he carried on, draining the water bag in the heat, and warming up with a tot of port and brandy when the icicles hung on the orange trees in the morning. He was pioneering his own piece of ground, and Val was his right-hand man, and they would succeed.

Some of the vines and trees weren't flourishing as they should be, and tests showed that their roots were wet, showing that the water table was too high. The only way to fix it was to put in some deep drains. They were necessary but would mean another expense that this time had not been foreseen.

It was time to reassess the game. They sat down together in a forced review of the situation. Aub drew out a drainage and irrigation line across the map of the block, taking into account the slope of the land. They needed deep drainage and irrigation pipes right across the property. He didn't blanch at the digging of six-foot drains, laying of pipes and sinking of sumps, but to buy the pipes he would have to lift to a worrying level the leverage the packing shed already held.

Young Roger Hollitt, who lived just down the road, was leaving school. He was a big strong lad and could certainly handle a shovel, so Aub employed him. The digging was too heavy for Val. They began the mammoth task of digging the drains by hand, through the heavy loam and stone under the topsoil, armed with six-foot crowbars, wide-mouthed shovels and trenching shovels, and solid steel pitchforks.

Each night, Aub would sharpen the shovel blades, and in the morning the edges would be shiny. By the following evening, they'd be blunt and dull, and he'd do it all again. The heavy work continued for months (through all weathers) whenever they could fit it in between other jobs. They dug to a depth of at least six feet six inches, and Aub in his usual demand for perfection measured carefully. The drains crawled across the sultana patch, and slowly crawled on. They found stones and snakes and aching muscles and bones, but the digging went on. All in all, the two of them dug a length of thirty-six chains, laying the pipes as they went. It was a huge improvement, all done by hand, in the absence of the mechanical diggers that were to be available in years to come.

All of the plantings improved over the next year and the results were worth the cost and the effort. Still Aub wasn't satisfied. To him, it was obvious that the soil supported sultanas, wine grapes and stone fruit better than some other varieties, and the slight slope of the land meant the irrigation could be made more efficient. He wanted to change the plantings and reset the rows to better suit a pipeline irrigation system. Of course, this would take years, and there would be less income while it was being done. If the new plan was to happen, it was going to happen right.

Val was tired. Although she knew he was right, the thought of more debt, when she never had enough money for mere essentials, scared her. It meant grubbing out, clearing, new trellising, planting, and waiting several years before the new crops were viable and they could see the returns. The sheer amount of work, as well as the usual picking, pruning, spraying and so on frightened the daylights out of her. And they would need a new tractor. It was never a thought in her mind to say 'No' to Aub, but it all seemed to be never-ending.

It took time and was mentally draining to look after Jenny, who was finding school very difficult, and of course she had to look after Marilyn, Aub and herself as well. She would drop the girls at school (because Jenny couldn't ride a bike) and pick them up unless it was a good day for them to walk, but she was never able to attend visiting days, or welfare club, or school picnics and sports days, because she was always working down the block. Anyway, she lived in her overalls and didn't have the clothes to wear. There was no time any more to sew for herself. Covering school books, mending and making clothes and such, always had to happen in the wee hours of the morning. The inconvenience of the old house with its bleeding ceilings, non-fitting floors and skirtings, archaic toilet, its excuse for a bathroom and laundry, together with a barely basic kitchen, would just have to wait, and the car was only just still running.

They had lost touch with many of their friends, other than perhaps running into them at the shop or the shed, and there was no time to go off seeing family. Fortunately, now and then some of them would call in on a weekend, knowing they'd find them working down the block. Val would whip a cloth on the table and make a cuppa with some eats, while she mostly hosted them in her overalls, leaving her rubber working boots at the back door.

To her extreme credit, she never questioned what Aub thought or said. It was how it was going to be. Neither of them was shy of hard work, and she just hoped that, somehow, they would get through.

The Bluff

29

The new plan needed new money, and it didn't allow for the doctor's advice to Aub that he should cut back on the work and do a bit less. In fact, he saw the message as a sign that he should do everything he could before his body might start to slow down.

He arranged with the packing shed to take another forward advance for development costs, and although it hurt to do it, it was a help. He'd paid Myrtle well ahead on the repayments, and she agreed for him to make interest-only payments until the principal balanced out. He arranged for his bank manager (whom he'd known for many years) to come and view the property as it stood, and to view the new planting plans. He wanted to keep them fully informed of his position. He knew he was raising the stake against their future once more, and there was always the risk of frost or storm damage wiping out a crop, and of losing the expected income that went with it. There was very little room for things to go wrong, and he just had to make it work. It was time to back his own hand.

He designed the plantings to run in long rows following the natural fall of the land. With wide headlands left for the tractor to turn at the top and bottom of the patches, this would mean much easier and more efficient working. The last of the open channelling would be replaced with a pipeline operated from an outlet set behind the strainer post on each row. Of course, this meant more trenching, more pipes and the casting of concrete to make the outlets. Besides this, the old tractor was prone to drift sideways down the row in the sand, which made it hard to drive for any length of time, and it was too heavy for Val. A new tractor was a definite priority.

Aub was young enough to feel enthusiastic about what was to come.

The first patch of vines was pulled out and stacked for burning down near the Puddletown lake. Sighting and measuring was done, and the rows of new posts could be seen from the kitchen window marking out the new sultana patch. They were very excited to see the plans begin to take shape.

Gruelling days in the heat and the dust, freezing windy days during the winter, times when bones and muscles ached beyond capability, autumns and springs, harvests, and prunings, and irrigations, all passed in a continued, frenzy of determination to keep going. Aub was a non-stop machine. Eventually sultanas (drying grapes), doradillos, gordos, grenache and malbec (wine grapes) filled the large attractive patches seen from the kitchen window.

He knew he couldn't beat the weather. The elements rule the land, the markets govern the prices, and prices govern the returns. There are always good years, better years and bad years when you live on the land. It was the ever-present unknown. In a violent storm, even in as little as half an hour, a whole year's harvest could be wiped out.

He would see the broody clouds stacking up dourly on the far horizon. He'd always said that grandfather Jury's horses knew if it would rain or blow over, and the bull ants were a good indication, depending if they were 'digging out' or 'filling in'. He'd hear the distant thunder, or feel the stillness, or feel the breeze lift, or be aware of the ache in his broken toe, and try to remember the signs, so he could gauge the rain as accurately as the old man had done.

Sometimes the seasons were kind. Sometimes the tail end of the northern monsoons would dip low, and sheets of pouring water would ruin a peach crop, or a severe hailstorm would strip the vines, leaving a mess of useless berries underneath. Or light sleety rain would coat the warm leaves, and leave them to be destroyed by downy mildew, or Jack Frost would visit, and leave his wizened calling card.

One year, the ground was white with frost for several days, a harbinger of things to come. Then, one early morning, ice dropped in shards from the wires, burning the new shoots on the doradillos in a vista of black waste. It had spread widely across the district, leaving catastrophic damage even to the citrus crops. Hail had wiped out the berries of last year's grape crop in a patchy pattern across the shiraz, and the tonnages had been well down. The hailstorm had gone through rapidly, on a narrow front, and Aub and Steve Wade had both been caught by its malevolence. That was a very bad year.

When strong winds and gales blew in the summer, dust storms were legend. As the winds lifted, the sky would glow in an ominous red swirling cloud that cut out the sun. Red sand lifted from the ground being cleared and worked-up in the Mallee, where there were no plantings to protect the topsoil from the howling winds. You could see it coming, and everything had to be shut down and put away. It would come with choking speed, hot grains of red dirt stinging and sandblasting legs and arms, stinging eyes and smothering everything in thick red grit. It got into every crevice and crack, caked into motors and pipes, and spread an eerie, evil red hue far and wide. Even inside the house, the kitchen would be pasted in a red film of gritty dust. It was awful.

The clean-up was awful too. What a job. Aub would start cleaning out the sheds while Val attacked the house, sweeping the dust off the cupboards with a small broom and dustpan before washing them. Everything you touched was rough and gritty. The trees and vines looked dusty and dirty and would stay like that until it rained. You could never quite get rid of it all, and household washing was a frightful job. Bathwater looked like henna, and their hair needed a thorough scrub until the water going down the drain was clear.

These severe weather events left crippling debt in their wake, and at times Aub would be in severe doubt about the good intentions of the Lord. In later years, these storms would be a thing of the past as the Mallee land was planted with crops.

The problem with the co-op agreement was that interest piled up on your debt and, as years were passing before final payments for fruit were made, it was a nightmare to clear it. New funds were needed all the time to keep the property working. It was like walking a tightrope, and there were lots of growers struggling with the worry. Little did they know that an even more perfect storm was brewing.

Europe had been repositioning and rebuilding after the war, and a European Common Market was being formed, a trade alliance (with member countries) that would change the current markets for Australian wheat, wool, goods and fruit. To add to this, the Australian government wasn't helping. Robert Menzies was still prime minister and, in general, Aub thought he was doing a good job. Now, though, he was angry, because the government had lifted an embargo and allowed the importation of Turkish figs into the Australian market.

His mate Allan Campbell weathered the storm for a while, but it didn't take long to see that his big fig property was a casualty. He was by far the biggest commercial fig grower in the district, and it was obvious that although he also had some vines, he would have to diversify further. He was devastated at having to bulldoze his perfectly good trees because the crop was no longer viable. Aub went down and viewed the destruction of the much-loved fig patch. The bulldozing and piling the trees together ready to dry enough for burning, and its effect on his mate, were too much. As the days went by and the job was completed, his angst grew into a concise and fiercely directed disgust. The senselessness, the waste and the despair all because of a stupid government policy.

He'd always been interested in politics, with little time for Labor Party policies, but he had never joined a party before. He took his anger and his chequebook and became a paying member of the Liberal Party, in order to have some say against such nonsense. From then on, he attended meetings regularly for the next few years. He never hesitated to state his case, based on a carefully thought-out position. He believed like his grandfather had told him, that landholders had every right to be heard in the formulation and development of government policy.

Money, or the lack of it, was still the ever-present thorn in his side.

Following the storms and the reduction in sales and prices at the packing shed due to the new Common Market, his debt levels were perilous.

The day came when two men from the packing shed arrived to discuss the matter. All three knew each other of course, which made the conversation even more difficult. Aub met them by the underground tank after he'd banished Val to the house, with the message that there would be no cups of tea offered. He knew they were only doing their job, but they got a wage every week, and didn't have to put their lives and their families' lives on the line to be able to afford a living. As far as he was concerned, they had better be very careful what they said.

After a very short preamble came the nub of the matter.

'Aub, you'll have to sign a lien against the property, giving us the right to sell it if the amount can't be reduced after the next harvest.'

'No, I bloody well won't! And since it is still my land, you can bloody well get off it!'

They left in a hurry, but the boiling anger didn't leave Aub. He was furious that anyone might think he couldn't pay his debts – he had never let anyone down in his life and he'd damn well pay them somehow. He'd always paid what he owed, always accepted his responsibilities, always been aware of the chance of failure, and had always somehow made things work out. There was no way he was going to go under.

It reminded him of the way he'd felt after his dad had died, worried sick about money. He was taciturn and morbid. By the very nature of the block work, he frequently spent long hours alone, and he would talk little when he came inside, spending the evening playing his sax if he wasn't going out to play for a dance. Like his mother before him, no one outside of the house would ever guess how close to the line he was. The shoulders were straight, and the head was up. He didn't realise how much like his mother he had become.

Val knew well by now that this was the time to keep quiet and just go on with the things she needed to do to keep the family in clean clothes and food, as well as doing the hand work down the block.

But Aub wasn't the only one who was upset; so was she. Jenny was often difficult, understandably throwing tantrums out of frustration, and it wasn't possible to reason with her. Every day brought conflict and stress, and it was difficult to know where to draw the line and when to discipline her. She would loudly say 'I'm the boss' and it was true. Marilyn would disappear up to play with the Harris children, and Val didn't blame her. Sometimes she would have escaped too if she could.

30

The reprieve came unexpectedly and unannounced, in the guise of a small, middle-aged, little Chinese man.

Aub found him walking around the block, or he found Aub – or whatever. He said he ran and owned a fruit stall in the Melbourne market, and had come to the area looking for a source of quality fresh mandarins, to be provided by someone he could rely on for supply. A common acquaintance of them both (in Melbourne) had recommended he see Aub, and he had come to the block to have a look for himself, to walk around the different trees, and to see if he wanted to deal with Aub. He had been let down before.

Aub was cautious and had it not been for their mutual friend he probably wouldn't have entered into any discussion at all. Being committed to the cooperative scheme it was a departure for him to sell fruit for cash, and growers had found themselves out of pocket before when the expected cheque didn't arrive. It wasn't something he'd thought about, and his friend hadn't rung him to warn him he might be approached. But his back was against the wall.

Val provided a nice lunch of course, and after a long discussion, a deal was made regarding quantity, price and transport. The arrangement proved to work very well, and it grew and continued for the following years while the buyer maintained his market stall.

The cash reduced the immediate pressure and meant the loan advances from the packing shed were gradually being reduced. Then as the new plantings began to produce crops, every extra penny went towards paying Myrtle's loan off first. At last they were beginning to see some results from their years of worry and work.

Believing in the continued development of the country, Aub was in agreement with the current policy that was bringing migrants in from Europe under the government migrant labour scheme, and Aub enrolled to take part.

With the new vines coming into production, extra labour was needed, but it was very hard to get local workers, as most were fully employed. Each grower was allocated men, but he must guarantee at least two months' living quarters, meals and work, regardless of their character or performance. The men were mostly Italian or Greek and some were Czechoslovakian or Yugoslavian, with a sprinkling of other nationalities as well.

Aub usually employed two men at a time during the grape harvest and arranged with his neighbour (Eddie Harris) for them to live in his picking quarters. All of their meals were shared with the family, but with two young daughters in the house, he was cautious about having them live in the home until he had a feeling for what sort of men they were. On the boats coming out, they were taught about Australian money and were also armed with a small translation book of basic words and phrases that was supposed to help them understand the language.

Over his several years' involvement with the scheme, men came in all shapes and sizes and temperaments, wanting to make a new start for themselves or to send money home to their families. The legacy from the war was a changed Europe with many people wanting to leave. Having travelled from the south and the north of Europe, and everywhere in between, there was sometimes bad feeling as the result of old simmering tensions between the various regions at home.

When the train arrived in Berri, they spilled out onto the platform clutching their papers in hand. The interpreters would match their name with the allocated grower. There was never much luggage, usually just one small case or bag.

They would arrive home with Aub from the train, and everyone would sit down in the kitchen for a cup of tea and some sandwiches and cake. The first job would be to introduce everyone. This wasn't easy, because it depended where they came from, whether their Christian name or surname came first, and it often took some time just to sort out what they should be called.

Mostly they had no English and, of course, Aub and Val had none of their language either. Sometimes it was possible to work out how many they had left behind in their family, and what their job had been at home, but mostly it was several weeks before this came to light. There was a lot of shaking of heads, shrugging of shoulders, hand signals, blank looks, and a little laughter. The migrants must have felt quite homesick, but Val did what she could for them over the ensuing weeks.

The language was a problem too in explaining the work to be done, but with the best will on the part of both parties and lots of hand signals, this was usually achieved one way or another. There was often a high degree of frustration on both sides, and tempers needed to be managed, and tensions released, with as little explosiveness and surliness as possible.

Aub was a fair boss who never asked anyone to do something that he wouldn't, and he was always working hard alongside them. Sometimes a good friendship was forged, and at other times it was good to see the pickers move on. For everyone involved, it was a challenging and character-building experience.

Aub was particularly worried one year when the two pickers were from the opposing regions of Trieste and Sicily in Italy, areas that had a traditional distrust of each other. The lad from Sicily was a pleasant, sunny, happy man who worked hard and interacted well with the family. He always sent money home to his mother for his 'littley' sister. The other migrant was a tall, fair Italian who looked down on his compatriot and belittled him at every opportunity. 'Cosimo, he animal,' he would sneer, accompanied by hand and facial gestures. Cosimo would continue his work and ignore the constant niggling and belittling, but it was nasty and, despite being warned, Ferdinand refused to modify his behaviour.

On a rare day off, Aub and Val went down to Katarapko Creek

yabbying, and when they came home Cosimo was sitting on the veranda sewing a button on his pants. At dinner time, the other man didn't appear, and when asked about him, Cosi shrugged.

Towards the end of the meal, the taller man arrived, asking if Cosimo had gone, saying, 'He animal. I not sit with him.'

Aub took a dim view of this and said, 'If you want a meal, you'll sit down.'

But he remained standing outside the wire door. Cosimo said he would leave, but as he approached the door his compatriot pulled out a knife saying, 'I kill him! I kill him!'

With the family at the table, Aub gestured to Val, and then pointed to the guns that stood in the gap between the kitchen cupboards. 'If you're going to kill him, don't do it on my property. Get out on the bloody road and do it. And see those guns – you move, and I'll blow your bloody leg off!'

Val called the police, and then pushed the frozen girls and Cosimo into the lounge room. With the aggressor frightened to move, Aub stood his ground until the police arrived and took him away. He spent the night in a cell, while Aub (fulfilling his obligation to provide work and living) rang around to find another grower who needed a man and would take him on. On the following morning (after his release), he took him and his possessions over to another grower at Monash.

A police warning had been issued, but Aub issued one of his own, leaving no doubt about not coming onto his property again nor about leaving Cosimo alone! Fearing reprisal against Cosi, they moved him into the house to live. He stayed for several months, became a friend, and in later years became a sugar-cane farmer in northern Queensland.

Another challenge came when the picker Sarantis, who was such a nice man, was so completely hopeless at the work in hand. He would smile away, and you couldn't dislike him, but he was smaller than Val and couldn't even pick up a sweat box. Aub needed someone who could do the work, but he had to meet his guarantees and couldn't afford to take someone else on as well.

Sarantis was very willing and would rush in and then get upset because he couldn't manage. He arrived one morning with his phrasebook and managed to get out, 'Mr Jury, very sorry, no good for farm.' He must have worked on it all night.

Clearly, everyone was stressed, so Aub made an appointment for them to see a government interpreter from the labour scheme. He learned that Sarantis had been an optician in his own country! No wonder he was struggling. Aub got the interpreter to explain that he would try to find a job better suited to him.

Two days later, he borrowed Arch Slaven's car and took Sarantis and his gear down to Adelaide. He had given it a lot of thought and took him to see the employing officer for Laubman and Pank opticians. Of course, they were sure nothing was available, and Sarantis would need Australian training and so on. Aub started discussing how hard the language problem was, and it got amusing, until he then asked how they communicated with their Italian clients, for example. Why didn't they have their own interpreter for something as difficult to assess as an eye test?

In the end, it was agreed that Sarantis would begin with them and would work interpreting for Italian clients, with some cost sharing by Aub. In later years, Sarantis was able to become an optician in his own right and settled successfully with his family.

31

Everyone was excited when the new tractor was due to arrive – a Fordson Major of course. On a clear and sunny day, Val and the girls dropped Aub in Berri at Murray Motors. Then they waited for him to get home to see the new addition. It took him ages, or so it seemed, but of course, top speed was around five miles an hour. He finally arrived on the shiny, blue, noisy and very big machine. Jenny was scared of it, but Marilyn was very impressed. There was a big toolbar on its short back, and a large shiny round radiator cap on its long front, with a great big seat in the middle. Two massive wheels (more than twice as tall as Marilyn) straddled the sides, and two smaller wheels were set at the front. Val wanted to learn to drive it straight away, and she and Aub went laughing down the block on the roaring big blue smelly monster. They were so happy, because this altered everything. Now it was so much easier to work the rows, to burst out ready for the water, to disk and to cultivate. The old tractor was lined up to become a permanent belt drive for pumping water into the overhead tank, so even that job was easier.

Being a perfectionist in all things, Aub was meticulous with his equipment. He was careful with how he set his implements up, and always made sure they were correct weights and so on. He had jointly purchased some new implements with his friend Horrie Mudge, and they shared the use of them. Horrie was practical but not so meticulous, but his son Barry made up for it, so the arrangement worked well.

A few months later, Val woke up 'thingy' in the morning. She'd had a dream during the night and had seen Aub hanging from the tractor. He was due to do some disking, and she was adamant that he shouldn't go. She wasn't normally given to this sort of thing, and he was cross about her being so ridiculous, and they argued about it over breakfast. Unusually again, Val got really sulky, and was upset and wooden-faced when he left.

At 10.30 in the morning, it happened. He was suddenly upside down, caught with his boot in the spoke of the steering wheel, with his head hanging down towards the disk. The tractor was still moving, and he knew if he fell he would die. He had no idea what had happened, but he knew that when he hit the walnut trees at the end of the row, he would be jolted down into the sharp plates. He could see the vines going by and the ground below him. His mind was frozen, and he couldn't think. He was desperate, kicking with his foot at the ignition toggle behind the wheel, scared his boot might slip out of its trap between the spokes. He was dizzy and disoriented, trying to grab something solid above him with his hands. By sheer luck, and in desperation, he managed to knock the motor toggle off, and the tractor stopped. He hung upside down in the eerie silence, with danger still only inches below his head.

Weak and spinning, he had to get himself out without falling on the sharp plates, and there was no one around to call out to for help. Gradually, scared of the sharp blades below him and shaking badly, he managed to manoeuvre upwards and to pull himself out. He lay on the ground exhausted, numb and blank with shock.

When he finally got to his feet and looked at the tractor, he was promptly sick on the ground. The assembly plate and seat mounting between the large side wheels had broken across the front and tilted backward, taking the seat with it. It couldn't happen – but it had.

He walked into the kitchen ashen, white, and couldn't even explain to Val what had happened. He sat sick at the table, while she got him a warm jacket and made a cup of tea with a shot of brandy to help stop him shaking. It had been a very close call.

When he could, he rang Murray Motors to tell them what had happened and they thought he was being funny. 'Yeah. Good one. No way. Couldn't happen, Aub!'

He coldly and quietly delivered the message, 'Get out here now'. He couldn't even swear.

The dealer, who was also a friend, was speechless at the sight of it. He phoned Ford in Sydney, and after getting to the right person, and acting on instructions, cordoned the area off, with nothing to be touched until the assessor arrived. Aub didn't even want to look at it – he knew how lucky he was to be alive. His number wasn't up.

The assessor went through the process of examining and weighing the disk and the toolbar, finding that none of the recommended weight limits had been exceeded. They checked everything, and it was agreed that the central platform had broken, and it was attributed to metal fatigue – a one off fault in a brand-new machine. Ford replaced the tractor immediately and delivered the second new shiny beast out to the block. They were excellent, but the gloss was gone, and although Aub knew it had been a one-off 'lemon' problem, he was never again complacent about driving his Fordson.

It was completely inexplicable that Val had seen the image in her dream, because she wasn't superstitious and hadn't believed in that 'rubbish' until now. Aub frequently made the comment that true life was stranger than fiction, and in this case it had been very true.

Playing It Out

32

Very occasionally on a hot evening (work permitting), he'd feel like a swim and he'd take the family down to Lake Bonney, as he couldn't take the girls to the river. He often thought about swimming in the river and he missed it. He was a very frustrated swimming teacher, because to him it was easy, and he couldn't understand why Jenny couldn't get the hang of it and couldn't just float. Listening to Jenny shrieking, Marilyn would get frightened of having a go, and the resulting fiasco was always unpleasant. Nevertheless, it was a real change for them, and afterwards they would all pile into the old buckboard and sing all the way home, with Marilyn perched on Val's knee in the single narrow cab.

Unfortunately, working all the time, coupled with the distance, meant there was not a lot of opportunity to see other family. Thora and Arthur would try to call up every six months or so, Clarrie would come to stay for a few weeks, and Val's mother would come over for a month

each year. Aub still didn't like her, and it was still mutual, but they observed a respectful truce and got on together without any unpleasantness.

It was always good to have Clarrie to stay, and she was much loved by Val and the girls. Age and the years had increased the differences in the way Aub and his mother thought, but they were able to accept this and to choose to keep away from those topics. Just the same, he had found some of her judgements over the years to be harsh. She was older now, though, and accepted that he was his own man, but he still felt her measuring him against his father Stan.

Clarrie loved being able to walk out and pick fresh fruit, announcing, 'The doctor said it's good for me.'

Of course, at the time the doctor hadn't realised she'd be staying on a fruit block. She was diabetic, and he was none too happy at her next visit after she got home. She listened to her radio serials each day, *Dr Paul* and *Blue Hills*, always with her cup of weak black tea, enhanced with a slice of lemon, and she wrote the day's recipe down in her red-covered book. She was slim now that she was older, but her piercing gaze was as clear and direct as always. The girls adored her and called her 'Meem'.

Dolly had remarried – a friend of Ivor's from the air force. Don Frey was very good with Ivor's children, and Aub was very grateful that Dolly was happy and well cared for, and he kept in touch as much as he could. Sometimes they would turn up out of the blue for a few hours, when the whim took Don to have a day's run in the car, and it was a pleasant surprise, and there was always lots of talking.

News of Bill (brother Athol) was sparse, and Aub missed him. It was expensive to phone, and the occasional exchange of letters was always welcome, but they never really satisfied Aub's curiosity about Bill's life and how the family really were.

Val's family were all in Victoria except for her brother Len, and again letters had to suffice. Len used to call in with his happy smile, his latest joke and his bits of news. He was a funny man with a witty sense of humour, and with lots of sayings he always brightened up Aub's day. He and Jean and son Lynton lived at Renmark, and Len owned the Renmark West grocery store that had the huge Rosella parrot painted on the side. One day he arrived with their brother Les, and Val cried. She hadn't seen Les for nearly twenty years.

The girls always spent Christmas in the Hilton home in the early years. There would be carols (with Dot playing the piano) on Christmas Eve, and some friends would come in. There were carols in the street too when the Salvation Army band played on the corner

outside the house. The girls loved Dot's pretty decorations, and Betty would help them to make some as well, to hang on the tree. The tinsel was bright and shiny, and there were coloured birds clipped on the tree, and Marilyn always thought it must be what Fairyland was like. Aub and Val would arrive in time to share Christmas lunch, and stay until evening. Myrtle would come in the afternoon.

Aub wasn't a great one for Christmas. Nana had died on that day and it had been a cruel loss for him. He was pleased that Val and the girls enjoyed it, but he'd find himself thinking about the fruit getting ripe on the trees.

The date was notable in the family too, because Nana and Grandfather had married on that day, and it was also Myrtle's birthday. Aub remembered all the years when he wouldn't miss going to church at Christmas, and he still felt the religious significance of the occasion but had no wish to pursue it.

Auntie Myrtle was known for her lack of generosity, both with family and friends, and she was certainly known for it on birthdays and at Christmas. She never gave anything away unless it was something she had been given that she didn't want, so it was no surprise when they opened the cellophane package for the girls to receive a handkerchief wrapped around a calendar dated several years ago. Aub, though, would always make sure she got some little bonus with his repayment in December, never forgetting that she had given him and Val access to a commercial loan when no one else would. They were still working hard to repay it as soon as they could.

Apart from his sax playing, his social life was simple. Occasionally they went fishing but he wasn't so keen to go shooting now because there were more people camping everywhere, and you couldn't be sure where they were, and what went up must come down, and he didn't want any accidents.

33

He didn't mind drying the sultanas, but they were labour-intensive. First they needed to be picked into the sieve-holed dip tins to be cold caustic dipped and drained. Then they took time to spread onto the wire racks to dry. After several weeks, they could be shaken down onto hessian, and then transferred onto sisal-craft sheets. These would first be raked over to remove the stalks and rubbish and then each night they were wrapped up to avoid the overnight dew and frost. Of course, each morning they'd be raked out into the sun again. The result was sweat boxes of beautiful clean dried sultanas. It was well into autumn before the process was finished.

One year, however, Aub's careful attention to things didn't stop his rack collapsing when it was loaded with fruit. Tons and tons of freshly dipped sultanas, crushed on top of each other – ten tiers of wires, over thirty-odd yards long, dumped unceremoniously on the ground after a massive crack as the strainer post gave way. All hands were needed to pull it up. Friend Barry Mudge arrived, the neighbours and Roger Hollitt all came, and the massive task began. Tractors reared up on their wheels as they struggled and strained to pull the wires back up. Tempers flared, and if you weren't doing something, it was best not to be an onlooker! The work was dangerous and tedious. It was a long, long, day, and complete disaster was only avoided because of everyone's help. One of the tractors had to be left standing sentinel at the top of the rack, chains attached, until extensive proper repairs could be made. It didn't help Aub's enthusiasm for drying sultanas.

By comparison, the wine grapes were picked by hand onto split wheat bags placed down the centre of each second row. Mostly a gang of about six people would be used to pick loads of around seven tons

at a time. The middle row was left clear for the tip truck to drive along while the bags of grapes were thrown up into it from each side. This was very heavy work that challenged every muscle in the body.

Val's job was to stand on top of the load and throw the empty bags back down. As the level of grapes in the truck increased, she stood higher and higher on the very slippery, dangerous load. The driver needed to be very careful that he didn't jerk the truck and throw her off. It was a dangerous job, and she was always relieved when loading was finished and they could all sit down to share a cold beer.

It was inevitable that after a few years the decision would be made to replace the time-consuming sultanas with wine grapes, leading to another section of the block being grubbed out, pipelined, trellised and replanted. Neither Aub nor Val could imagine how technology would change the way digging, pruning, picking, processing and irrigation would change over the next fifty years, but for them, in these years, it all had to be done by hand.

The citrus trees were easier to manage. The dead wood would be cleaned out regularly, blood and bone would be spread and irrigation would be carried out in the usual manner. When they were picked, Val packed the fruit by hand into the boxes ready for sale. Oranges, though, were no longer worth much for sale, being replaced on the new European Common Market by citrus from Spain, Portugal and other Mediterranean countries. Another group of plantings needed to be removed.

The soil was particularly suited to apricots. Aub was scheming and his plan was to have five hundred trees of two different varieties, one ripening earlier than the other. It would require a special cutting shed, trailer tooling, pruning platforms and a considerable gang of workers in the summer. Trees took around seven years to come into full production, so the plantings would be done a section at a time. He was picturing cutting benches, trolleys and sulphur boxes in his head and planning for a large drying shed to go over on the dry block. He was excitedly planning his project, totally absorbed with what he was doing and driven to get it done.

It seemed to Val that all they ever did was keep starting again and again. It was wearing a bit thin, and she was finding it harder to cope with the back-breaking work and the heat. She was getting older and finding she didn't quite have the same energy and thought, 'God only knows where Aub gets his.' She could see the improvements they'd made, though, and when she thought back to where they'd started, she found it hard to believe how far they'd come.

An unexpected pleasure (and reward for Aub's fastidiousness in all things) came in 1954 when the new young Queen Elizabeth came to visit Renmark. The local packing shed was asked for the best dried apricots in the district to display on the dais and they chose Aub's beautiful Moorparks. These had the top rating as five-crown fruit, still perfectly round, and of good colour and perfectly clean and weighty. Of course, no one else knew or even thought about it, but Aub was silently very, very pleased. He always wanted to supply the best quality that he could, and this was a heart-warming recognition as far as he was concerned.

The visit itself was a long day with all the schoolchildren and local people grouped at the oval waiting with their flags and flasks and sandwiches. It was windy, and a pale Queen arrived having been very airsick in the very small plane from Adelaide. The sound of the speeches blew away in the wind, and after a brisk circle of the oval the Royal couple were gone. There was no doubt she didn't even notice the fruit, but Aub didn't care because *he* knew it was there.

The irrigation roster ruled the calendar. You applied to the department for a water allowance and were allocated an amount, usually metered by time. The date was set and generally couldn't be changed, because it messed up everyone else on the rosters. Jackie Mules (the water joey) would come round on his horse and cart to check that everything was booked correctly and that handover of the main stream to the next grower was efficient and timely. Water was expensive, so the best possible use had to be made of it each time.

For Aub, it was a necessary evil. The new pipeline serviced the whole twenty-three acres now, and watering took about three days and two or three nights, depending on what time the stream was handed over.

The bursting out of furrows would be completed in preparation, with four furrows between each row, and the concrete outlets would all be checked. Each patch would be watered separately so pressure was maintained. The water would be sent down the first furrow until it reached the bottom and then it would be cut over to the next furrow in turn. As the rows were long, this was a two-person job, with one at the bottom end signalling, and one at the top of the row cutting over.

At night of course, a hand signal was useless. So Val would be at the other end of the row with a tilley lantern waving a yes or a no. This needed to be done every four hours, meaning the whole twenty-three acres would be walked many times in the eighty-odd hours. With broken sleep and other daily things to do, it was exhausting. Nevertheless, it was one of the most important jobs of all because no water meant no crop, and no matter how urgent something else might be, the water always came first.

Tired when they were finished, Aub would take a couple of days to read. It was always something constructive. He liked to know about new things that were happening, new gadgets and implements that were being invented, politics, insects and pests, new ways of irrigating and in fact anything at all that was part of the technology and science of the changing world.

He read all he could about the newly developed rocket range at Woomera, and about the Blue Streak and the other rockets. He knew there was atomic testing happening at Maralinga, but there was little information about it and it seemed it was all being kept quite secret.

The Wild Card

34

The stench was stultifying. Like a putrid fog, it descended over everything, seeping into the senses and the very pores of the skin. Like the foul smell of dirty rags left too long in stagnant water, it assaulted the nose, with a dead, revolting stink. 1956 had been a dreadful year on the Murray.

The heavy rains had come early, and first this was good, but word came down from the Darling in March that the big rains in Queensland were feeding a high river. The Murrumbidgee was running a banker, and the water volume below the junction was going to be huge. There'd been floods before (the highest being in 1870), and there was reasonable confidence that lessons learned from the 1931 flood would help people to put plans in place to manage the situation. These floods didn't happen without warning, so there was plenty of time to prepare.

For three months, it poured, dumping annual rainfall and swamping the district. Some of the citrus growers in the area couldn't get on the ground to pick their crops. The river rose in April and again in May. Many of the locals thought the increased rainfall was because of the atomic tests at Maralinga, but of course, there was no proof of that.

The Renmark flats were low-lying and obviously at risk. Levee banks were rising around the district as quickly as they could be built. Tractors and graders came in and raised banks in places chosen by their geography and by the degree of urgency to protect them. The water level rose. The news from upstream was dire, and it was clear that this would be no ordinary flood.

People everywhere were filling sandbags, with men and women and older children all working together. All available tip trucks and anything that could capably carry dirt was utilised. Appeals were out across the state for wheat bags, manpower and trucks. Food was needed for the volunteers, and for many of the local families, as access roads were gradually becoming creeks.

Aub and his mate Allan Campbell went to the Hilton home in Renmark with a load of forty-four-gallon drums and long planks. It was just a precaution, Aub said to Dot, as the news was getting more and more worrying. They set the drums up and made a platform across them with the planks. All the non-essential furniture was loaded up on the platform, leaving room for the rest to go up in the event that the flood banks should break. Ern was not a well man by this time and couldn't do any lifting himself. He was of course too proud to ask anyone for assistance, and he was grateful that Aub was taking charge of the situation.

Cousin Betty, who was still living at home, joined the workers on the levee banks. While filling sandbags, she met Luke Monaghan, who had a block at Cooltong. They got along well, and ultimately married after the floods.

The Renmark schools were underwater, and students were billeted out into the Berri and Barmera districts. Those towns were flooded too, but parts were still accessible. The drains around the town backed up and ran free as the water table rose. As the hospital began to drown, patients were evacuated to other district hospitals in a logistical nightmare. Only essential services were allowed in and out of the town via a Bailey bridge put in by the army.

On the block, Aub was quite safe from flooding but, like everyone else, he was dismayed by the levels the waters reached. The ferries were of course unusable, and the locks had been open for weeks. For the whole length of the lower river, communities and properties were isolated. He thought of all the families he knew in the district – people he had called on while working for the T&G. In all his years, he had never seen anything like this, and could never have imagined in his wildest dreams the relentless destruction the river could wreak.

He felt some guilt that so many were suffering while he and his family were all right. He was greatly saddened for the many businesses that were going broke; he had had his back to the wall himself over the years. These poor beggars could do nothing to stop it, like Val's brother Len, who handed out groceries from his shop to people who couldn't pay, knowing as he did it that he would go broke.

The water kept rising, swallowing roads, vines and trees, houses, packing sheds, wineries and businesses. The creeks had disappeared, monstered by the insidious swirling waters that had claimed the land. People were being rescued in small boats and were evacuated into emergency shelters. Some, with their pets, were being billeted with friends, relatives and strangers, and the local radio was broadcasting constant alerts. In August, the waters reached the highest levels in the Murray's history, and many of the banks that had been holding gave up in a catastrophic sea of mud.

The impacts afterwards were enormous. The water lay across the flats for months, stagnant and stinking. The damage and devastation was everywhere. The logistics and costs of the planning and rebuilding were massive and daunting. Many people had no hope of starting again because of their age, or health, or lack of money and resources. Snakes, washed out of their natural homes and left in unfamiliar areas, were a real hazard, and the putrid smell filled the air no matter where you were.

So many people were destitute that money was urgently needed, and morale was low. Dean (Rocky) Page contacted Aub to say he was going to run some benefit concerts for the flood victims. Rocky was a country and western singer, a hypnotist and an entertainer. He was gathering a group of actors, singers, musicians and local comedians to put together his programme. Aub immediately said yes, of course he would help. The clarinet and the sax went off with him each night for rehearsals in Berri, and the show gradually came together.

The star was undoubtedly Rocky. He was a real entertainer, but Aub did have some concerns. There was a part of the show where

Rocky hypnotised himself and proceeded to show the power of the mind over the body. One of the acts involved him putting his head on one chair with his feet on another, and his body stretched between the two. He would then have a heavy man stand on top of his suspended body. After this performance, someone would have to bring him out of his trance, and Aub most certainly didn't volunteer to do it, but sometimes he had to. He was always afraid that for some reason Rocky wouldn't wake up, but fortunately he always did.

There was some excellent music, and singers and actors with skits, and the show was very well received. Many of the local people were generous with their time and their talent. They played in all the river towns, and throughout the Murray Mallee, and raised a good amount of money. The pleasure they gave people was a breathing space from the problems on their minds and helped to lift morale in the district. It was a credit to Rocky.

As the flats dried out over the summer, there was an increase in the mosquitoes, gnats and sandfly population. When it came time to harvest, the vinegar flies would rise in a cloud from the fruit into the hot sky. In some places, there were ridges of salt showing white on the clay as the pans dried out, and there were salinity problems throughout large parts of the district. Aub was very glad he'd put his deep drainage system in, and his block was looking pretty good.

Sadly, there had been a more personal blow for the family that year too. On 16 August, Clarrie, Aub's mother, died suddenly from a cerebral haemorrhage. The event had stolen her away quietly and quickly. She was only sixty-nine and had lived for thirty-three years missing her Stan. She had always said it was 'better to wear out than rust out' and she'd achieved her wish by dying suddenly while she was peeling potatoes.

It was a dreadful shock for everyone, especially Thora. Clarrie had lived with Thora and Arthur for almost their entire married life, and they had given her a wonderful home, sharing their love and their company, and their girls. It was a very sad gathering in Adelaide for the

funeral, and the years rolled back for Aub, to his very first memories as a small boy.

With no belief that there was anything after death, Aub again felt saddened and diminished by the loss. He didn't know if he had actually loved her, but he knew they had shared an extremely strong bond, and that he had the utmost respect for her, her strength of character, and what she had managed to do.

She had instilled a strong ethic of hard work, honesty and integrity, and a genuine concern for others in him and his siblings. She had been a strong advocate for education, saying it had the power to change lives. He had never seen her willingly do a bad turn to anyone, and although they didn't see eye to eye on many, many things, he had respected her opinions, knowing that they were based on her experiences from earlier times.

Her directness and no-nonsense approach to things was in a large part responsible for him having learnt not to outwardly express his emotions, and to hide them in silent moodiness. He had found her a hard taskmistress in his youth, and so a tender love had never been forged, but he had cared for her deeply.

As he'd grown older, he had begun to appreciate just how great the loss of Stan must have been for her, and just how much the direction of her life had been changed forever, when she was just thirty-six.

He was a bit confused by his mixed feelings, and he felt aged, in a subtle indescribable way.

Taking a Trick

34

Always up for a new interest, and being an experienced shooter, he joined the Barmera rifle club. As always, he had to have all the equipment, so the big shed housed a special vice for balancing stocks and barrels, measuring tools and so on, and often someone from the club would be there working on their guns. Aub liked the company, and the competition, and sometimes he would come home very happy having won the Cock of the Walk, and sometimes he would come home with a splitting head, and everyone would be very careful what they said. Often he'd present Val with a silver cake dish or a teaspoon that he'd won as spoils of the day. Surprisingly, given his poor sight, he was a good shot, but he developed tinnitus over the years from the noise. The ringing and whistling meant he always had company.

1958 was a better year on the block.

Many of the growers were now needing to replant due to salt damage, and because the changing market demands were making different varieties of fruits more viable. Aub had been a bit ahead of this, and the block was now a mix of wine grapes, and a very large proportion of newly planted stone fruits. There were good markets for all of them.

When the new trees began to produce, the work pace in the summer was frantic. Eight hundred apricot trays had to be washed and stacked in the cutting shed. A gang of up to twenty cutters and pickers was employed, and the days vanished in a haze of heat and work and work and heat. There was a camaraderie that survived long hours, criticism, praise, chiacking, rubbishing and the need to get the job done quickly.

The scorching temperatures would ripen the fruit, leaving it hanging like jelly if it wasn't picked. Each trailer load went up to the cutting shed and the tins were stacked into Aub's vertical steel frames, up off the dirt. Sometimes the ground would be too hot to walk on, even in working boots, and the pickers would join the cutters in the shed until the cooler part of the day. The water bags would be perched around on wire hooks, starting out like distended udders, and finishing the day looking like wrung-out bladders. There would be jokes and yarns and friendly one-upmanship. Morning and afternoon tea were provided by Val, and at night after a full day's work she'd begin cooking cake and biscuits for the next day.

On Boxing Day, everyone would listen to the test cricket while they worked. 'Richie Benaud has come in to bat, and the seagulls are rising on the ground in a magnificent sea of white' – the dulcet tones of Charles Fortune from South Africa, together with the Australian and English commentators, would float across the shed. The boys would bring another load of fruit up from the baking patch and Aub would declare it was '45 degrees in the waterbag'.

In his typical way, he was not happy picking from the trailer or the ladders, as was the norm. He set about designing a special picking and pruning trailer which had height adjustable platforms that could be swung around into the trees, making the whole process much easier. This was very successful and the pickers bragged about Aub's swings, because no one else had them.

The apricots were cut and laid straight on the trays to avoid them wobbling, and were then exposed to the fumes from burning sulphur overnight. When the boxes were opened in the morning, the hit of the sulphur fumes up the nostrils and down the throat made everyone's eyes water and stole the breath away. (Aub reckoned it had burned all the hairs out of his nose, and he'd been well and truly immunised from colds for the rest of his life, and strangely it seemed to be true.) The trays would be spread out in the sun to dry and, once dried, the fruit would be scraped off the tray into sweat boxes and sent into the packing shed. In one year's harvest, three and a half tons of dried fruit was produced, and money was now coming in.

With both of them being stretched to their limits, sore and tired, Aub and Val would get 'a bit short' with each other about how something should be done. Val considered that she was in charge of the cutting department. Aub couldn't understand why she was getting so snappy and he could retort quite nastily sometimes. Fortunately, the people in the shed had come to know how this worked between them, and so they didn't get involved and let it pass.

It was wonderful having neighbours like Enid Harris and her children involved, and everyone worked very hard. As usual, Aub demanded that a high standard of care and cleanliness be maintained for his fruit. If it was picked just right, and cut just right, and dried just right, it would be beautiful in shape and colour, and would make you want to eat it just by looking at it.

Aub asked Massey Harris, who lived next door, if he could borrow his car to go to Renmark. He packed the family into the little Austin and off they went. He dropped the girls at Auntie Dot's and he and Val went to see Myrtle. She was pleased to see them and asked how things were on the block.

'Not too good, I'm afraid.'

She hadn't heard Aub admit this straight out before and was very concerned about what was coming.

'They're only good enough for me to pay you out.'

They were very, very excited as Aub handed her the final payment for the loan on the block.

Myrtle didn't know how close he had been to losing the block several times. She didn't know that the men from the packing shed had once come calling asking him to sign a lien against the block for what he owed. She didn't know how much Val had gone without, or how many nights Aub's working day had extended to providing cash for food and clothes by playing his instruments, or why the worn-out old buckboard was still the only car, or why the old house still didn't have a decent toilet or a bath, and why Val still didn't have a kitchen sink. None of it mattered to Val and to Aub now. Their debt to Myrtle was paid, and they were grateful she had given them the chance to own their land. Aub felt years younger with the weight of the debt off his shoulders. The arrangement had suited them both well. They had the block and Myrtle had received a good interest rate and timely payments on her investment.

With Aub, as usual, being a no-fuss person, Val cooked a nice dinner eaten after a couple of frigid beers, some smelly cheese, and some pickled yabby tails. The block was theirs, all theirs, and it was very, very, sweet.

35

Now the focus could change to working the property and improving the living conditions as money would allow.

In 1959, Aub bought the first family car, a second-hand Vanguard Spacemaster. The old buckboard had become totally unreliable. The starting motor would go, and the car would have to be rocked backwards and forwards, until a loud 'sproing' announced it was back in place. The crank shaft no longer lined up with the engine, and the old canvas hood was tattered and torn. What a marvellous job it had done over the years to keep going as long as it did.

Wally Wescombe had announced one day, 'At least, Aub, you don't need to worry about anyone pinching it. No other bugger could drive it!' There were no sentimental feelings about it when it went.

The new car was luxury. It was dry, and warm. It even had flippers for turning signals, and windows that wound up and down, and everyone had a seat. Now Aub and Val could call and see friends in the district and for the first time in years could travel to Adelaide in a car of their own. This was now important for Aub, as his eyes needed more attention than the local optician could provide. His accountant had moved to Adelaide too, and he didn't want to change to someone he didn't know.

He had long held the dream of buying a new sax and clarinets. In typical Aubrey fashion, he began to research the instruments in music magazines and with instrumentalists that he knew, and started to seek out the best available. He rationalised to Val that they were tools of trade for him, and that this justified the cost. She knew that the new instruments would make him happy and she certainly didn't begrudge him having them. As far as she was concerned, he had well and truly earned them.

He bought the clarinets first. A symphony pair (A and B flat) of wooden Selmer clarinets made in France. They arrived in their beautiful case with the plush burgundy lining, and he was almost afraid to pick them up. He honed his best reeds with a little red wine on his special stone, and then left them for a day. When he began playing, the tone was full, and round and mellow in the lower registers, and pretty, clear and fluid in the top. He was in love, and from that time he played them at least a little on most days.

Then he bought his Selma E flat alto sax. It was shiny, gold and sexy, embodied with a honeyed ambient resonance, and he was in love all over again. He would pick it up and his eyes would light up, and he'd race off a riff before he settled into playing.

He loved music, and playing these beautiful instruments touched something in his soul and to a degree answered the needs of his moods and the edges of his inner melancholy. He would be absorbed into a world of his own, escaping from his worries, and the family noticed that he was less moody now that he was under less pressure.

He started playing dance music with a small group (piano, double base, violin and drums), and they were booked regularly throughout the Murray Mallee. At the end of the harvest, the balls and dances were held in the local halls and town institutes. The children would be spread on the theatre seats around the edge, with couples dancing in the middle of the floor, a couple of tables of card players in the corner, and the usual few helpers working in the supper room.

The pianist's husband always did the Mallee driving, and then

Aub would pick up his car at Loxton and phone the punt man at Berri to came over and take him across. It was always the wee hours of the morning before he got home but he was still up at first light to start his day's work.

He was cheery and good company when he was out, happy and hugely entertaining with his dry and witty humour. Dressed in his black suit and bow tie and wearing his patent leather pumps, he enjoyed the company and the jokes, and provided more than his fair share of the entertainment.

They called him the 'saxophone man', the player who could play anything. He could change the mood of a room by what he played, almost making his instrument talk. He loved taking requests, particularly if someone asked for a classical piece, and he could always oblige. The music world was a huge part of his life, and it became a life apart from the family, and apart from the block. It gave him a breathing space from his worries even when he was tired, and he embraced it fully.

He felt a bit guilty, though, because Val was always on her own. She never complained and still used the time to do any chores that were needed. She managed in the old house as best she could. When she was feeling a bit flat and had a little spare time, she'd move the furniture, or get out the paintbrush and paint something a bright new colour. This was the only way that she could escape from her unchanging scene.

Aub organised weekly band practice with the pianist, drummer and violinist. Sometimes there would be a couple of other instruments as well. These practices were held in the lounge room, and a small set of drums now sat there permanently. His idea was that he would be home on these nights and not leaving Val on her own, and this was true. It meant for her, though, that she had lost another part of her lounge room, and she always needed to cook for supper. With typical resilience, she enjoyed the company and coped, and as usual Aub was oblivious to the compromises she constantly made.

Then, of course, there was photography. The end of the kitchen table was taken over for weeks. There was the reading and evaluating of cameras, lenses, light meters and so on; the comparisons of shutter speeds, apertures and focal lengths; the study of polarising filters, hot shoe flash equipment and cable release timers, and of course the quality and types of film. Finally, the new 35mm Leica camera came home, and was disassembled on the kitchen table. Val was very scared that it might never go back together again but she didn't say so.

He was fussy with his photos, and close-up lenses and prisms meant he needed a larger camera bag. He wasn't satisfied with the commercial processing, so home came all the equipment for that, and the pantry was turned into a dark room. He set up studio lights in the lounge room for the taking of portraits and bought a twin-lens reflex Rolleiflex portrait camera. Next of course he needed slide mountings and a dual slide projector for both slide sizes. He still did all of the block work, but now he had some new obsessions as well.

Val was quietly working around it all, and when he started going to camera club, she went with him, fully understanding the precept that if you can't beat them, you should join them.

Every activity and piece of equipment had a book, and every book was read and studied. When a new fridge eventually came home for Val, the thermometer hung in it for the first two days, while Aub made sure the temperature was exactly what the book said it should be.

But nothing, other than music, surpassed the study, testing and fastidiousness that went into making and bottling home brew! Aub read up on it, got the best of all the equipment and ingredients, cleared a section of shelving in the large walk in pantry and, of course, proceeded to take over the kitchen table. He knew that Val was partial to a 'brown lemonade', so there was no opposition to the boxes of bottling gear, bags of hops and so on coming into the house. Together they worked to produce the first brew and together they waited for it to be ready, with Aub testing it studiously during the process. Finally, the first bottles were ready. Of course, they had to be at exactly the right temperature for Aub to test, so he put two bottles and two glasses into the freezer. You couldn't serve beer in a warm glass.

Val put some cheese on some biscuits in the evening and got the new special opener that didn't damage the caps. Aub opened the freezer and she needn't have worried about the caps. Both bottles were frozen and broken, sitting atop bags of vegetables. Aub said it was Val's fault because the freezer shouldn't have been turned up that high. She said that he was the one who regulated the temperature, and perhaps he shouldn't have put them in the freezer. The evening was not a success.

Later, the beer making became an art and the froth was just right, the colour met with Aub's standards and the taste was excellent. He enjoyed entertaining many friends for years with his excellent home brew, and even mounted a dartboard across the upper part of the kitchen to passage door, so everyone had to stoop to go through every day. It stayed there for about four years.

Testing the Play

36

There were other matters that Aub found frustrating. They came in the shape of his two girls. He freely admitted he didn't understand girls and always said bringing them up was nothing to do with him, as that was Val's job. At the same time, he held very strong views that Val was often on the receiving end of. This meant that when the girls asked permission to do something, she quite often replied, 'Don't ask me, ask your father – I have to live with him when you're gone.'

He was an austere parent. The girls had never cuddled or sat on his lap, and he had never really played games with them. He loved them both dearly, but as his relationship with his mother had not included the soft cuddles and gentleness of a tender bond, there was no precedent for him in showing it. He left it to Val to handle the day-to-day parenting, knowing that had they been boys he would have taken charge and that they would have well and truly known how to handle a shovel.

In those years, he didn't allow comics or women's magazines in the house, as he considered that any reading matter had to be constructive, or there was no point in reading it. Music was an allowable outlet, but sport was not. As Jenny couldn't take part Marilyn was not allowed to either. Films were a waste of time, and circuses and such were of no value. The only real outing he thought worthwhile was attending the annual concert when the symphony orchestra visited Barmera, and the whole family looked forward to it every year.

Jennifer found high school very difficult and worked hard to cope within her limitations. She excelled at English and at Latin, and Joe Perrin who was her subject teacher helped her a lot. At the same time, the sewing teacher demanded that Jen sew, which of course she couldn't do. In fact, she shouldn't have been forced into sewing classes at all. Maths, history and geography made no sense to her at all. By about seven o'clock in the evenings, there was always an upset as the stress of the day came out in tears and tantrums. Invariably, Val would give in to the current issue, Jenny would get her own way and peace would be restored, but when Aub was home, he was angered and dismayed by the whole performance. He worried terribly about what lay in front of her, feeling no capacity to improve things and having no answers to the situation.

Jen left school and began to work for Bill and Mavis Campbell. (Mavis, née Shaddock, and he had kept company in their early years.) Jenny answered the phones and did the books for their plumbing service and helped Mavis in the house. She kept up the work book, answered inquiries and followed up payments up for Bill. It gave her a little bit of independence, and she found that there were things she was quite good at, and that in turn helped her confidence. But Aub knew that the challenges would be with her all her life, and that her inability to compromise was always going to be a problem, not just for her but for others.

Marilyn was another matter. She generally lived in her own little world, was bright and had a vivid imagination. She would go up to her friend's houses as often as she could to play and to ride her bike. She would tell lies, generally a story she had made up about something she had seen or heard. Val would tell him it was her way of escaping from the tension in the house and was a means of getting a bit of attention herself, and that it would pass. (She did, in fact, grow out of it completely in her late teens.) She had a quick mind that needed to be kept occupied, and she needed company. Bullying at school was more of a problem for her than the work itself, as she didn't really fit into any of the sporting or loud social groups.

She had begun to learn the piano and showed some ability. She worked hard, starting practice at five each morning and practising until about seven. If Aub was inside and listening, he would call out

'That was wrong,' when she made a mistake, and he was cross that she would sometimes flounce off and slam the piano lid instead of staying to get it right. Although she did well, he always thought she could do better, and when she passed her Leaving Honours music exam with ninety-six per cent, he castigated her for the four per cent she had lost. His standards were exacting, and he expected the same from his daughter.

He had not had the opportunities in life that he would have liked, and although he wanted the girls to have them, he never read a school report or attended anything at the school, even when Marilyn was debating in inter-school competitions. His assessment was that he knew his children better than any teacher did.

Against his better judgement, he allowed Marilyn to join the Girls Life Brigade (which was run by his friend Mavis). This went well for the first couple of years, and she enjoyed the annual camps at Barmera immensely. But when she reached her intermediate year at school, he decided she couldn't go. Mavis herself entreated him, but he was adamant. 'Music and school are quite enough for her to cope with, as well as the jobs at home and it's not a point for discussion.'

Earlier in the year, brother Bill, who lived in Hobart, had come over to stay. As always, they got on well together. They were ideologically opposed politically, so they stayed away from that, each respecting the other's view. It was nostalgic for Bill to be back in his old territory, and it was warming for Aub, seeing him and feeling the old closeness with the younger brother he had cared so much about over the years.

Bill's wife Sally talked him into letting Jen move to live with them for a while to give her a new experience, and as a nurse with a knowledge of handling people, she felt she might be able to help her.

Val, who was showing some signs of the long-term strain of years of 'managing' Jen, was upset, but agreed to let her go provided she could come home whenever she liked. Jen did go, and she got a job working at Nestlé as a clerk. She liked her job and enjoyed her cousins John and

Michael too. She loved the mountains and the harbour, and the pretty sights of Hobart. She wrote long letters home. For the first time, Aub felt happy for her, glad that she was doing something she had chosen and that she had found something she felt capable of doing. It was a turning point for them all, and now Val had some more time to spend with Aub.

37

It was time to do some work on the old house. The kitchen walls were pulled down, the huge stone door step was torn up, and a new kitchen, laundry and bathroom were built in their place. The chip heater in the bathroom, with its hissing and spitting, gave way to a large hot water service and was never missed. The kitchen was fitted with built-in cupboards, and Val, at last, had her shiny new sink. In place of the old green Metters wood stove stood a resplendent White Chef (run on bottled gas), and everything was painted, shiny and clean. The bench tops were Laminex in Val's favourite colour of bright yellow. The linoleum was replaced with black and yellow inlaid tiles, yellow curtains framed the view down the block through the new western window and the old vegetable tidy was resplendent in a coat of green enamel paint to match the mantelpiece. The square four-foot table was dressed in yellow Laminex, and Val was thrilled.

The other rooms had new ceilings and were painted throughout in soft tones, except for the lounge, which had a bright cyclamen feature wall at the end. The man from Solomon's was called in to fit the rolls and rolls of A1 Axminster carpet that completely transformed the rooms. New gold curtains graced her windows.

The huge fireplace in the lounge remained unchanged, and Aub continued to burn the remains of the old walnut tree and the large posts and stumps from the cleaning out of the block. It amused him that often he had everyone lined up along the back walls of the room trying to escape the heat.

The house was a pleasure to live in, and he was surprised by how pleased he was. He remembered the little galvanised house in Renmark, the bush hut in Monash, the old house they had moved into, and now this lovely comfortable home, and he felt a great sense of pride and achievement that he hadn't expected to feel.

The Berri Hotel contacted Aub asking that a group be formed to play dinner music on regular Saturday nights and for special functions, including Christmas and New Year celebrations. This would be on a five-year contract basis, and although it meant he wouldn't be home on Christmas and other special times, it would provide good additional income and so he accepted.

A group formed comprising drums, piano, sax, clarinet, and often a violin and double bass, depending on the occasion. He was paid under the Musicians Union rates at the time, being three pounds eleven and fourpence for the three hours eight until eleven p.m., with overtime of three shillings and ninepence per fifteen minutes. They were an instant success, and entertained a diverse audience including visiting West Indian cricket players and notable visitors and entertainers from overseas, as well as a regular audience of local people.

There was a young girl who used to come up for dinner (from Galga) with her parents, and she wanted to sing. So the band got her up, and with her pigtails down her back, and with plenty of confidence, she fronted the dining room and sang. Wow! Aub was amazed. This lass had something very special indeed. After that, she would sometimes sit on the back of the piano stool with her legs swinging and sing along with them. Her name was Julie Lush, and she had a lovely voice, great rhythm, a wealth of natural talent and a delightful young personality. She later became known as Julie

Anthony, and her wonderful talent and hard work earned her the lead role in the musical *Irene* in Australia and later in London. Aub didn't ever meet her again, but he followed her career over the years with a very keen interest. He loved to see people make a success of their lives, and she certainly did.

The family drove to Victoria to see various members of Val's family. It was a long time since they'd been together and they all slipped back into the old closeness they'd always shared. Aub liked driving, and he was in his element looking at the farming country and checking out the crops.

In Hopetoun, Val's brother Norm, his son Teddy, and Aub went down to the local dealers to have a look at the brand-new Falcon that had just arrived. He'd been a Ford man all his life, and it grabbed his attention immediately. All the way home he talked about it, and explained to Val that even though it was automatic you still had actual driving control of it. She was pretty sceptical, but sure enough, after a test drive a few days later in Berri, they went in and ordered a brand-new, two-tone green automatic Ford Falcon! They had to wait for it to arrive and it seemed the day would never come. It was finally delivered, shiny and beautiful, and it immediately went off on a trip to Broken Hill to 'run it in'. Their years of hard work were paying off.

A new pianist moved into one of the distillery houses with her husband and children, and she and Aub met at a concert they were both taking part in. They formed a duo and began working together. Eileen was a classical pianist who could play anything, and she matched Aub with her talent, so they were always in demand for weddings and other functions. It was a real boost for him to be accompanied by such an excellent pianist, and sometimes at home they would play classics, or jazz, just because they could, with the two families tapping their toes.

Really, Aub had a life of his own apart from the family. He was a social person and a people person, witty, amusing and entertaining. Val knew that he loved her and that he wouldn't cheat on her, but she spent many nights at home on her own with just the radio for company and finally, when it came in, the television. The isolation meant that she was losing confidence in herself and was becoming withdrawn from mixing socially. Aub didn't see it at first, because he'd just assumed that she was happy. She enjoyed the new comforts in the house and was a warm and generous hostess. No one got out of her kitchen without a cuppa and a piece of cake or a beer and some tasty titbits, but she didn't want to go anywhere, and it slowly dawned on him that there was a problem.

He gave it some thought and came up with the answer. Saying nothing, he went into Berri and arrived home with two sets of Ben Hogan golf clubs, resplendent in their shiny bags, each one mounted on its trolley. Val was cross, couldn't see any sense in it and badly did not want to play. He asked her to go out to the little Winkie golf course on a non-club day with him so that he could have a hit, and his plan was an instant success.

As she had been years before at tennis, Val was a natural. Gradually she met others and soon they were playing on club days. Aub had done well. They both enjoyed it, but she was definitely the better player of the two. He didn't care. He had gotten her out of the house and she was mixing with people. Later they joined the bigger club at Berri, and it was a shared interest for them, but it never did work for them to play together as a pair.

Perhaps the greatest pleasure for Val came unexpectedly. Aub always littered the kitchen table with papers when he was preparing the year's tax information. This process was fully understood by the family. No one made any unnecessary noise, talked too much or asked questions, until it was finished. He was good at figures, but there would be loud exclamations such as 'God bugger my eyes' (Aub's only real swear words), and the mood would be grim. For some unknown reason, the budgie always seemed to pick up on this and would choose to shriek as loudly and shrilly as he could. Val would move his cage onto the veranda while Aub threatened loudly to 'kill that bloody bird if he doesn't shut up'. When the figures were done, they were off to Adelaide to see the accountant.

There were profits coming in now, and the accountant (who had known them for years) suggested that the 'permanent man' should become a partner, in the interests of tax splitting. So this year Val officially became a partner, and her name now appeared on all of the paperwork together with Aub's. She felt very excited knowing that now she was acknowledged as the owner too, even though she knew Aub's word would still rule. He was pleased too, because he knew how hard she had working alongside him over the years, and there would have been no way to stay on the property without her. In a two-handed game, she was the best partner he could have had.

38

The next few years were comfortable and enjoyable. The neighbours (all of long standing now) were a nice companionable group of good people who all got on well together.

Wally Wescombe (from Renmark days), lived with his family two blocks up. They had known each other for many years, and Aub had known Ivy too before they were married. Wally had always been a rival right from their swimming days, and he had never lost that competitive edge, but he was a good mate. He was a keen reader who went to the library regularly, unlike Aub, who liked to buy and keep his reference books, and never read fiction.

Ivy had a vegetable garden and some chooks. She had a cheerful nature and was a good cook. They were fiercely proud of their three children and quite unknown to them (and to the lad) Aubrey had tagged Roger 'Wonder Boy'. Ivy earned the tag for him by always saying how good he was at everything, and how 'Roger did this, and did that' until it was almost expected. Roger was a likeable lad who was very good at both sport and school subjects, and Aub was fond of him. The magpies in Aub's big tree, though, didn't like Roger at all and would swoop on him as soon as they saw him. He even had to go to school the long way around Puddletown when they had eggs in the nest, and Aub was highly amused. Roger was to grow into a capable young man, and Aub missed him when he went off to New South Wales.

Wally and Ivy's older daughter Helen was a pleasant person with a happy disposition, always bright and cheerful. She was always the same, and Aub used to have a joke with her. She was keen on tennis and enjoyed all sport and there was no nastiness or pettiness in her. Their younger daughter Kay had a cheeky spark, and looked like she might take some 'keeping up with' over the years. In fact, she kept everyone on their toes, and Aub liked her ready smile and cheery manner.

Eddie and Enid Harris and their four children lived next but one, with Eddie's father Massey Harris in the house next door. They were a lovely family. Enid was a gentle lady, perhaps even slightly shy. She enjoyed her tennis and was a devout Christian. They regularly worshipped at the local church, and Enid was a supportive member of the school welfare club. Eddie had been in the same fields of the war as Bill, serving in both the Middle East and in New Guinea, and Aub had a real soft spot for him. That, however, didn't stop him from playing the odd joke on him. Once, when Ed had gone off for lunch, he dropped a dead snake into a deep hole that Ed had been digging. Eddie was very scared of snakes and when he saw it he yelled for Aub to come and kill it, not knowing of course that it was already dead. Aub had a good laugh at Ed's expense.

Ready for Guy Fawkes night, Eddie was the leader of the pack making the guy. (He and Enid had taken over hosting the night from Wally and Ivy, who had done it for years.) He would get all the children together and help them make the straw man, wearing his old clothes and with a straw hat on top of his cloth head, the man of the moment. Aub wouldn't have got involved with the children like that but he could see they all relished it. 'Good on you, Ed,' he would think. 'You're a better man than me.' The old stumps, posts and burnables from the blocks would be piled up to make a huge bonfire, and everyone would arrive with food and drinks and the fire would be lit. Once it had burned down a bit, the guy would be thrown on to frizzle, sizzle, crack and burn. There would be a few crackers, and everyone would go home happy and tired.

Trevor was the oldest of the Harris children. He was a quietly spoken lad with an intelligent and gentle disposition, and Aub liked him a lot. He was good at drawing and colouring and had entered lots of competitions as a child. Now he was talking about architecture, and Aub thought he'd make a good career for himself. Judy was a petite little girl and was a bit of a tomboy, perhaps because she was growing up with three brothers. She was a very happy little person and seemed to go along with whatever was happening, and she could cope with a fair bit of teasing, which Aub liked to dish out. Ronald was always making something, or building something, and had a very practical mindset. Even as a youngster he had a dry sense of humour to match his easy-going manner. Young Colin was very quiet, and Aub didn't know him very well. He was just a bit young yet to 'get a handle on'.

Aub was fond of all of the children and took a genuine keen interest in each of them, and this continued for the rest of his life.

On the adjoining block, Steve Wade and Muriel lived with their son John and daughter Eileen. Steve had been a competitive footballer but had come home from the war with his fitness in tatters. He always put in a full day, and he and Aub worked quite well together. Aub had some reservations about Muriel, though, and was careful what he said when she was around. She always seemed to know what was going on, and liked to share it.

On Christmas mornings, the neighbours would arrive to share good wishes, a drink and some snacks, and it was a tradition that Aub and Val valued very much. Sometimes there would still be people there into the mid-afternoon, and Val would serve lunch after they had all gone.

One particular year, fifty-four people came on the one day. The talk ran well into the afternoon, and the family didn't sit down for lunch until after three o'clock. Val had been alternating things on the stove and stalling the serving as long as she could. The pork and trimmings were excellent, and plates almost empty, when there was an almighty blast. Everyone stared in shock at everyone else to see if they were all right. The kitchen was peppered with small pieces of shot! The pudding in the pressure cooker had boiled dry, and the lid had bent and blasted off! The dried-out pudding had turned into pieces of shrapnel, and Aub said Marilyn should get a returned soldiers badge because she had been sitting closest! The clean-up took the rest of the day, and it was a Christmas lunch never to be forgotten.

39

For years, despite lots of pleading, he had been saying there would be no dog. But at a sale in Loxton, he sighted this small black, tan and white mongrel pup and arrived home with the piece of wriggle in his jacket. It was all ears and had a quizzical way of tipping its head on the side to see what it was looking at through sparkly brown eyes. It was an unorthodox mass of features – short stubby legs, longish solid body, long sturdy tail, long nose and large, attentive ears. Aub loved him because he reminded him of himself; somehow the stunted body didn't quite fit the dog. He reckoned it most probably had an Alsatian grandfather, a Dachshund grandmother, and parents who couldn't spell 'pedigree'.

The pup was bright and intelligent, and the tilted head always meant he was thinking something out. He learned quickly. Named Skipper, he set about the business of always being at the helm of the ship. Convinced that he was a necessary part of the scheme of things, whoever came out of the door got escorted by Skip. He liked everyone, and Aub duly pronounced him to be a wonderful watchdog: he watched them come in, and he watched them go out.

He was a happy dog because he was a working dog. His forte was to climb the apricot trees during picking and pruning, and one day he nearly made Grant Thiele (who was picking for Aub) fall off the ladder when he dived his head through the leaves and licked him on the nose. Grant had never seen a dog climb a tree, but no one had told Skip he was a dog.

In the heat of a summer day, he would disappear for a short while and come back dripping wet. He used to drop off the footbridge into the irrigation channel and pull himself out at the bulkhead, just having a swim to cool off.

There were many escapades over the years. He ran into a grape truck while chasing birds, and the burly truck driver was in tears as he carried him down the row to Aub, and once he nearly drowned in the creek when his stumpy little legs couldn't carry him against the current, but whatever the situation, Aub was there to rescue him.

Skip's real talent, though, was his innate understanding of people, and in particular his understanding of Aub. He had a levelling gaze that clearly said, 'No, it's you and me.' He had a sense of presence and of worth and it was a true partnership. Aub was leader of the pack and Skip was his disciple.

Aub was approaching his sixties with virility and purpose, feeling good about who he was. The block was producing well, with mature trees and vines as the result of all the replanting. He was winning the game.

Final fruit payments were still intermittent. The system had not changed with the cooperative winery, so monies were delayed and estimating what your final income might be was impossible. The Greeks and Italians (who were now buying blocks) were not happy to accept this and wanted instant payments. They didn't understand that the original growers had built an industry and a market by forgoing payment until future years. This caused a lot of friction and Aub was very concerned about some of the hot-tempered incidents that were arising more and more often around the district.

He had bought a smaller block of a few acres across the bottom road from his property. This was good soil, and he planted a crop of tomatoes, as they had been in short supply in the previous year. The prolific crop flourished, with fruit of good quality and size. The timing was unfortunate, and it proved to be a poor decision, as everyone suddenly seemed to have beautiful tomatoes in large quantities. As a new grower in a plentiful year, he couldn't get a quota for his fruit, so he let it be known they anyone wanting tomatoes could come and pick their own. From the house, he could see the block on the rise, and over a couple of weeks there were always cars there, some with trailers, and many with families all picking as hard as they could. While he wasn't making money, at least he wouldn't have to waste them and disk them in. No damage was done to his outlets or boundaries, and some people rang to thank him and tell him how good their latest batch of sauce was.

What it did prove was how good the soil was, so he and Val trellised it up, and planted young Doradillo vines, which were in demand for the winery. This little block proved to be a star, with heavy crops every year, and was the most lucrative little acreage Aub had.

His diligence, hard work ethic and desire to do the best he could at things meant he would often take longer to do something than some of his neighbours. If he was knocking up a lean-to to store wood (or something similar), a solid foundation would be laid. Posts would be set in concrete after being measured meticulously. The designed frame would be built, with over emphasis on the spirit level, and with the sides tacked on with nails all at the same level, as set by a string row. The neighbours would watch this knowing that this was 'just Aub' and knowing too that they would have just knocked something up in a couple of hours and that it would have done the job just as well.

At the same time, he looked after his block with careful attention, and regular practices often took precedence over its general neatness and appearance. He was very annoyed one day when it got back to him that Johnny Wade (next door) had said his tractor work was always behind everyone else's. He had the pleasure of pointing out to Johnny that, had they checked regularly, they might not have lost a shed to white ants, they might have avoided having codling moth in their apricots, and a few other very pertinent things besides. He did not accept criticism easily.

Aub was a good boss, and the boys liked working for him, both the older ones and the new local lads coming along. He never asked anyone to do something he wouldn't do himself, and always paid a little over the expected rate if they 'put in'. For all his perfectionism and obsessive enthusiasm, he was fair and commanded a great deal of respect from most of those who worked for him. There were a few of course who couldn't stand him, often people who had been on the end of his criticism and incisive wit or had been victims of his 'black and white viewpoint. With Aub, there were no shades of grey, and once his mind was made up he didn't change it.

Then, just when everything seemed to be going along well, something happened that challenged his ideas, and ultimately changed his lifestyle.

Rubbish Cards

40

The Beatles happened. Aub's whole musical expertise and grounding had been classical, incorporating tonic solfa, fingerboard harmony, and correct chord progressions. He had taught Marilyn the chord structures – major, minor, augmented, diminished, augmented sevenths and so on – and he couldn't stand to hear incorrect chords. Melodies had structures and chord progressions, and cadences should follow accepted patterns. That was why good musicians could jam and play jazz, even if they didn't know the tune itself, and why music soothed something in the soul, because there was no chaos.

Along came the Beatles, with a new sound, often misusing a few basic chords in their early days, and Aub couldn't stand it. It wasn't music as far as he was concerned. They were a disaster with their long hair and their unconventional harmony and he couldn't stand seeing them on the television.

The younger crowd took to them, however, and it annoyed him when people began requesting that the group play Beatles songs. They were easy to play, but the drummer had to become loud and unrelenting in his rhythm to satisfy the crowd, and the tunes were basic and repetitive, in his opinion. When a Beatles song was played on the radio, he would turn it off. And besides, he didn't even like the silly lyrics.

A group of young lads from Berri formed a new group calling themselves the Four Berries. He didn't think that they had any real musical expertise, but as long as they played Beatles songs, no one but him seemed to care. The young crowd loved them, and they achieved immediate notoriety. It was the turning of the tide to a new popular trend and sound that would sweep the world.

He was angry, and his burning fuse festered like an infected sore.

He was being made to feel old and out of step by people who had no idea of what music was about. The beautiful haunting tones that could evoke emotions of sadness and melancholy, the frisky, playful upper registers of scores that made people feel happy and joyful, and the lovely satisfying cadences that settled the soul were being superseded by a poor imposter. As far as he was concerned, the Beatles songs were rubbish, and while they were at it, they could go and get their hair cut!

It annoyed him so much that he called it a day, and stopped playing dance and dinner music, living out the adage that 'if you can't stand the heat, get out of the kitchen'. Many people in the district were upset and so he agreed to continue playing at private wedding, anniversary, birthday and party engagements with Eileen as pianist. It had always been some of the best of his music, but it still left many hours and evenings free that he'd not had to fill before.

His beautiful pair of symphony clarinets were still his favourite instruments and he played them at home most nights, challenging himself with old classics and specialist instrumental pieces.

When he was asked to teach woodwind at the Glossop High School, he wasn't in the mood for it and declined. Val was glad to have him home, but he was moody, and she thought perhaps he'd 'cut his nose off to spite his face'.

Aub missed the social aspects of the music scene too. He was engaging company, and liked people, and had many friends in the district who he'd become used to seeing at events he'd been playing at. Now it wasn't the same, but somehow, he didn't equate it with how Val might have felt over the years. After over thirty years, he was missing a whole part of who he had been, and he wasn't coping well with it. He knew that if he had been living in the city, there would have been plenty of musical avenues for him to pursue, but he loved the river and that wasn't an option.

Then Eileen's husband was transferred to Nuriootpa, and when they had moved his top pianist was gone, and that was the end of playing in public for him.

Now he bought a reel to reel tape system, placed it on the kitchen cupboard and started collecting his kind of music. Like all of his interests, it became a passionate pursuit, and the collection of tapes grew and grew, only to be replaced in later years by a top-quality sound system and a collection of cassette tapes, followed in turn by a collection of compact discs.

He hadn't been a great fan of television, but now with more time to fill, he found there were some interesting programmes that he began to follow, mostly instructional ones of course. He liked documentaries, couldn't stand movies, watched the news and was a fan of *Four Corners*.

One day when driving home from Monash, he came round a bend and froze as everything in front of him reeled into slow motion. On his side of the road, the truck advanced ever so slowly, and he wondered how long it would be before the crash. In fact, it was only seconds, and there was nothing he could do. There was noise, and the car was on its side in the dust, and pumpkins and pieces of chrome, and glass, and metal were all over the road. He crawled out, unaware of the cuts, whiplash and bleeding, but lucky to be able to stand. He was numb when he looked at the remains of his shattered car, and the people who had stopped began to speak to him, and he couldn't hear what they were saying. He was kept at the hospital for a while, but he just wanted to go home. He was disorientated, his glasses were gone, and his head ached. One of his friends drove him home to Val.

The suddenness of it left him vulnerable and shaken, and it was several days before the shock began to wear off, and the deeper bruising began to come out in maudlin colours. It was sobering and, as his injuries began to heal, he realised that there was more to coping with these 'minor' happenings than he had previously thought. He wasn't well enough to work, and now didn't have a vehicle, so he and Val decided to take a holiday.

Years before, Marilyn had gone to Adelaide to go to teachers college. The morning she had left, Aub had told her that if she got into a financial mess, he and Val could help – making it quite clear that any other sort of mess wouldn't be supported. She had later married a teacher, and they were now living on Kangaroo Island.

Keen to see the island, Aub and Val made the crossing on the *Troubridge* from Port Adelaide to Kingscote, the short sea trip being the first either of them had ever done. Marilyn and Allan met them at the wharf and took them home to the little weatherboard house on the banks of the Cygnet River.

There was no fence, and an anteater had made his home near the clothesline. There was no reticulated water, nor 240-volt electricity, but there was a hand lift pump from the rainwater tank and a generator in the old broken-down shed under a massive grizzled gum tree. Possums danced on the roof at night, making dull thumps to add to his snoring. There was no red dirt. The air smelt moist and fresh, the noises of the birds and sheep were a complete change. It was real 'country' and he began to feel like he was expanding and could breathe again.

The island was pretty, and green, with spectacular bays and lighthouses on the headlands. He enjoyed some excellent day trips and, with his love of local history, and his camera in hand, he learned what he could about the place that had been the first settled in South Australia.

Marilyn's husband was a keen angler, and together they knew all the best places to go to catch a feed. On the shore, they fished at South West River, off the rocks at Cassini, on the Kingscote jetty, and at Stanley's Rock, where they caught 'double-headers' of sweep. Aub met one of the local commercial fisherman in the hotel bar and arranged a day trip out with him. The breeze blew up his nostrils, and the small craft pitched in the waves as they set and pulled the nets and he had a wonderful day.

It was the first holiday they'd taken, and Val loved every minute of it. Now she could imagine where Marilyn was when they were on the phone, and apart from the isolation she thought the island was beautiful. Aub now had a new interest to research and to learn about.

Over following years, these fishing holidays would extend to Yorke Peninsula, Eyre Peninsula and the south-east of South Australia as various postings moved them around the state. In between trips, Aub would acquire new rods and reels and practise casting outside the big shed. He was the keenest fisherman on dry land.

41

A whole part and purpose of Val's life had changed. Aub had always clearly come first, most particularly since the girls had left, but the reality was that he had always had other interests in life. Besides, his toys tended to be large, and they were all over the house. She was finding it hard to put up with. Her sweet nature had been tempered and tested over the years, and where she had never really questioned him (apart from jobs on the block), she became argumentative, and a bit terse around the house. He retaliated nastily, and sometimes the arguments got quite heated. Why was she getting so argumentative? He did whatever he wanted to do, and she was welcome to join in, it was up to her. He loved her, and it didn't occur to him that she might not have enjoyed his pursuits as much as he did. For her part, she had grown tired of always fitting in, and began to say sometimes what she thought. This different Val bewildered him.

Gradually he became concerned that he hadn't seen her happy smile for a while, and a couple of friends had asked if she was all right. They had the chance to go on a trip to the Mediterranean with friends, but Val didn't want to go and he wouldn't go on his own. He guessed it was too far away from Jen for her, but he was disappointed. He had always read about Greece, Italy, Spain and Portugal and it galled him not to go. He didn't push, because he wasn't really sure they could afford it, but otherwise he might have been more persuasive.

They went on driving trips to visit family, friends and new places, and he was keen to get a caravan and travel further afield. Val couldn't think of anything she wanted to do less, knowing that because of his poor sight she wasn't too keen now on his driving. Of course, she didn't say so, but she showed a complete lack of enthusiasm.

They still played golf, and Val was playing well, but Aub found he was losing interest, so they didn't go out as often as they had in the past. He was a generous person by nature, and he would have given Val the world if he could, just so long as he knew what she wanted and it suited him as well.

His reaction to all of this was to come home with a set of bowls, and to enroll them both at the Monash Bowling Club. After a bit of arguing about whether she would play, Val reluctantly went off to bowls. Aub's choice, and his perseverance, proved to be a masterstroke and was the start of years of happy bowling for them both.

Val proved to be a natural bowler, and she liked the company of some women whom she had previously expected might be bossy and unfriendly. She began to enjoy herself again and looked forward to the companionship she had been missing. She developed a solid friendship with her pairs partner Florrie, which continued for several years until Florrie was killed in a car accident. Bowling was never quite the same again for Val.

Aub loved his bowls. It provided an interest that was to last for well over twenty years. He got into the science of the game and bought several books on how to, why to, and when to. He enjoyed the social interaction immensely and was soon playing against other clubs and meeting people he'd known around the district years ago. At various times, he was a member of each of the Berri, Monash and Barmera clubs, and was active not just in playing, but also in maintenance jobs and working in the bars. 'It's the best social game in the world,' he used to say, and he meant it. 'Where else is it possible to get so many people together in such a small space, where both sexes can play, where there's good competition, and everyone can have a good time with a bit of a social mix-up afterwards?'

He had a very dry quick wit and was somewhat of a wordsmith. He loved using long illustrative words, making up his own adages and sayings and often embellishing the ones he'd learned while down on the farm with Grandfather. He remembered poetry and ditties and they often shaped his turn of phrase. He was witty and entertaining, and his faultless spelling meant he was very quick with puns and word reversals, and canny little sayings.

He wrote his address on the back of envelopes as Knot a Cent Towers, Frosty Hollow, Poverty Ridge, South Australia, and it was only when people said it aloud that they got the message.

While he was good company and was interesting, he needed to be a little careful that he didn't come over as a know-it-all, because he actually did know so much, about so many things.

In the community, he was mostly liked. He was often elected onto committees, and more often than not was also elected to hold office. He could weed out the rubbish from the substance, and was widely respected for his honesty and integrity, and his ability to organise. This, of course, could be divisive and bring conflict too, but it wasn't a good idea to pick a fight with him because he could cut an argument down with a few incisive and articulate words after beginning with 'You think that, do you?'

There was a disturbing and upsetting happening at one organisation while Aub was president, and it caused a lot of upset and a lot of lost sleep and worry. It became apparent in an audit that money had been embezzled. When the culprit was proven, the board discussed it at length, as a decision had to be made on how to proceed. The person concerned was extremely well known and well liked in the community and was a member of a family with children. It was decided that, in the interests of the family, the matter would neither be reported nor made public but that there should be no doubt that documentary proof would be presented to the police if there was any hint of such a position being abused again. The board met and a decision was made that the person would be fired, the reasons would be clearly stated to them and there would be no comments to the wider community. Aub, of course, had to do the firing.

Next day, there was a very angry call from the perpetrator's partner, incensed that they had been fired for no reason, and demanding reinstatement. Over several days, there were calls from many people blaming Aub for taking such action without good reason. He could only say that the matter would not be discussed, and the board would not be making a comment. It caused a wide and angry split in the community and that was something that Aub had to wear as president. The person's partner, who had been a friend, never spoke to him again. Some people were vocally abusive, but the board held to their decision to be discreet.

For Aub, the saving grace was that they had preserved a family's integrity, and that a partner and children could still hold their heads up in the community, as they had done nothing wrong. He had little respect or concern for the culprit.

He had always been a man of his word, and had always tried to be fair, and it was a horrible thing for him to know that people now openly questioned his integrity, and he felt scarred by the experience. He'd known it, but it proved again that you soon find out who your friends are.

Val was very, very angry. They were attacking her Aub, and she would have loved to tell a few people just what it was all about, but of course that was out of the question. She knew she couldn't say anything, but people didn't mind what they said to her, and she avoided going to the shops for a few weeks unless she really had to. She would have quite cheerfully thrown the book at the person concerned after dobbing them in to everyone!

All in all, it was a sad time, but the person concerned was careful and honest from then on, and continued to care for family, and work in practical capacities within the community. They had made a wrong, poor choice, but Aub noted that in ensuing years the best use of the second chance was made.

42

As a Boy Scout, Aub had developed an interest in astronomy and, reading as he did, it was natural that he followed the space programme. He and Marilyn had stood on the front lawn and watched the first Sputnik go overhead in 1957. It was such a far step from the first missile that had been launched from Woomera rocket range in 1947. In 1961, Yuri Gagarin made the first manned spaceflight on *Vostok 1*. Then astronauts Borman, Lovell and Anders were the first men to leave earth and orbit around the moon and return safely in 1968 in the Apollo 8 spacecraft.

'Just imagine what it must be like to travel through space and feel weightless and look back at earth.' He subscribed to a magazine on the space programme and read everything he could find, buying books on astronomy and regaling the family with stories about galaxies and black holes.

Unsurprisingly, his next toy was a celestial telescope. He read the brochure and put it together, mounted on its large viewing tripod. It remained set up in the main bedroom and he carried it outside and peered through it for hours on clear nights. He was at a complete loss to understand why Val wasn't interested in the stars. For that matter, he was surprised at golf and bowls (and among his friends) to learn that most of them had only a passing interest in it. As far as he was concerned, there was great relevance for everyone, and they should all follow it in detail.

Then in 1969 he had spent the day with Val in front of the snowy Chrysler TV screen and watched with the rest of the world as Neil Armstrong took the first steps on the moon. Here we were. Walking on the moon. He knew he would follow the space programme for the rest of his life, with a real thirst to know where it would lead. He would have liked to be part of it. At the same time, he felt bewildered that man had learned nothing in so many ways and yet was so advanced in others. How could we come so far in some things and be so backward in others?

When he ordered his new Ford Falcon, he had a specially built trailer made for transporting fruit to the cannery and the car was custom-fitted for the job. He had applied and received a quota for fresh fruit and intended to use it for a few of the apricots and all of the peaches. Peaches were the most unpleasant fruit to dry. In the heat, the prickly peach fluff settled inside elbows and crevices and mixed with perspiration and dust causing itching and burning. Drying peaches was no one's favourite job, and now canning was an option. In the past, he had sold some fresh in Adelaide at the East End market, but the round trip took at least seven hours including loading. The new cannery was only six miles away and two or three trips could be made in a day.

One day, he had been to the bank in Barmera and when he got home, he parked the car at the back door ready for Val to go straight off to bowls.

She made him a cup of tea, said her goodbye and walked out with her bowls bag. Next thing she was back. 'Where did you leave the car? It's not in the shed.'

'Don't be silly. You walked right past it. It's at the back door.'

'I'm not that stupid. There's no car there!'

They walked outside and looked. No car. It wasn't feasible, but they had to admit it must have been stolen. They were feeling incredulous. Three miles off the main highway, five hundred yards from the service road, and ten yards from the kitchen, while they were both there! They had seen and heard nothing. Aub rang the police, and the long, anxious wait began.

Over the next three days, the news came in dribs and drabs, as there were sightings from different places and the police worked to track the car down. Two juvenile absconders from McNally Training Centre (in Adelaide) had walked up through the blocks to the house. They had seen the car, jumped in and taken off. It was fortunate for them that they hadn't gone into the house.

The car was spotted and tracked in Berri, Loxton, Pinnaroo, in the Murray Mallee, and along river tracks. On the third day, it was seen heading from Berri to Barmera, where the police set up a road block, but the lads gave them the slip and raced towards Kingston along the Sturt Highway. The police gave chase, firing shots at the car tyres as it raced around the backwaters at Cobdogla. It rolled on the famous S bend and was a complete and total wreck. The police rang to give Aub the news and to tell him that both offenders were all right.

He was absolutely furious! They had come to his property, stolen his car, completely wrecked it, and the police were glad they were all right! Well, if he could get five minutes with them, they wouldn't be all right. They were lucky he couldn't. He was disgusted and angry, and he would have been very happy for a chance to 'sort them out'. He could just bet they had never done a hard day's work in their lives. Besides, why were the police firing shots, when the car had to stop at the punt crossing two miles down the road at Kingston anyway?

The insurance company replaced the car, but not the additional tooling and fittings for the cannery, and he was inconvenienced until the new car came. He was still out of pocket, and was livid with anger when the lads received what he considered to be a 'slap on the wrist' as punishment. He only had to think about it to feel his blood pressure going up. He couldn't believe what the world was becoming and couldn't understand why so little seemed to be important any more.

The world had only made Antarctica a reserve ten years ago. There was a war being waged in Vietnam, and terrible things were being done to people – again. In 1961 the Berlin Wall had risen to divide a Europe that people had fought to keep free. The Aboriginals, who fought in the world wars alongside white Australians, hadn't been given the right to vote until 1967. The White Australia Policy of 1901 restricted entry by

Asian migrants, and this had only begun to be dismantled in 1949, and the prejudice from it still hadn't been got rid of. And in America President Abraham Lincoln had issued his Emancipation Proclamation in 1863, but prejudice still existed, and the Ku Klux Klan was still active.

Information about chemicals and pesticides flowing into rivers and polluting streams, about huge companies not caring about the land or the people in the countries they worked in, and about natural habitat for the world's animals shrinking by the day, was being presented regularly in the *National Geographic* magazines. How could these things be allowed? It outraged his sense of human justice. He had been brought up to 'do unto others as you want done unto you', but now it seemed that a lot of people only worried about themselves.

He had been a Freemason, and the lodge had been important to him for many years. The fellowship and the working together, and the working for good, all fitted with his outlook on life. One of his good friends, though, had done something that the Freemasons didn't agree with, and he had been treated badly as far as Aub was concerned. He knew what had happened, and when his friend was excluded, he resigned, seeing it as an injustice. He packed his apron, case and medals away in the back of the lowboy, and told them he no longer wanted to be any part of it.

Since the advent of the contraceptive pill, 'they' talked about 'free love' as if it was acceptable. The bodgies and the widgies dressed like nomads, blew their minds with magic mushrooms and smoked 'weed.' God forbid! He had been raised, and had raised his girls, with the words 'There's no substitute for good speech, good manners, and good deportment.' Good morals and behaviour had just been an expectation that didn't even need to be stated. Being clean and presenting yourself well was as basic as working for a living, and some of this new breed didn't seem to care too much about that either.

He could work harder than most, was fitter than most, and knew more than most, so why was he being made to feel that he was out of step?

The current state of political affairs annoyed him too. He was no fan of Gough Whitlam. Aub did think he had been right as prime minister to introduce an Aboriginals Land Rights Bill into Parliament, but other than that he considered him a disaster. When he was ousted, Aub thought it was a good thing, believing that the Liberals would do a better job.

The older he got, the more he was questioning things. He had grown up to value his principles, to back his word, and to be true. Now so many things seemed to be changing, and the community he lived in seemed to be relaxing so many of the standards that he thought were important. He didn't like any of these unpalatable changes, but it didn't occur to him that perhaps some of his own standards and expectations should be reviewed to help him avoid the danger of finding himself the only one in step.

Beating the Odds

43

Johnny Wade from next door made an offer for the block. This was unexpected and Aub was taken aback, and in truth a bit put out, that Johnny obviously thought him decrepit enough to make his retiring an option. Johnny had no immediate time frame in mind, but wanted to put on record that if, and when, Aub was ready to sell, he would like to buy. The two properties had an adjoining boundary, and he was taking over his father's block in the next year.

Aub's response was a flat no, and he even had a bit of a sulk about it. Then Val floored him by asking how long he thought they could keep working like they were. That aspect hadn't occurred to him and didn't concern him at all. He was still strong and had grown up with the farming ethic that you left the land in a wooden box, with your boots on. He was shocked that Val would even ask. There wasn't going to be a time when he wouldn't be able to manage the work. As far as he could see, it was more likely that Val wouldn't be able to manage, and he wasn't ready to think about that either. He'd always wanted a son, but there wasn't one, so the expected line of succession wasn't going to happen. He couldn't imagine being without his piece of land, and he had no intentions of living anywhere else.

Of course, nothing ever stays the same. First came the hernia operation, then a prostate scare, and then the blood pressure tablets. Aub was beginning to think his body needed a rebore, but never that it was letting him know he should slow down.

Val was suffering badly with arthritis and was walking with difficulty. Her mother had been practically bedridden for fifteen years with the same condition, and he didn't like what he was seeing.

After much deliberation (with himself), he came to the conclusion that he definitely didn't want to move, even if the block was sold. So he set the wheels in motion to have the house and main sheds divided off the property. It took many years, and lots of solicitor's bills, before the legalities were complete, but eventually the house and the main shed were transferred onto their own title.

By the time it was finally done, Val's arthritis meant she was not able to walk easily and was often in pain. Aub felt that he was strong, but his body was sending a different message, the property was in good shape and he didn't have the same enthusiasm that he'd had when he was developing it. Grudgingly, and unhappily, it was time for discussion with John before the block went on the open market.

Surprisingly, Johnny made a reasonable and fair offer for the home block, the Loveday block and the dry block in total, but excluding the plant. Aub and Val discussed it. She was so pleased that he would consider it, and they eventually accepted the offer.

Val would have preferred to live in the new units at the lake's edge in Barmera, but since she wasn't asked, she didn't venture an opinion on that. She was worried enough about how Aub would cope without his big piece of land, and thought it was just as well the house and shed stood on the larger than usual home block that he'd had surveyed off, and he would still have all of his tools. There would be no easy adjustment for either of them.

They sold the block for thirty-three thousand dollars, and there were still final grape payments to come in over the next few years.

There was no great excitement for Aub over the sale. He could still look out of the kitchen window and see 'his' land, and when he walked outside it was all around him. That was the good part. He knew every yard of it like the back of his hand. He liked Johnny and always thought that Steve had been a fairly hard taskmaster for him, so he was pleased to see him have the chance to be his own boss.

The bad part was that he didn't agree with the way Johnny pruned the trees nor how he worked the rows up on the tractor, and he would get agitated if he saw him spraying. Aub had been prepared to let the weeds grow, so that when they were turned in they put some nitrogen back into the soil. Johnny always worked it clean, being more concerned about how neat everything looked.

Aub had long ago read and considered the research on sprays and poisons and had decided that he would opt for more natural controls of pests and diseases. He had used copper sulphate to counteract downy mildew on the vines after summer rains, and blood and bone to fertilise, but he was concerned to see other chemical sprays and fertilisers going back onto the ground. He was in a thoroughly bad mood every time he saw the spray vat out behind the tractor.

Fortunately, after a few years there was an upturn in proceedings. John was an excellent golfer, and his wife Sophie had wanted to live in Berri for a while, so when the chance came, he took a job at the Berri golf club. The blocks were all sold, and the new owners moved in.

Bob and Marlene Kennedy had been farmers on Eyre Peninsula and had no previous experience of fruit growing. Bob's father-in-law, who was also involved, had a farming background too. Of their four children, three were sons. Bob realised that Aub had a wealth of knowledge that he was only too happy to share and could see that letting him feel involved would be beneficial for them both.

This worked well for Aub. He would show them how to prune the trees, and discuss with them at what times, and how, things needed to be done. They didn't always take his advice, but they ran the block as a business and were intelligent and keen and hard-working, and this gained his great respect.

Here was a whole new interest for him in the latest implements they were using, and how they worked out what improvements they could make. He was amazed by the money they were prepared to spend to set things up and couldn't help but think how far the industry had come since he and Val had started with their original meagre plant.

He was happy to see the land valued, the best advantages taken of the soil and the topography, and the genuine effort being put in to improving production from the property rather than just ripping

everything out of it. He could walk around a few acres at a time and know that it wasn't resented, and he often drove down through the block on his way out to just to see what was happening.

Val found things were much better because Aub was much happier. Bob and Marlene and her parents were lovely, and they were good company. Then little Emma arrived, making five children running around with their squeals and laughter, and it brightened her days.

A new family had moved into Eddie's block on the other side too, so Aub wandered over one day and introduced himself. They were Andy and Slava, of Eastern European background, and it was obvious that Andy was the boss. Aub welcomed them and asked them to come over the next morning to meet Val. They arrived shyly, but over a cuppa and a chat Slava told them about their family and Andy talked about their background experiences.

Sometimes, Andy would come over and ask Aub about something, and now and then Aub would lend him a tool for doing a special job. Aub, of course, had all the right tools for everything. They were well looked after, and lived in their own special spot in the toolshed, each hanging on a nail.

Andy was meticulous about returning things, always knocking on the back door and handing them back with thanks, and thanks, and thanks. One day, this extended to bringing a bottle of his home-made wine and a couple of cinnamon sticks. He asked Val for a saucepan, dropped the cinnamon sticks in and proceeded to heat it all up together. After a chat, while it was cooling, he proudly poured a glass each and downed his in one hit.

Aub swallowed one mouthful and nearly choked. He flew outside gasping for air, got red in the face and sat gasping on the back step. Poor Andy was mortified, but he got the message that this wasn't his finest hour, that he could borrow anything he liked, and that he should leave his bloody wine at home.

A new normal gradually descended for Aub. Life continued with a pattern of bowls, dinners at the club, seeing friends and having frequent visitors, going to the things he was involved in, playing his instruments, listening to music on his sound system, and of course keeping a watchful eye on the work that was happening on the block.

But change was afoot yet again, because you can't rely on anyone to do what you expect.

44

For the life of him, he couldn't understand how someone who seemed to have a modicum of common sense could be so stupid.

Marilyn and her husband had arrived for the weekend, bringing the news that she was leaving, and moving into Mt Gambier, with the girls. He didn't want her to go, but they had apparently agreed a year before that when he got his next Education Department move, due at the end of the year, she would not go with him. Now, although the new move had been delayed for another year, she had decided she would not stay.

Val was distraught. She was genuinely very fond of her son-in-law and couldn't imagine how any of them would cope. Marilyn was working at an aged care complex for thirty hours a week, and financially it was going to be an absolute battle, and she worried about the girls missing their dad.

Aub was just wild. He was losing the white-haired boy, his good fishing mate and a steady bloke with a good earning capacity. He talked with him about it up in the shed, but he didn't talk to Marilyn. His only comment to her when they were leaving was to say, 'You don't move out from security.' He was shocked by her calm reply that there were various types of security. What did she bloody well know about life?

He remembered his mother working hard to bring up the family (always worried about money) and he himself had worked and worked for years and years to provide some financial security for his family. Here she was throwing security away. And furthermore, she was rejecting them and not moving back to the Riverland close to him and to Val. There was no doubt about daughters.

He was so angry that he virtually wiped her off, and wouldn't discuss it with Val. He just couldn't believe what she was doing, and she wasn't a topic for discussion in the house. If she rang and he answered, he would hang up, but if he was out and she rang, she and Val would have a chat. These rare chats kept Val going, and she was becoming angrier and angrier with Aub as the year drew on. She missed her loved son-in-law, and she grieved for Marilyn and the girls. Aub was having none of it.

Jenny had married Geoffrey Salman and surprisingly they were supportive of Marilyn regarding her move. She had made no indications of her feelings, and on visits over the years had not made any comments that might prepare them all for this. But like Val, Jen knew she would have her reasons, and couldn't understand why Aub was so unrelenting in his attitude.

For her part, Marilyn made no derogatory statements about the girls' father. He was a good person who was capable at his job and was successful at sport. He had been a good father to the girls, but there were differences between the two of them in their natures and their values. Years before, her doctor had told her to leave, but she had stayed because of the girls. Now she was seeing signs that they were feeling the tension and it was time to go. She had not discussed this with Aub, Val or Jen, but had expected Aub's reaction.

The stand-off continued for twelve months until the day when Marilyn rang and told Val that she was going into hospital for a major operation. She had friends whom the girls could stay with. However, she thought that they might like to come down, and Aub might like the chance to see the girls and get to know them while she wasn't there. It was up to him.

Val for once was adamant. There was only one way this was going to go. It was the first time she had really stood up to Aub about anything but stand up she did. There was no reasoning with her, so they went. They stayed with the girls in Marilyn's little house, and all went well.

Unexpectedly, though, the neighbours, and some of Marilyn's friends, told Aub things he hadn't known, and he got a somewhat different picture of things.

He rang to arrange to see his fishing mate and was given the run around by his new partner. When she asked who it was on the phone, he replied, 'Tell him it's General Jackson.' This had been somewhat of a joke between them and he knew the message would instantly be understood. There was no return call. Aub made no comments, but from then on, his attitude changed, and he did give Marilyn credit for the way she was managing in a difficult situation.

It appeared she had some very good friends, two in particular being Elizabeth and Ken Norton. They were older than her and were wonderful in the way they looked out for her and the girls. They were ever willing to help, and Ken had taken responsibility for cutting her lawns. Aub thought he was a top bloke and in fact he found he liked all of her friends.

It was clear from their comments that there was very little support coming from her ex husband. Initially, Marilyn had asked him up for meals and helped him where she could, as he genuinely found the break-up very difficult. For a start, the girls went down on some weekends to stay, but his new partner didn't like them and made no secret of the fact that she didn't like having them in her house. Aub was mightily unimpressed by what he saw as a lack of backbone in not standing up for, and supporting, the two children who were there before she was.

When Marilyn crunched the front passenger door of her little yellow Mazda Capella against an unyielding stobie pole, Aub chased up a door from the wreckers and got it fixed. He paid for her subscription to the RAA, and sorted out a box of useful tools for her to use around the house. These were practical things he could do. She was grateful, and appreciated it.

Neither of them ever discussed the awful lost year. Aub was still aggrieved, and hurt, and confused, but he did have more grudging respect for his daughter. He had seen a different woman with a side that he hadn't known, and he admired her strength.

45

Now he had more time to enjoy his four grandchildren. Marilyn had two girls, Kristin and Sue. Jen and Geoffrey Salman adopted two boys at birth, first Andrew and then James. (Ironically, Geoffrey was the son of Harry and Joyce Salman, and it was Harry who had beaten Aub all those years before to gain the scholarship to become a pharmacist.) The children were the light of Val's life. She would feed them, knit for them, and sew for them, and think about them all the time, living for their visits.

Aubrey would star in his witty manner, telling funny stories and performing minor miracles by manipulating his fingers, his ears and his tongue. He would recite the alphabet backwards, makeup ditties, mix up words, recite poetry and present puzzles on the kitchen table using matchsticks. His real forte was his phonetic alphabet: A for horses, B for mutton, C Forth Highlanders and so on.

He was not a 'cuddly' grandfather, and he enjoyed the children

more as they grew older and their personalities began to show through. They loved it when he would do a riff on his clarinet and then play, or especially if he played the saxophone for them. They got a bit bored with his many slides, on nights that seemed to go on forever, and sometimes when he was trying to get them interested in the stars (or something else), their eyes would start to glaze over after twenty minutes or so. But he was a favourite and they loved to see him.

They all loved the tractor too. It was big and noisy and smelly and went where the car wouldn't go. The big shed was a treasure trove of bits and pieces and interesting things they didn't see anywhere else.

Most of all, they loved the Monash playground. There was no other playground like this. Huge steel slippery dips, massive swings and all manner of inventive climbing apparatus, and in fact any exciting thing you could think of, had been massed onto one square of ground that was pure excitement. There was no other playground like it.

Grandpa had crinkly hair and couldn't see anything without his glasses, and his favourite things were music, fishing, and eating smelly cheese. He would buy gorgonzola, mash it up with a fork and put it in the fridge in jars. When the lid came off, the dirty socks smell would be overpowering, and everyone would groan and complain. Grandpa loved it and told them it was 'no good unless you had to chase it with a net'.

They would all come up for Christmas, and the four grandchildren got on well. Marilyn would take over most of the cooking, as Val was finding it harder than she used to. There would always be a couple of barbecue dinners out on the front lawn and Aub easily slipped into his role holding court as head of proceedings.

He and Val made a trip to Tasmania and were transported to a different world by the beautiful scenery. He couldn't live there, though, saying the weather was only fit for 'frogs and toads'. Best of all was seeing brother Bill in his own environment and, as always, they got on so well.

It was satisfying to see that Bill had made a good life for himself, and Aub marvelled at how active he was in the community. They had such a lot to talk about and to see, and Sally and the boys made them very welcome. It was good too, to see where Jen had lived and worked, and overall it was an eye-opening and very enjoyable trip.

Aub continued his overseas travel when he disappeared into the pages of the *National Geographic* magazine each month. Television was starting to show him the wonders of many places too, and he'd put up a huge tower with a booster on the antenna at the top to receive a better picture.

Next, he bought a Quintrex runabout boat and a good outboard motor from a marine store in Port Adelaide. With typical attention to detail, the safety equipment, life jackets, spare globes and tools for the trailer and so on were all carefully packed and stowed. It was a nice size to launch and fish from comfortably on the river, the creek or the backwaters. He was at peace again being out on the river. The birds were still there, the sounds and the colours, the big open skies, and the whispering reeds. There were fishing mates too who enlivened the days, and he reckoned this was the best little boat he'd ever owned.

He had lost his appetite for shooting. He'd only ever shot to put food on the table, and the killing aspect of the sport didn't interest him. As he looked at the 'roos and the ducks and pigeons, he wished he'd never had to shoot any of them. He'd never felt any affinity with them, nor thought about it. But as he got older he found more interest in watching them, and he learned that they seemed to have a pattern or code that they lived by, and some order of community law. They would think out where to go as water and food sources changed, what to do with approaching danger like flood, and would take action against a rogue animal in their midst. He had a new respect for them that he wished he had had when he was younger.

Rabbits were another matter, and he had no respect for them. He'd stopped shooting them when the government had introduced myxoma virus to control their population. Though the effects of the disease were dreadful to see, it was effective at culling them, but he didn't want diseased rabbits for dinner.

In his own way, he had been a bit of an environmentalist for years, without even realising it. He had stopped using chemical sprays long before he'd sold the block and had used natural methods to feed and build the soil. He'd bought a little Honda hatchback as a runabout vehicle and had chosen it because it had the first of the new built-in technology for pollution control. The house had twelve-foot ceilings, and he'd had additional secondary ceilings installed at the ten-foot height as well, to provide a double barrier to help with heat control. The whole house now ran on rainwater, showers and all, and he was quite proud of it, thinking he was helping the environment. No one seemed to worry much about the world around them, but he did.

There was another thing he was reading about that seemed a bit like something from science fiction. It was called a microchip. Chips had always been made of wood as far as he was concerned, so he had to learn about this new silicon chip by reading whatever he could find.

They were saying it would change the world when it came to the fore. The sky was the limit and all that sort of thing. He didn't discount it, because he had seen things change from the first planes to the space programme, and from the first silent movies to television, and he knew that scientists were making discoveries every day.

Apparently, once these chips came into common use, nothing was ever going to be the same. He didn't understand a lot of it, and there didn't seem to be many around who could explain to him just what the application of it might be. He was told that new calculators had a chip in them, as did lots of the new machines. He couldn't understand why anyone needed a calculator anyway. Figures had always added up in seconds for him. Everyone was talking about computers, and Marilyn worked for someone who was aiming at having a 'paperless' office. How the hell could that ever work?

He broke his rule and read a fiction book called *All the Rivers Run* that had been written in the seventies by Nancy Cato. He didn't normally read fiction, but he knew that she had spent a lot of time with Pearl Wallace (Norm Collins's sister) getting information, and a bit of it was based on fact. Pearl was a friend of his, and had been the first woman skipper on the River Murray, and she was a very nice woman too. He found the book interesting and watched Sigrid Thornton in the television series and enjoyed the excellent shots of the river scenery. He was very disappointed, though, when he heard through Norm (whom he still saw occasionally) that Pearl had not even been acknowledged in the book. He'd not noticed it when reading it, but if it was right, he thought it was very poor on Nancy Cato's part.

There was a world in reading and television that he would become absorbed in, and invariably, with his inquiring mind, it would lead him on to something else. He couldn't resist books. It was legend in the family that he couldn't walk past a bookshop and not go in and browse, and always came out with a book. The grandchildren reckoned Grandpa had a book on everything!

He was a *Readers Digest* man, who often ordered from their promotions. He bought binoculars, pens, records, books and magazines, and numerous other items. He bought their big new atlas each time they reissued it. These were his favourite books, and he pored over them with his large magnifying glass for hours at a time. He bought dictionaries too, and his prize was a Webster's tome that was as thick as his hand and so heavy it could only be used on the kitchen table. When the *Australian Geographic* was published, he bought that as well, and read each edition from cover to cover.

It was hard to find people who could discuss things with him, though, and he missed the fortnightly games of chess he'd had with George Milne years ago. George had been the local primary school headmaster, and he too was a great reader. They had shared an interest in poetry and football and many other things, and sometimes there had been more talk than chess.

Playing On

46

Marilyn had met this bloke, David, and was bringing him to meet them. He didn't want to meet him. She'd been on her own for seven years, and he'd got used to that, and as far as he was concerned a new bloke wasn't welcome.

They arrived on a Friday night with the girls. Aub ignored him. He talked to everyone else and went to bed early, and it was obvious David was the elephant in the room. In the morning after breakfast, Aub rose from the table (still ignoring David) and announced that he was going up to the tool shed, and that anyone who was interested should 'present themselves'. David had been summoned.

On the bench in the toolshed, David (who was an electrician) found the electric barbecue waiting for repair. He looked at it and said that whoever had pulled it apart had 'buggered it'. Aub announced that he had pulled it apart. David pointed out that it was him then who had buggered it up!

Next came the challenge with the new fishing rod and magnetic reel, to see who could get closest to the privet hedge. Aub wrapped it hopelessly into the hedge and David lobbed it just short. The ego was bristling, and Aub was not pleased.

He learned, though, that David in his forties, and having always worked with men in mills and on the shop floor, was not going to wilt, and even had a sense of humour. By the time they left on Sunday, he'd thawed out a little in spite of himself.

In his late seventies, he was only about as fit as the average sixty-year-old. He thought he'd slowed up a lot since he'd sold the block and had no idea that he was remarkable for his age. A couple of his friends had had heart attacks; two had died of cancer, two of his brothers-in-law and a nephew had died as the result of a cerebral haemorrhage. There were others too. He missed them all, and it saddened him, but he saw it in no way relating to him and the age that he was.

He didn't cope well with sick people and didn't go to the hospital to see his very good friend who was there for two years following a major stroke. To him, sickness was a weakness, and when cousin Betty could no longer manage because her fingers were painfully twisted and curled with arthritis, he couldn't understand why she just 'didn't get on with it and do things'. It was a complete lack of understanding from one who was so fit.

His attitude was challenged, though, because of what was happening to Val. She had painfully arthritic feet and was finding walking difficult and could no longer play golf or bowls. The increase in pain had been gradual, but now it was forcing a change in lifestyle. He understood that she was coping as best she could with it but couldn't understand why it was happening to her, as he knew she wasn't weak.

Her doctor sent her to an orthopaedic surgeon. He explained that she could have the bones in her feet altered. Some would be removed, and a Y shaped prosthetic piece would be inserted instead. This should provide stability, and the top piece of the Y was designed to flex in the same way as toes. Dr Pope explained that he felt this should be successful for her, and that there was no other long-term alternative for managing the pain and keeping her walking. Val had the operation in Berri and spent the first two weeks with her feet under a frame on the bed. Gradually she got up, began hobbling around, and then was allowed to go home.

He didn't mind that he had to do pretty much everything. It was just that he had always referred to the housework as 'squaw's' work and had kept out of the way, not noticing that she had always waited on him hand and foot, even laying out his pyjamas each night. Val didn't like anyone else meddling in her kitchen but now by necessity he was thrust into this new role. It looked like an eternity to them both.

Nevertheless, he coped and he began to realise just how much Val had always done in the house and was starting to wonder how she'd managed when she was working long hours on the block with him.

There were some things he just wouldn't have put up with if he'd been doing the job, so inevitably some of the equipment and appliances got smartly changed for the better. It didn't dawn on him that while he had always had his 'toys', Val had gone without quite a lot of simple necessities.

She got onto her feet sooner than expected, and although she had to be careful, with a good result, she was mostly pain-free. Six months later, Aub had a renewed Val, who was happier and mobile again, and they were both able to get back to golf, bowls and better things.

When they could, they went fishing, usually in the river or up the Ral Ral Creek. Sometimes the callop would be biting, sometimes it would be bream, and on a really good day, a couple of nice cod would flap in the bottom of the boat. On a bad day, they'd have to settle for the scenery and the peace of the river, without getting a bite.

Yabbying was a favourite pastime too, mostly down at the Katarapko Creek. It was relaxing, plying the muddy banks with short baited set lines attached to tent pegs. The line would be drawn up slowly, so the yabby didn't skit off, and the dab net would be swished behind him so he was caught as he backed off. At home, the old copper was fired up and the catch would be dropped into the boiling water, creating a frothing broth as they changed colour. The warm yabbies would be taken in, spread out on plastic on the kitchen table, shelled and cleaned out, and put into jars of vinegar to chill. The meat was eaten cold with a beer, and Aub always told yarns and sang ditties and held court at the table when the yabby tails came out.

Val's mother Mina died in 1978 at the age of ninety-three. She had been virtually bedridden for the last few years with arthritis and had been almost blind for several years with glaucoma. They went to Swan Hill for the funeral and then spent some time seeing parts of Victoria where pioneering Jurys had settled in the early years

Lois Jury from Kadina, who had married a cousin of Aub's, had begun tracing the Jury family tree, and Aub had become involved too. His excellent memory allowed him to recall many people, and he could picture just how they had looked, their movements and their sayings. He often thought of old Henry, and of his uncles, and his great grandfather and they were as real to him as when they had been together. Now he developed a totally new train of thought. His interest in reading, knowledge of South Australian history, fascination with his pioneering forebears, and enjoyment in meeting people, all combined to drive an obsessive interest that would last for the rest of his years.

A paper trail was amassed and discussed with Lois. She was very good at tracking information, and when another cousin, Don Jury, visited England, he sought out birth and other records and returned with photocopies of pertinent certificates. Together they compiled a wonderful record of the family's history from the birth and arrival in South Australia of the four Jury siblings. They had been true pioneers in a new colony that had only just begun. Aub's great grandfather had arrived in February of 1840, and when Aub was born the colony was only seventy-three years old. This short span made it much easier to trace exactly what had happened since settlement.

A fascinating story was emerging, with facts mostly good and a few bad. He learned new things about people he had known. A couple of out-of-wedlock children, a conniving scoundrel, and a couple of previous marriages and families came to light. He found the causes of death interesting, being everything from accident to senile decay. Some died from an illness that Aub now knew was diagnosed as diabetes and heart failure, and this could be traced through to several family present day people. One family member had been murdered, several had died in childbirth, some had drowned, others had died at the war or because of it, and so it went on.

Other traits appeared like sketchy random cobwebs linking one generation to another. Irish forebears had been talented and notable musicians, with one being a violin maker and another holding a

university chair in music. Poor eyesight had been especially notable, and the crinkly hair had clearly been handed down from Jewish heredity before the 1800s. For their times, his ancestors had shared a high degree of both fitness and intelligence, and overall, they were a family of good people who worked hard and were held in high regard by their peers. Some had been farmers, some politicians, some had run businesses, and some had been educators. Mostly the men had been well over six feet tall and had been good at sport.

He approached the task with the thoroughness that he applied to everything. There were boxes of family sheets, boxes of letters, boxes of photographs, handwritten notes, books of contacts and phone numbers, and regular contact with Lois. There were records, handwritten in the Hart family album, and photos in the leather Hilton photo album, that his mother had given to him. Some of the people now had faces. There were no convicts, as South Australia had been a free colony.

Aub devoured it, and he was so intrigued that he couldn't understand why his girls only showed what he would call 'a mild amount of interest'. Perhaps it was because they were girls. The regret he felt at not having a son was heightened by the fact that now he was more than ever aware that no one in his line was going to carry on his name.

In 1990, a Jury family reunion was held in Botanic Park in

Adelaide, celebrating 150 years since the family had settled in the colony. There were descendants from each of the four Jury siblings who had first arrived, and some had come from other states of Australia. Don Jury had done most of the organising, and Aub and Lois had been responsible for most of the 'tracking down'. It was surprising to see the family likenesses in lots of people of all ages, including the distinctive dark wavy or crinkly hair, and the pale washed-out grey-blue eyes.

Aub was in his element. 'How are you, my old boy?' 'You don't look any older than your grandfather.' 'If you run off and get the horse and cart, I'll meet you down the lane.' 'Come on, sing me a song.' 'You're as beautiful as ever.' 'Don't you remember him? He was only two or three generations ago.'

It was an emotional day for Aub as he thought of his father and mother, and the grandparents he had known. He could picture now how and where they had cleared and farmed the land, helped build shops and businesses in the towns, and fought in two world wars. He thought of the women and the challenge they had faced in having to cope with different climate, insects, snakes and lack of water as they fought to raise their children and support their men.

He pictured them all with their horses and their drays, in their Sunday best going off to church, and now everyone had arrived here in their shiny cars.

47

The family was so important to him now and he was finding much more pleasure in his grandchildren than he had ever expected. They were intelligent, bright interesting people and he realised they were the continuation of the family, even though they would not be carrying on the family name.

Grandsons Andrew and James were making their way now. They were both interested in cars like Geoff was. They had jobs, and they worked hard and displayed good work ethics. As children, they'd both had paper rounds and had worked for the local butcher. They had played tennis and made full use of the beach a couple of streets away. Andrew showed more of a leaning into the clerical side of things, and James was more practical and hands-on.

On a trip to Melbourne, Aub saw Val's nephew Stuart, who was home from Antarctica. He had spent most of his working life there on one base or another, and had regularly sent Aub copies of *ANARE*, the *Antarctic News* publication. They had plenty to talk about, and Stuart had some amazing photos of the ice, and Aub found plenty of questions to ask.

Stu had a large seagoing yacht that he had built during his home leave times. He was a good sailor and had been a crew member in several major yacht races. His beautiful yacht was moored on the second deepest mooring at Williamstown, and he arranged a day's sailing. It happened to be the day of the fleet sail-past and the bay was full of craft. Aub sat on the side, relishing the wind in his face, the smell of the air, the noise of the sea and the sirens, and was surprised that Val enjoyed it as much as he did. It was an absolute treat of a day and he wished he'd had a go at sailing in his youth.

In 1989, Kris asked him to extend his grandfatherly duties and give her away at her wedding to Peter. Now, he didn't have much time for drummers, but he had to make an exception here. Peter was a talented and qualified drummer, and he seemed to know what he was doing in his field. Apart from that, he was personable, intelligent and likeable and had Aub's seal of approval. With great pride at having been given the honour, he was absolutely delighted as he walked his granddaughter down the aisle.

There was sadness that year too, with the brutal blow of Bill's death. His little brother was now also gone. He hadn't enjoyed good health and had had great challenges in caring for Sally in the later years, after a car accident. He had lived his life well, and Aub knew that Stan's and Clarrie's ideals had lived on in the way he had conducted himself. As brothers, they hadn't been able to spend a lot of time together over the years, because of geography and the cost of getting together, but he knew Bill so well, and he would miss him forever. They hadn't been expressive in their love for each other, but it was all there. Another ache to add to the others.

Several years later, when Sue married Glen Winkler, another bright and impressive lad came into the family. Glen was a graduate in business marketing and knew a bit about logistics. The wedding was a happy get-together, and there was plenty of opportunity to do some talking.

Aub never ceased to be amazed at families, though. Kristin and Peter had sadly separated in the preceding months. Peter had been close to Sue and Glen, so the party of eight wedding attendants included both him and Kristin although they were not paired with each other. There were people at the wedding who found this surprising, and several of them asked him what he thought about it. His reply curtly put them in their place. 'I suggest you ask the bride and groom,' he said, knowing that none of them would.

He liked that he could have a good in-depth, intelligent conversation with these young things and their friends. Sometimes when they talked amongst themselves, though, he couldn't understand the jargon they used, but they all seemed to be acquiring a bit of sense, and he wondered what his two grandfathers Alf and Henry had thought about him at the same age.

His nephews and nieces were also special to him. Thora's girls had grown into lovely women, as had Ivor's two daughters, and he took great pleasure in it when he could see them and talk to them and find out what was happening in their lives. He very much liked Lindsay, who was in the building trade, but had seen more of Ivor's younger son Michael over the years, as he had sometimes come up to stay in the school holidays as a boy, and the closeness had continued.

Bill's two sons lived in Tasmania, and although he'd met Michael he didn't know him very well, and would like to have spent more time with him. Bill had spoken highly of him, and called him his mate. John, who was occasionally in Adelaide, had kept in touch often and he treasured this. John was the one in the family who had shown the most interest in the family tree and, as this was dear to Aub's heart, it pleased him no end.

They were all making good lives for themselves with careers, partners and children, and the branches on the family tree were growing leaves.

48

As he was growing older, he found himself confused by his conflicted views. He'd always been so sure of what he thought.

These days, he said he was 'no religion' and he felt sure in his own mind that there was nothing after death. And yet he felt the weight of his ancestors, whom he now knew so much about, of his parents and siblings, his grandparents and the older uncles he had grown up with. It was in his memory that they were close, and his memory was excellent. It was only now that he was realising just how much of their lives he had absorbed. But he had no sense of them being close in spirit. They were gone.

He did believe there was a God, and his basic beliefs were Christian. But he also thought that, had he been born somewhere else, his beliefs would probably have been based in the Islamic or the Buddhist or some other faith, and that would have been fine. His extensive knowledge of the Bible was still quite clear, and he could quote sections at will, and he did accept them as a code for him to live by, but not as the only code for others. For the rest, he didn't know. His extensive reading into scientific and evolutionary findings meant there needed to be a leap of blind faith that he couldn't make. His mind was as active and questioning as ever. He felt no need to go to church and didn't see why there should be denominational splits within the Christian faith.

He was confused about other things too. People didn't use good grammar any more. They mixed up tenses, and put verbs and adjectives where they shouldn't be, and worst of all it didn't seem to worry them.

Once, everyone had worked for everything. Now a sense of greed, and loss of the will to help others who needed it seemed to be creeping in. It was a scramble to get volunteers for things. Young Glen was a volunteer firefighter in the Country Fire Service but, like all organisations, they were constantly having trouble trying to recruit new volunteers. In Aub's day, they would have been lining up for any such community service.

The world had reeled at the news of a nuclear meltdown at the power plant in Chernobyl. It was hard to know exactly what the implications were. Reports had been heavily censored and there was no precedent for assessing the extent of the damage and pollution nor the time and method of cleaning it up. There had been evacuations and the ongoing situation was grave, especially for Europe itself. There was talk of radioactive clouds and acid rain. Having lived through the years when the atom was split, leading to the development and the use of the atomic bomb, and having seen the development and harnessing of nuclear power, Aub had always had grave misgivings about how smart man was getting, and just what the cost might prove to be. Perhaps we were about to find out.

He was a big advocate for the wonderful advances that had been made in medicine, and had seen for himself what they meant. His dad would still have been alive if they'd had sulphur drugs when he was ill. But in 1986 the first test tube baby had been born. Now that wasn't smart, it was a step too far.

He wondered what we'd really learned from the mass exterminations in Europe, Vietnam and Cambodia over the years, and thought about the capacity for man's inhumanity to man. Would we ever be able to overcome such base behaviour? He said there would be no peace until the world was 'brindle' and the fighting over religion, power, wealth, land and water finally stopped. He lived in hope that education and integration would one day solve most of these problems. A man can dream, can't he?

Val was slowing up. She was limping around now with an arthritic knee and, once again, bowls and golf were a thing of the past.

Shopping and outings were difficult for her, and she was largely confined to the house.

He couldn't understand why she thought he should tell her what he was doing. She would make a cup of tea for him and limp up to the shed with it, only to find he was not there and the car had gone. Then she'd be annoyed that he hadn't told her he was going, or even asked if she'd like to go for a ride. There were no close neighbours and it didn't occur to him she might be lonely. Sometimes he'd just gone for a ride around the block, or to see friends like Bob and Marlene, or Barry and Janet, what was wrong with that? He was happy to help by doing the shopping and, in fact, he enjoyed going into Berri or Barmera and having a chat to whoever he saw.

For the life of him, he couldn't see why she was getting so snappy. Over the years, she'd always gone along with things. Now, more often than not, she was arguing the toss about what was happening.

Finally, fed up with pain and isolation, she had a knee replacement. The rehabilitation period was long and painful, and he did everything he could to keep things going and was proud of the fact that he never served a meal without a cloth on the table.

Thora died in 1994. She had been ill, and it was expected, but that didn't help. She had been his sister for eighty-three years and they had been great mates together, in their early years particularly. They looked alike too. He remembered sliding down the gables with her, walking to school across the vegetable gardens in Torrensville, and then across the clay flats in

Renmark. He could see her, devil may care, with her bush of hair, down at the river with Carmen and Lois, as a young teenager. He thought of her wedding day, and of the homes she had lived in. He thought about the children being born, and

how happy they had made her. He could see the way she turned her head, and even the shape of her fingernails.

He felt very sorry for Arthur. They had been a close couple, and he too was getting older. He could not imagine a life without Val, so he knew that this was an unthinkable horror for Arthur to face now. It seemed the older one got, the harder things seemed to be.

He kept himself busy. He often played his clarinets, but not so much the saxophone. He always read, and still enjoyed his photography and fishing and pennant bowls. He thought it a little 'soft' that they didn't play once the temperature hit forty-four degrees, deeming it too hot for the 'old boys'. He, of course, was not one of those, even though he was well into his eighties.

He put pop-up sprinklers in his lawns, and kept them mowed, and kept the bushes trimmed. He always found jobs to do in the tool shed, and occasionally Bob would ask him to go down the block to prune the odd tree.

He had never lost his love of, or belief in, the power of exercise, and kept active and fit. There was no time for puzzles or crosswords or the like, as he viewed them as a waste of time, and preferred to be doing 'something constructive'.

He was always keen for new experiences, and something both new and constructive that he'd never thought about came along unexpectedly.

Kristin had been explaining to him about new word processors and, always a gadget man and always up for new technology, he had a good think and of course read what he could about them. He didn't understand these flash new computer things, and in fact, when he talked with people who said they did, he often thought that they didn't understand them either. But it got him thinking about all his family history records and who might want to read them over the years. He thought if he could type the family sheets up into folders, he could store them better. Now they were in boxes and piles and drawers all round the house.

He went off to Berri and arrived home a couple of hours later with a large box and excitedly told Val how pleased she was going to be. Out of the box came a new Smith Corona electric typewriter! He had a new toy, and he was delighted.

He set up in the kitchen on the table, and became absorbed with the manual, while Val inwardly groaned, knowing that she'd lost the space until he was good and ready to give it up, and however long that took, she better not move anything. It took weeks.

With his typical diligence and enthusiasm, he taught himself to touch type, sitting at the table with an instruction-manual alongside him. 'The quick brown fox jumps over the lazy dog'. Val continued to work on the other side of the table. Aub proved he was never too old to learn new tricks and was soon proficient enough to start typing up his family history sheets. Finally, they set up a table in the lounge under the standard lamp, and he worked there, on and off, for well over a year.

Most problems that arose were because he would pull pieces of the typewriter apart when something went wrong, and then he'd have problems putting them back. He would have ribbon, and keys, and other odd-looking pieces around him, and would be loudly telling them how useless they were. Nevertheless, he got great enjoyment and a sense of deserved satisfaction from his typing, and the printed family history sheets mounted up rapidly.

49

Val's body continued to show the results of her years of hard and heavy physical work. Arthritis claimed her hip and her back. She was limping and moving around the house again slowly and in pain. Although it could be done, she didn't feel that she could cope with an operation on her back, which apparently would need to be done first to maximise any rehabilitation of her hip. She wasn't afraid of pain, but just didn't feel she had the energy to cope. Aub found this difficult to understand, and he hated to see her so restricted, as his vibrant, energetic Val had faded away. She was given medication for pain management, and had drops for her advancing glaucoma, and she managed as best she could.

It was difficult when her sister Win died in Nyah in Victoria. Val and her sister Meryl were the executors of the will and needed to go to Nyah to clear and pack and prepare Win's home for sale. Aub didn't know how they could do it with Val as she was, so Marilyn and David took time off work and picked them up to take them over.

They found that Meryl and Les had arrived from Melbourne a couple of days earlier. They too were in their eighties, and the whole situation was somewhat overwhelming. Aub and Les looked at the size of the task and decided that they best tackle the outside and the sheds first. It was a very trying and upsetting job for them all. Win's house was within a lane's length of Mossgiel, where Val had grown up as a child with her grandparents. The long association with the place over the years, as well as Win's death, hit her very hard. She had loved Win and she missed her already. To the others, she seemed vague and distracted.

Win's leg had been amputated as the result of her smoking, and they found a cupboard housing her unused single shoes and her false leg. Aub choked as he and Les burned the spare single shoes out in the yard. He had been close to Win and had a very tender spot for her, and burning her shoes was almost a step too far for him. He had promised Fred before he died that he would always see that she was all right, and had found a warm kinship with her over the later years. Now the price seemed too high to cope with.

In the evening after the funeral, they all sat up together talking until nearly five o'clock in the morning. It provided some relief from the stress of the last few days, but it was a sad parting the next morning. Val was no better, and Aub was realising that she was getting old, and he felt the world was a lesser place because of it.

Over the next few months, she continued to be vague and forgetful. Sometimes she would fall in the garden, and she often got dizzy at the clothes line. He was worried and would often leave her in bed while he went shopping, feeling she should be safe there. In fact, she was mostly restricted to the house now, and didn't get out much at all. Living on the block next door, Bob and Marlene could see that she was lonely, so they'd pop in and see her for a few minutes and have a chat as they were going down the block. There were others who called, and she was always pleased to see them. Aub was very worried. He was doing as much as he could, and of course she thought he wasn't always doing it right, although she was very, very grateful.

Marilyn and David came up every fortnight if they could, and cooked and left food in the fridge, and cleaned. David would help with the lawns, and Val always wanted a little hole dug to bury some 'past it' food. Aub was frequently heard saying, 'Of course I couldn't dig a hole.' He was bearing an increasing load and, being fiercely independent by nature, was refusing help from friends. He thought they were coping just fine.

He would climb up and clean out the gutters or tackle any other thing he wanted to do. Bob used to keep a worried eye on him, and he would just happen to appear and lend a hand quite casually while he talked. Aub appreciated Marlene and Bob for their thoughtfulness, their sense of humour and their company. He fortunately didn't realise how much concern the neighbours and the family were feeling.

This concern extended to his driving. He had been driving for years, and he knew perfectly well that he was an extremely good driver, and that he was very careful. He would go very slowly, right down the middle of the road, in his little iridescent blue Honda Accord, and he liked the way people made a definite and special effort to wave to him! Marilyn had a couple of calls from neighbours suggesting that she get him 'off the road'. There was no chance of that.

Joyce Hollitt (Roger's wife) phoned too, to say how worried she was about Val, and wondering what could be done. Joyce and Roger had been particularly close to Aub and Val, and they thought of them both like their own parents.

Aub would slip off in his car to have a look at the blocks or call on someone and have a chat and a cuppa, and it was his escape. Sometimes he would go down to the shop and get the paper and come home to sit in the car and read in the sun. He reckoned it was the warmest place in winter.

Val had regular appointments with her eye specialist in Adelaide, so David would go up and get them and bring them down to stay for a few days. Aub certainly couldn't drive the distance and Val couldn't manage on the bus. Aub enjoyed these trips and found he always learned something and was keen to talk with everyone. Jen and Geoff always called out, the grandchildren all came in and they were good times.

The trip in October 1997 was no different. There was the usual 'Where's so and so?' followed by 'Next time I'll pack my own bloody case!' heard coming loudly from the spare room. This threat was never acted on of course, (although he'd been making it for over thirty years). Val was tired and a bit cross and was unusually quiet on the first night.

In the morning, she got up and, feeling dizzy but saying nothing, she walked against the passage wall to make sure she didn't fall. They went to her appointment and found that her vision had deteriorated badly. She didn't seem well, so Marilyn took her to the doctor that evening, and from there into emergency at the Royal Adelaide Hospital. It was busy and cramped, and was obviously going to be a long night, so David and Aub went home to get some dinner, and left Marilyn to ring when she needed to be picked up.

After some preliminary tests, the doctors felt that Val had had a mild stroke, and she was to be admitted as soon as there was a bed available. She chatted now and then with Marilyn while they waited, and apart from her now customary vagueness, she didn't seem to be too concerned. Marilyn went home when Val went up to the ward several hours later, pleased to know that it appeared medically that she was going to recover quite well.

In the morning, though, the news was bleak. Another stroke in the early hours of the morning had left Val unconscious, and while it was not yet possible to know what the effects would be, they were expected to be grave.

The Frozen Pack

50

Aub was numb.

The days rolled by like a kaleidoscope of horrors.

Val didn't wake.

Val woke, but didn't know him.

Val wasn't Val. He didn't feel like Aub.

He hated the hospital. He just wanted to go back to how things were. He knew that he was not himself. He had hammers in his head stopping him from thinking. Perhaps that was good?

He felt like he was outside looking in at everything. Hearing things from afar. Viewing things through glass.

He was so racked with pain for Val that he couldn't even cry. He couldn't talk about it, and he just wished everyone would shut up.

Marilyn kept saying it might help Val if he went in to see her, but he didn't want to. Not like that. It wasn't her.

He had never realised what it had been like for some of his friends and family when this had happened to them. He felt insecure, like a child again, scared. He felt lost like he had when his father died.

The days dragged on into weeks, the weeks into months and the hurt into agony.

Then gradually Val began to improve. She knew them now, and she had her speech back. They were teaching her to stand, and trying to help her to walk, and she was making some progress. Nonetheless, it was clear that she was never going to be able to live back at home.

The axe had truly fallen, and Aub felt cut off at the knees.

The discussions began with the doctors about what the future might hold for Val. The most pleasing thing was that her memory was now improving, and she no longer seemed so vague. The doctors explained that one of the medications she had been on for pain management had been the cause of her vagueness, and they had written a letter to her doctor addressing the issue. This was an even more bitter pill for Aub, because he felt they had unnecessarily been robbed of a better two years together. He was pleased she could remember things, but what use would it be now?

The decision had to be made about what was to happen next, and what a horrible choice it was. Val needed to go into care either in the Riverland or in Adelaide. If she and Aub went back up the river, she could be placed in any of the towns where there was a bed, but he would want her to be in Berri. This would mean him still needing to drive. He was eighty-nine now, and the driving issue had been coming to a head for a long time. Aub was sure he could drive for years yet but, from the reports of friends and neighbours, Marilyn knew this clearly wasn't so. She didn't say so, hoping that the issue would resolve itself.

She did, though, say that if he wanted to go back to the river to live, they would help him to move into the town, as they couldn't continue indefinitely to support him as they had been. Besides that, he would then be able to better support Val. He was fit and could walk long distances around the streets and would have more company with people around him.

He didn't need this ultimatum and he wasn't the slightest bit interested in their logic and didn't want to think about it. He wanted to walk outside and see 'his' block, and to be able to tell by the smell of the air what weather was coming, and what jobs Bob had been doing. He wanted to be *carried* out of his house wearing his *boots*, and the 'wooden' overcoat. The alternative, having Val stay in Adelaide and him living with Marilyn and David, wasn't at all attractive. How could he live without his river, the land around him, his friends and his interests?

But he loved Val; she was his other half and his loyal partner, and for the first time in his life, he really made the decision that was best for her. They would stay in Adelaide because he knew that the family could support her more solidly if that happened. There was no doubt in his mind that they would be helped by friends and family if they went back up the river, but he knew that the same level of constant daily support could not be expected nor relied upon.

He absolutely, just couldn't stand the hospital social worker. It wasn't personal. He just wasn't interested in what he had to say. What did he know about their situation anyway? Words, words, words.

'Don't start telling me what to do. You're still wet behind the ears. Just do whatever she says,' he shouted, pointing to Marilyn. She held enduring powers of guardianship, so had the authority to make any arrangements, and he was damn glad that she did. Coming to terms with any of it was impossible for him and, in fact, he never did.

Marilyn got Val into Resthaven just near their home. She had a single room with an en suite, and a small sun porch, in a group of five separate bedrooms, with a shared lounge and dining room.

The Resthaven aged care complex sat on the banks of the River Torrens, and there were reeds and ducks and gum trees. Walking now with a frame, Val could get around, but she needed a lot of care, medication and assistance. She had recovered some of her mental capacity, now remembering most people and places, but she wasn't able to work things out, and often got confused trying to manage simple things like changing channels on her television.

Marilyn and David had seen her every day since her stroke, and sometimes Aub had gone too. He was angry, though. He knew it wasn't her fault and it wasn't of her choosing, but he blamed her having the stroke for the complete change in his life. He had made his living decision for her, but couldn't put down the boding resentment against the whole situation, and honestly, sometimes he just didn't want to see her like she was. He didn't want to live in Adelaide, but here he was.

The most difficult time came when they went back to Glossop to get some things for her room. Marilyn chose some small items of furniture, including the favourite small brass table, the mirror from over the mantelpiece, pictures for the walls, vases, photos and personal

items. Aub spent a few hours in his toolshed, walked the acres, felt the familiar warmth of his home, and broke his heart.

Val was delighted with the bits and pieces, and in fact was very happy with her room and her surroundings. She said she had everything she needed and knew she couldn't have managed with any more. She seemed to have no thoughts about home, except for missing her friends. There was a definite gap in her grasp of the change, but it seemed to help her acceptance of her new home.

There was a real highlight for everyone when Jen's son Andrew married. His bride Susannah Jacob looked beautiful, and it was a very pretty wedding. Val shone, getting around on her walking frame, and didn't mind the spitting rain a scrap. She loved Andrew and James, and this was a great day for them and for Jen and Geoff. The reception was a real treat, and they took her home happy and tired.

For Aub, it became a bit easier to see her once she was a little settled, the surroundings were more pleasant, and she was more like Val, but he didn't want to be on his own with her. They would take her out for drives, bring her home for meals and afternoons, and make sure she was there for any family gatherings. She always enjoyed it, but surprisingly was also always ready to go back, and never complained.

Aub struggled with the loss of his wife, companion and friend, taken from him so suddenly and unexpectedly. She just seemed to accept that he was there and didn't appear to have any sense of the loss he felt so badly. He remembered how tiny and beautiful she had been, her green eyes and her dazzling smile. He had called her his 'sandy cat' in those days, and even though they had finally grown to argue a bit, she had been by his side for nearly sixty years, and now he felt adrift and incomplete.

A room came up in Val's block, and she couldn't understand why he wouldn't live there with her. There was no way he was going to do that! He was battling as it was, in a situation not of his choosing, and he certainly wasn't going to live there in residential care. Val had no concept of this, and nagged about it, so he kept his distance and didn't go in for a couple of weeks, and by then a new resident had moved in.

It was proving to be very difficult. They had brought his desk, sound system and television, bookcase and books from home. There was a comfortable bed and plenty of cupboards. There was plenty of room in the house and the garden included a pool and a nice outdoor area. All this was very well, but what the hell was he going to do with himself?

He walked around the streets getting to know the area and the neighbours. He went for a ride in the car every time it went out. He spent some time on his own at his desk working on family history, or photos or whatever. He did a thousand steps everyday on the stepping machine. He read the paper. He watched television. He couldn't get interested in anything.

There was no more improvement in Val's condition, and the house at Glossop had to be sold. That was the end of everything he'd wanted and worked for. He was bewildered and overwhelmed.

The Single Hand

51

Marilyn now owned and ran her own business and was able to arrange time to suit the circumstances. David took holidays, and the three of them went to Glossop with heavy hearts, Aub's heaviest of all. The impact of the task was massive, as they began tearing the fabric of his life apart to prepare his house for sale.

Marilyn was working in the house, trying to pack as many of his interest items (for him to keep) as she could, but there was so much. Then the cleaning out began, and the kitchen and the pantry alone took several days.

Aub was generous and gave away items like the microwave and washing machine, and a few things were sold. The big family kitchen table went to Marlene and Bob, and many memories went out of the door with it. He thought of all the family and friends who had shared meals and laughter around that table, and they were sweet memories that warmed him, and he wanted to cry, but men didn't cry, as boys hadn't either.

When it came to his tool shed and the main shed, he couldn't believe what was being called junk, and what was disappearing to the dump. Pieces of old pipe that might one day be good for something, bits of rope, pieces of bag, old brooms and hats and gloves, old paint tins, old bottles, bits of tin and so on. David was piling a lot of it on a low-loader and dumping it, sometimes a couple of loads a day. They said to pick out the things he wanted – didn't they understand he wanted all of it? He was so angry.

Gradually, they got together instruments, fishing gear, books, photographic equipment and a myriad of other pieces of his life. He gave away a lot of his valued tools, his compressor, vices and ladders.

He wasn't going to be able to drive in Adelaide, but he didn't know what to do with his little blue car. One of Thora's grandsons had bought his big Ford, and he felt quite good about that, so he was pleased when the lass who was going out with Bob's son made an offer and bought the Honda. Well, he was pleased about who bought it, but not about having to sell it.

The disgusting dismantling of everything took about three weeks, and then, of course, an agent had to be chosen to sell his home of fifty years. Two trailers were loaded to go to Adelaide. Barry Mudge took one, and David the other.

In Adelaide, his things were fitted into his room, the tool shed, and another small shed that had been added near the pool. They tried to do it so that he could find everything, but he never really used a lot of it again. Too much had changed.

After a few months, the home at Glossop was sold. The last trip home was very distressing, and he couldn't look as they drove away.

He had grown up through an era of land being developed, and his farming relatives had all owned land. As pioneers, their attitude was that you were no one if you didn't own a bit of land. You had no identity. He had a lot of time to brood on this, and for the first time began to have an inkling of the huge and great disconnect the Aboriginal people must have felt as their land was taken over. He had never thought about it before, always believing that we were improving things for them, but now he could see that perhaps he had been wrong. He spent several weeks pondering this, and read some articles and began to feel more empathy and more understanding than he had felt before for the Aboriginal people.

The days were long, and even longer when David and Marilyn were both at work and he had to find something to fill the hours. They lived in a nice spot and had a nice garden with a mix of native and ornamental plants. There were plenty of good spots to sit and contemplate or to read, but you had to be in the mood to want to do it.

Ron and Ruth Hewitson lived across the road, and Aub grew very fond of them. They had a garden of native plants, complete with nesting boxes for the birds, and they were not far from the River Torrens. There were lots of birds, and this did interest him. He had known the ones along his river, so now he set about getting to know about these new local birds.

All of the rooms had large windows dropping to the floor, and as they had reflective security film on them, there were no curtains drawn during the day. He could sit unobserved anywhere in the house and couldn't be seen even by a person walking directly past the window. He found he could observe both the happenings of the day and the habits of the birds. He would see them come into the bird bath, and his favourites were the small honeyeaters that arrived in a noisy cloud and splashed the water all over the place. He used the large Simpson and Day bird book for identifying them all.

There were common birds, like pigeons of different types, and of course sparrows and blackbirds. There were willy-wagtails, and silver eyes, and swifts. But there were some small birds he'd not seen before. The magpies he was quite familiar with, as he used to have warbling conversations with them up on the block, and they had got to know each other quite well. These magpies wouldn't warble back to him, so he didn't think they were very smart. There was a piping shrike that would come and drink and then stand on the sill admiring himself and preening his feathers for the bird in the window. The lorikeets from Ron's nesting boxes would settle in the trellis around the veranda and chatter away, and two sulphur-crested cockatoos would call regularly and drink when the flock flew over squawking each morning and evening. Next door's cat would come, and it had a peculiar habit of sitting on the bird bath and cupping its paw to drink from. He hadn't seen that before.

Gradually, new patterns began to take over his day. He would do some exercise, read for a while, watch the birds, play his tin whistles, have lunch, go for a walk, visit Val, and then settle down outside for a drink with David.

On hot evenings, he would go in the pool, but it surprised him that

he couldn't swim the laps that he thought he should be able to. After all, you didn't go in the river unless you were going to swim over and back again, and it annoyed him and didn't occur to him that perhaps the fact that he was nearly ninety had something to do with it.

The house was always busy with family and friends calling in, and often people from the river would arrive, and they were always the best days of all.

Jen and Geoff came out regularly and it was good that Val would come out for meals, and even better when they all went for a drive in the hills or down around the coast.

Slowly, acceptance of his situation began to seep into the days and the weeks, but things could never be the same. He was happy with the care Val was receiving, and he was grateful to Marilyn and David for trying to make this his home, but he missed his river and his piece of land.

He was doing his best to play the new version of the game, but it was a very poor second to the old one that had been so familiar. Sometimes he knew he was being a bit nasty. He didn't mean to be, but he'd spent a lifetime hiding his feelings. So when he was feeling vulnerable, something had to give, and lashing out with anger and nastiness was the defensive emotion that was the easiest to show.

City people didn't talk the same language. For the first time in his life, he was bored.

52

The bombshell dropped when Resthaven rang Marilyn at work to say that Val was behaving strangely, and they were sending her by ambulance to the Royal Adelaide Hospital. Marilyn got there at the same time as the ambulance, and it didn't take long to work out that something was very wrong. Val knew her, but she was talking with her deceased mother one minute and gabbling strangely the next. She had had another stroke and was admitted to a ward immediately.

Aub took the news badly. Was there any other way to take it? 'Poor little bugger' was all he could say.

The next morning, the news was worse. Overnight there had been another much more life-changing stroke, and she was no longer conscious. She was breathing and swallowing and was not being kept alive with support, but she was effectively in a coma.

After several days, she recovered consciousness, but she was now in a quasi-world, where she recognised no one and had no idea who or where she was. Going to see her was dreadful, and on most days Aub didn't feel he could go, although Marilyn and David did.

It was terrible to see her reduced to this. She was vacant and staring, with dull eyes, and there was no recognition of people or surrounds at all. She could move her right arm but could not direct the movement, she had no speech, and made no noises, but she was breathing on her own. The prognosis was that she would never know the family and would need full nursing home care.

When she was moved three months later, Resthaven placed her at Leabrook, which was only a short few kilometres away. The staff were lovely, and the care was good, and gradually and unexpectedly, Val began to respond. She began to get excited when they came in to see her, and would make conversational noises, with the only distinguishable words being 'yes' and 'no', with both being used in the wrong place. She would look at them earnestly, and in a conversational tone would say 'woos, woos woos woos', clearly believing she was talking to them.

Everyone talked to her with normal conversation, and gradually they could see that she was understanding some of what they were saying. Soon too, she would recognise them coming towards her, and would make a movement to wave to say 'hello' as they got near. Between them, someone saw her every day. It was important to them all that she didn't feel abandoned.

After a while, Aub felt that he could go each day too, and he soon made friends with the staff, who all enjoyed chatting with him, but he never stayed with Val on his own again.

He fully appreciated now that his Val was gone and was so grateful for wonderful memories of the years when they had shared so much. Her smile became her main means of communication, and the staff loved her. She still had some of her slightly wicked sense of humour and began to recognise when something around her was funny.

She had always been quietly determined, and when her mouth was sore, her false teeth were lost for days. They were finally found, hidden underneath the top mattress on her bed, and goodness knows how she put them there with one arm. She blessed them with her most wicked smile as much to say, 'See, I tricked you. You weren't putting those in my mouth.'

She couldn't stand, walk, or talk but she had recovered most of her awareness and some of her personality. The family bought her a waterbed barouche so that she could be very comfortably moved around and taken home in an access cab, for special occasions.

She must have had some awareness of how she looked because she still liked to have her hair done and kept tidy and would get quite cross if it felt too long on the bottom of her neck, and she still always liked to wear a neck scarf.

Aub wasn't happy, but Jen and Marilyn arranged a small family celebration in a pretty, intimate room, in the nursing home, on the day of their sixtieth wedding anniversary, and Val looked lovely and had the widest smile of all. The stained-glass windows threw some pretty lights and shadows, the flowers were beautiful. She was very happy, perhaps thinking she was in a little church. Certainly, she knew what it was all about, and happily ate the cream puffs.

Aub could clearly remember the day they'd shot off to New Residence and married and not told anyone. He felt they'd railroaded him into this, but it was quite a nice celebration and he even agreed to a couple of photos being taken. It had been fifty-five-odd very good years as far as he was concerned, and it was just this last few when the wheels had fallen off that he could have done without.

53

In July 2000, when he was fifty-seven, David was made redundant in a company restructure. This was not a good age, or a good time economically, to be looking for work, and Marilyn was building a new business, so they faced a difficult, financial situation. For David, it was a huge challenge. He had always worked without taking sick days and had earned positions of some responsibility.

Aub went with him to the nursing home each day and Marilyn changed to working long hours and would see Val in the evenings. It was never really decided that things would stay like this, but although David was actively seeking a job, it seemed there were no employers looking for a man of his age. Fate stepped in again, changing family matters and forcing the hand, as it so often does.

Sue and Glen, who had been married for some years, came in glowing and excited, and the news bubbled out that Sue was three months pregnant. They were expecting twins in December. Great excitement for everyone. There were several sets of twins in the family, born over several generations, and here were another two little people to meet at the end of the year. Aub immediately delved into his family history sheets to track back across the family's sets of twins.

He had never seen ultrasound photos. He found them astounding, and Sue explained what was what and who was where. This was new technology he hadn't known about, so he read all he could about it. Pregnancy had always been a 'women's' thing as far as he was concerned, but now he followed the progress of these new family members with great interest. New things to learn again at the age of ninety.

Kristin had a new partner, Geoffrey. Aub found him an interesting man and he liked him. Geoffrey was a lawyer, and he got on well too with Sue

 and Glen. When they were all there together, there was plenty of noise and interesting conversation, and they always brightened his day. He was keen to ask them how they felt about things, because they were a from a different age group. Like voluntary euthanasia, for example, and the ethics of abortion in some circumstances, and what did they think about politics. The questions were numerous and diverse. Sometimes, this floored them a bit, as such topics were often best left alone. Grandpa, though, was always thinking with more emphasis on the euthanasia issue than most of the others. He was greatly in favour of voluntary euthanasia and thought there should be a little pill you could take at a certain age if you wanted too. Why should anyone else have a say over what you wanted?

Marilyn told Val that Sue was expecting twins, and Val smiled, and smiled, and smiled. When Sue went in to see her a week later, the first thing she did was to reach out and try to rub Sue's stomach. They were all amazed. She had not only understood, but she had also remembered.

As the pregnancy progressed, Sue couldn't drive and couldn't be left alone, so it was David that spent the days with her. When the capsules were fitted in the car for the babies, the man asked him if he would be at the birth, and David replied sagely that he 'didn't think so'. The fact that he wasn't working was a very real help at this time. Perhaps his retrenchment was meant to be.

Marilyn worked very long hours and in her fifties began studying for a second diploma. This was a long study course, and it wouldn't have been possible if David hadn't taken over the house and almost pushed her meals under the study door. She was earning enough at this stage to keep the family in modest circumstances, but she sometimes felt a bit disappointed that she couldn't do more of the family things. She was going to be the largely absent grandmother.

Aub, however, was somewhat impressed, and somewhat

unimpressed, by David's new role. In his day, all being well, the women did the housework, as Val had, even though she worked on the block every day. Here was David washing, cooking and even ironing. Aub had done this too, when he was baching and when he'd had to, but he found it hard to get used to the reversed roles in this house. He knew that Marilyn was building the business, but perhaps didn't realise how much the family finances depended on it.

Aub reckoned there was a great hullabaloo when the twins were born three days after Christmas. The little girl and boy now bore the Winkler name. He wasn't a baby person. People had babies every day, but he was very pleased to know that they were all well, and that there were no complications. They were tiny, and he wasn't too keen on holding them for a start, feeling he was all fingers and thumbs. But when the little boy was named Josh Aubrey, something that had never entered his mind, he was surprised to feel an immense rush of pleasure and pride. He had always been very close to Sue and got on well with Glen, but this was the first time a child had been named after him. (Cassandra Eva got her second name from Glen's mother, who was also delighted.)

It seemed that everyone swung into action to help with the double handful. Sue was very capable but was also very tired. Kris altered her working hours to a later start, so she could go over in the mornings to allow her sister time to have a shower and something to eat. David went up each day to do the extra things needed, a bit of shopping, cleaning up and so on, and Marilyn tried to call in if she could in the evening.

Aub watched all this, saying he'd never seen a family 'bat' for each other so much. He didn't realise that perhaps it was he who had always been at arm's length while these things that he viewed as 'women's matters' were happening. Anyway, it was a mighty big change in the family.

On Christmas Days, Val would come out by access cab,

comfortable and safe on her big barouche, and there would be quite a gathering at Kristin's and Geoffrey's home. Aub took pleasure in these days with Val, and always enjoyed seeing Shirley and Jim Adam (Geoffrey's parents) and Marilyn's and David's friends Gordon and Leslie. He was pleased to see Val so happy. She would look out and wave to them all like the Queen, as her access cab left to take her back to the nursing home.

Jen's son James had grown into a nice young man, and Aub was impressed by his work ethic and found him easy to talk with. It was obvious that he had followed Geoff's interest in cars and mechanics, and he seemed to be a practical young lad. Jen's older son Andrew, and his wife Susie, had a daughter Madelaine, followed by twins Evie and David. Now there were five great-grandchildren.

As usual, there was to be no fuss for Aub's birthday, but he always enjoyed a picnic, so they celebrated him turning ninety-one in Hazelwood Park. A chop, and a sausage, with bread in hand, was one of his favourite things. The smell of the gum leaves, and the warmth of the sun on his shoulders was welcome. He didn't feel 'excited' about being in his nineties. He had outlived his siblings and many of his friends, and nothing was the same any more. He was ready to leave it to 'you young blokes'. He announced loudly that he was ready for 'the wooden overcoat' and expected that it wouldn't be long before he was wearing it. But they remembered he had thought that when he was in his seventies too.

Geoffrey gave Kris a cocker spaniel the following Christmas, and she named him Toffee because of his colour. As they were both working long hours (usually until eight or so at night) and you can't leave a pup on its own all the time, they dropped him off each morning, and picked him up each evening, as they went by. So now there was a dog. He was a cute little bloke, but he had a habit of getting under Aub's feet, which would result in a loud roar. He chewed things too. Took the tops off all of David's sprinklers, and did it again every time he replaced them just to prove it hadn't been a fluke.

Aub was not good at putting his things out of the way. With the exception of his shed, where everything had had a place, he had always left things just where he was using them. (He didn't know how frustrating Val had found this over the years.) So, when his three-thousand-dollar hearing aid (one of a pair) went missing, Toffee got the blame.

It was a nice gristly little morsel, with a little wobbly tail, and any self-respecting pup who saw it sitting on the coffee table would know it was a chewable treat left just for him. When David found it chewed and discarded in the yard, they binned it and said nothing. It was replaced, and a spot was reserved (for the pair) on the mantelpiece, so that Aub would always be able to find them.

Toffee grew into a loving, sensible fellow with a white streak across his brow making him look very distinguished, and Marilyn christened him the 'Toff'. He was always 'on guard' and ruled the yard if anyone thought they should come in, but otherwise didn't bark much, and spent his days patiently waiting for his walk and sleeping in the sun. Aub referred to him as 'the long-handled trotting dog', or 'the four-footed quadruped,' reminiscent of his days with old Henry on the farm.

Aub ate everything and wasn't fussy. The variety, though, surprised him, and he was introduced to foods he'd never eaten before. He enjoyed this new pasta stuff, and always referred to it as 'dough'. He liked Marilyn's pizza too, and always pronounced it as 'pisssa.' After all, that was how it was spelt. Stir-fries were new, and rice wasn't just to put in custards, and cappuccinos were a bit better than the old coffee and chicory essence they used to have in his day.

He found a new appreciation for flowers. He'd never thought much about them, always being too busy growing crops, and certainly hadn't been guilty of giving them to anyone. He could see now, though, that some of them were quite remarkably beautiful and he began to understand the pleasure that Thora and Arthur had found over years of growing them. Arthur had even developed a strain of gladioli and for many years had supplied flowers to the stallholders in the Adelaide market on Friday nights.

His passion for exercising the body and the mind was as strong as ever. He did finger exercises and breathing exercises and practised patterns of coordination with his hands and his feet. He stretched and bent and did half squats. Then he would do his daily dose on the stepping machine.

He bought a yoga manual called *KISS* (Keep It Simple Stupid) and it became his new talisman. He read it and read it again. He chose parts of it to practise and learned passages that he thought were most important. One of his favourites was the Turtle, and he would talk about it at length. The yoga book was always on hand from then on, armed with pieces of white paper sticking out to mark things of note. For his age, he was remarkably fit, with little arthritis or illness. His memory was long and accurate and amazing for his age. He and Arthur had taken gingko tablets for several years, and whether they had done the job, or if it was just in his genes, didn't matter. He could remember and visualise people and places and happenings quite clearly. In memory, he could even reproduce smells.

Perhaps the downside was that he had always had vivid dreams, usually of the scary kind where lions and tigers or people were chasing him. He would wake up hot and frightened, and he knew he'd been right there. He had dreamt like this all his life, and he didn't like it. That was something you were supposed to grow out of, wasn't it? Some sleep guru would probably have told him what it all meant, but he didn't think he wanted to know, thanks.

54

In November, when she was eighty-seven, another stroke robbed Val of all that had been left, and this time there was to be no recovery. The doctor felt she would only live for a couple of days, and had carefully explained that although she was breathing, she was in another place.

Aub was glad for Val, that she no longer had to live as she had been, but he himself was completely devastated. He had thought that as he'd already lost her he was mentally prepared, but he hadn't been. He was ninety-two, he'd had enough, and he just wanted out.

Marilyn sat with Val every day and evening, day after day. Jen and Geoffrey went to see her and found it very difficult. Aub did not go in, but after five days, it seemed that perhaps she was lingering to see him before she went. There was no way to know. So, reluctantly, he walked into her room, and it was better than he had expected, but terrible nonetheless. She lay sleeping, her face quite relaxed, her soft hair curling around on the pillow, and she showed no signs at all of knowing he was there.

The doctor called each morning, surprised at her strength, and Marilyn sat with her for another five days. She died in a peaceful release, on the evening of 12 November 2002.

Somehow, Aub got through the funeral and the days around it, but it was all changed for him now. Bad enough before but, with your partner completely gone, there wasn't anything as far as he was concerned. His grieving for all he had lost was profound. There was plenty happening around him, but he wasn't part of it. He thought perhaps he had made a mistake by staying in Adelaide, but underneath he knew that he hadn't. He liked to think he'd still be driving around and seeing all the people he knew if he was still up the river. Many of them had died, but in his mind he still saw them there and believed things hadn't changed in his absence.

He thought about all the things that might have been different, but it was too late now. He lapsed into hours of quiet reading, and exercise, and walking, and drank more red wine these days than he used to. Somehow, he made the best of the days that he could. After all, you played the cards that you were dealt. He counted himself very fortunate. Val had been beautiful, and he could never believe how lucky he was that she had wanted him. She had been the best thing that had happened to him in his life, and there had never been anyone else for him once he'd met her. He thought of Val as soon as he woke each morning, and she was always his last thought at night.

The Long Game

55

He was cross, and he felt (wrongly as it happened) that no one thought he could do anything. When Marilyn and David were working in the garden he would say, 'Of course I couldn't do that', and yet no one was stopping him from pitching in. Marilyn thought he might like to take charge of some pruning out the back, but he replied that he couldn't do that because he wouldn't do it right. That was rubbish, because he knew more about pruning than anyone else in the house. It was really just a way of expressing his uninterested state of mind.

He kept in touch with his friends up the river, and Marilyn had ordered him a copy of *The Murray Pioneer* to arrive each week. He had known the early owners of this paper and, as a young teen, he had pulled Mrs Taylor's weeds. He'd been reading the *Pioneer* since he was about nineteen or twenty and still found plenty of interest in it.

Surprisingly, water was becoming a problem up the river. The locks had been supposed to fix all that. Now, though, there was more water being drawn by the other states upstream, and there wasn't enough coming down to South Australia.

The growers had already had to improve their irrigation processes in an effort to reduce evaporation and to get the water more efficiently to the plantings. Aub had seen things change from open channels to pipelines, from furrows to overhead sprays and then to drip irrigation. Now growers were selling their water allocations for cash.

Stations in Queensland and New South Wales were growing cotton, and were buying all the water they could get – or, in some cases, steal. There was an ethical and political bunfight going on, and no one seemed to be policing the rules. Once you sold your precious water allocation, you would never get it back.

He heard that on part of his old block Darren Kennedy was trialling trout farming, growing fingerlings in large tanks. He had never seen such a thing coming. They had worked so hard to build a viable fruit industry, and now they were having to diversify wherever they could.

He spent the days living with his memories as constant friends. He used to think about the boats he'd owned.

The old rowboat that he and mate Frankie Gaynes had kept on the river bank by the Renmark pub. The little punt he'd used for fishing and the day he'd rowed up to call on friend Don Bruce when he'd come back from the war. His loved gun dog Mack had been overjoyed to see him and had swum behind the boat trying to follow him home. He'd had to take him back. Broke his heart, and Mack's too, but he couldn't take him away from Don after four years.

He'd had a long narrow wooden rowboat too for years, and kept it floating in the underground tank so it didn't have to stay out of the water. People used to look at it quizzically sometimes when they walked past, but they just didn't understand about wooden boats.

Then he'd had the Quintrex runabout. Now that was a boat. They'd had some good hours with her. He'd drift off into musing about this fish they caught, and that day they did this... He'd sold it in the end to young Ron Harris and was very amused to hear that they were waterskiing behind it. Never occurred to him and Val.

Sometimes he'd remember the way he and Val used to argue regularly about the weather. It would be the middle of summer and blazingly hot, and the air would be heavy, and forebodingly still. The day's work would be done, and everyone would be tired and worn out. The apricot trays would be spread out to dry.

Val would cast her eyes skyward and shake her head. 'I don't like it. I think we should stack the fruit and cover it.'

He'd be too tired to even think about it, and when he said no, the argument would be on. They'd go back to the house, and he'd lie on the lounge room floor to stretch his back, and Val would start making lunches for the next day, and her face would match the thunder clouds.

He remembered one night when there was a fearful storm, with thunder and lightning all around, and they were out at two in the morning trying to beat the rain, stacking trays as hard as they could go. Roger Hollitt arrived to help because he'd heard the storm and he knew what would be happening. It poured and blew for a couple of hours, and by four a.m. they were all exhausted, but most of the fruit had been saved.

It was only now that he realised how often, after they had finished work, Val would begin cooking and washing and ironing and would often work until midnight and still be up by six in the morning. 'Poor little bugger', and now she was gone. At the same time, he would forget how achingly tired he had been on many nights when he had had to go out and play the sax.

So many things he thought about, and he was never lonely with his thoughts. It was a comforting thing, and he was grateful for it.

56

He did like the house and the yard. He used to think how wonderful it would have been if they had had a place like this when they were growing up. He liked to sit out by the pool and contemplate, and sometimes the blue-tailed lizard would sit and keep him company and they would both fall asleep in the sun. There had been a blue-tailed lizard when he was a kid.

Occasionally, he'd find himself a job to do in the shed, and he never let the kitchen knives get blunt and would hone them on stone and steel. He'd always done this, and he remembered one day at home when he'd had a dozen big knives lined up on the kitchen table for sharpening and the new water man had called in. He'd eyed them off warily and hadn't stayed long. Aub hadn't put him out of his misery by explaining why they were there and had enjoyed the concerned look on his face.

Marilyn and David took him for a cruise on the *River Murray Princess*. It was great. The colour in the cliffs was as familiar as anything, and the smells along the river took him back years. The reeds and the birds, the gums and the willow trees, the backwaters and the sunsets filled his soul. He found plenty of people to talk with too and spent a bit of time in the wheelhouse with the captain, talking about river boats, river captains he had known and river people. He was forty again.

He still didn't think of their suburb of Campbelltown as home; he was just biding his time there. He had friends and relatives call in, but they were all a bit younger than him, and most hadn't kept a connection with the land.

The Riverland was only two and a half hours away, and Aub would love to have gone, but Marilyn and David didn't make any move to take him. She went up regularly for work, but she knew they could never take him back. He would have wanted to see the block, and the house, and the neighbours. But the house was a wreck. The young couple who had bought it had moved on, and a middle-aged group of less desirable people had moved in, and let it run down badly. There was an old car, and a caravan, left in the thigh-high weeds where the lawn had been, and the shrubs were gone, Val's prize magnolia tree was no longer there, and the bushes at the front, that she had hand-watered for years were being swallowed up again by the scrub. The big shed looked derelict, and one of the large sliding doors hung sideways proclaiming to the world that nobody cared. The overhead tank stand had fallen down and the house roof was a mass of rust. There was loose rubbish everywhere. They couldn't let him see that his fifty years of love, work and care had been totally wiped out.

Now in his mid-nineties, the changes in living standards, morals, dress and manners absolutely staggered him. In his day, you were rich if you had a wooden or linoleum floor. You never answered back. You were seen and not heard. You treated people the way you wanted to be treated. You spoke the Queen's English. You respected people's dignity and property. You didn't need to lock your doors. You didn't go out without a hat and a tie. There was no substitute for good speech and good manners.

He didn't understand so many things that were happening, and he seemed to have got lost in the game, somewhere in the middle.

Despite everything, he thought that negative thinking had limited the things he'd done, and that what he had done wasn't quite good enough. Marilyn said he should be proud of how he had lived his life, and that it was the exacting standards and expectations he set for himself that made him feel like that. He had a word for it – pigsbullshit! He was fed up.

Humour had changed a lot too. The old jokes they used to tell, (and he still thought they were funny) weren't considered funny any more. You couldn't call women sheilas or squaws because these days that was sexist. There was this thing called 'political correctness', and it seemed to override into all sorts of things. He didn't think of himself as racist, and he'd had Aboriginal friends and other coloured friends too. Some of the words he'd grown up with like 'darkie' and 'half-caste' couldn't be said now without someone getting upset.

His mate Frankie Gaynes was the son of Tom Gaynes, who was a British citizen and was also West Indian. He had been one of the most liked and trusted men in Renmark. Aub's dad Stan had referred to him as the 'whitest man in Renmark', and had meant it as a great compliment. Now Marilyn was trying to tell him that Tom could perhaps have taken it as an insult to his colour and his forebears – that it could have been taken as suggesting that only white men could be true and honest. How anyone could put that construction on it annoyed and confused him completely. He knew old Tom had been close to Stan and was sure he had taken it as a compliment. He himself had never agreed with the White Australia Policy, having known some of the Chinese people who'd descended from the prospectors, so he didn't see that he was in any way a racist.

Communications and news moved at a startling pace, and by such various means. He sat down with Sue and Glen and saw the base at Mawson, in Antarctica, on the computer screen. The picture changed hourly, and you could follow exactly what the weather was there, in real time. By satellite too, he was able to see pictures of Maidstone in Kent, where his great-great-grandfather had emigrated from, and they were quite clear. Instead of telegrams, now messages just appeared through the air, as email, from people far away. He couldn't get his head around it.

He had thought that the coaxial cable was amazing when it came in, but now they talked to him about this place called cyberspace. With all of his reading about astronomy and space, he had never come across this place. Marilyn couldn't explain it to him satisfactorily, and neither could anyone else.

He didn't like change, but he'd had to go to a new optician once he moved to Adelaide and, as he knew his eyes were quite a challenge, he wasn't keen about it. As it happened, the local optician was very good indeed, and a good rapport and respect developed between them.

He went to David's doctor at the local clinic, and that was all right too, although some of his blood pressure tablets were promptly changed. Soon he found that this helped some of his headaches and he was sleeping better, so that got the thumbs up as well.

All these things now assumed a greater importance in his life, where they had been merely incidental to him before. He was beginning to sense the old man in himself, and now he was past the lifespan of 'Old King Billie' who they had all had to salute on the farm, when he was a boy.

Ever since the war years, he had had a severe problem with the control of his bowels. The parasite from the swimming hole in the tropics had left him with long-term problems, and he needed daily medications. The local chemist at home had always made him a concoction referred to as his 'cork' medicine. Now they wanted him to take tablets that didn't have quite the same firepower. It sapped his confidence when it came to going out, as he knew he could easily find himself in trouble.

He thought about a night years ago when he and Val had gone to stay with Win and Fred at Nyah. He'd forgotten his medicine and had to get the chemist in Swan Hill to mix some up for him. This had meant the pharmacist contacting the chemist in Barmera to find out what was in it. He had some concern because it contained opiates and so on, but he made it up because Win had worked in his shop for many years, and the Barmera chemist assured him Aub had been taking it for years with no ill effects.

That evening, the four had sat up late talking about life insurance, and dying, and wills, as you do. When they went off to bed, Val poured him his medicine, and he drank it down.

'How much did you give me?' he asked. 'It seemed a bit thick.'

They looked at the glass and discovered that, being tired, she'd poured him a double dose.

He rang the pharmacist, getting him out of bed, and said, 'What if I took double the dose of that cork medicine you whipped up for me today?'

He could still remember the expletive from the other end and was told to go to the hospital and have his stomach pumped. He wasn't having any of that, and ordered Val to make sure he didn't go to sleep.

Val, worried sick, sat up all night shaking him and saying, 'Aub, don't go to sleep, don't go to sleep,' while he snored his head off and she couldn't wake him up.

He was all right in the morning but let them all know it was the last time they'd discuss life insurance.

He remembered the time too when they had slept in the Ford, with the lay-back seat, on the beach at Rapid Bay. They woke up to a beautiful sunrise and a host of interested onlookers peering at them through the windows. A ship had come in through the night, and some of the crew had taken the chance to walk down from the conveyor jetty to the beach. They'd just had to stay in bed till they all took off, so they could get up and dress. Nowadays, the front seats of sedans could all be tilted back but didn't go flat like the old ones that you could sleep on. People had panel vans, combi vans and caravans instead.

Apart from the war years, he reckoned that he'd lived at the best time of all. They'd been great years to be a kid, and the river had been the best place of all to grow up.

57

Marilyn and David had been talking for a while about altering the house. For the life of him, Aub couldn't see why, but they seemed to think that changes would be needed in a short while. David had been diagnosed with prostate cancer and the prognosis had not been good. It was very aggressive and was already in the surrounding tissue. He had undergone hormone treatment, and then ray treatment for seven weeks, but Aub couldn't see much difference in him. Marilyn thought he was very pale and tired, and the family had been making a bit of a fuss of him, but Aub thought it would all blow over. Indeed, David did improve, but there was no remission, and he would remain on treatment for the rest of his life.

The real complicating factor about the house, though, was that by 2007, and in need of a hip replacement, David could barely walk. Furthermore, it looked like the other hip would be as bad within a year or so. Due to the state of his health, the specialists would not operate, so the possibility that he would soon be in a wheelchair was very real. He had had a back problem for several years, with calcified discs, and now with hip problems his movement was quite restricted and was severely limited by pain.

Marilyn still needed to work to bring in income, and the beautiful garden was now too big for them to maintain. They had a builder friend look at the possibilities for modifying the house, but there were inherent problems in making it wheelchair accessible. In fact, when Ron (David's ex-father in law) was living there and had had a stroke, the ambulance officers had needed to fireman's lift him out, as they couldn't get a barouche down to the bedroom.

Lovely as the house was, and practical as it was under normal circumstances, the change was being made. Aub didn't want to move. It had taken him long enough to get used to this place, and he was now turning ninety-eight, and he didn't want new neighbours either.

For his birthday, the family bought him a new stepper. It was easier for him to use than the old one, and he still liked to do a bit on it every day. He couldn't understand the computer thingy on the front, but otherwise it was easy for him to adjust, and he thought it was a pretty good present.

He had never been gracious about receiving presents and would usually make some comment about wasting money. It was normal for him to feel, shake, smell and put down anything he was given, and then to open it when there was no one around. The grandchildren had always been very frustrated when they gave Grandpa a present.

He was a generous man himself, but he preferred to give a present when it suited, rather than at Christmas or birthday. He liked to give something that someone wanted, or liked, and always enjoyed the pleasure they got out of it. He always insisted on paying his share of anything, and he didn't like those blokes who had 'death adders' in their pockets. He was never mean and there was a warmth about his generosity that made it really appreciated.

He was a bit shaky on his legs, and unhappily considered it the ultimate indignity when he needed to use a walking frame while he was outside. The only good thing about it was that he always had a seat with him and could sit down wherever he was. He hadn't expected to live long enough to come to that. The 'wooden overcoat' was taking longer than he'd thought.

Marilyn and David were excited about a house only a few streets away, and took Aub see it. He walked around and had a look, but he didn't take in much of it at all. It was modern, and just looked big and open and large, and he couldn't get a grasp on it at all and couldn't see himself living there. But the die was cast, the momentum picked up, and the packing boxes began to appear.

He found it very unsettling. David couldn't do too much, and with Marilyn working, there was a bit of tension in the air to get everything done, All of them had sentimental feelings about the happy times shared in the family home they were leaving. For Aub it was sad. It was the last home he could picture Val being in. The skips and boxes reminded him of the horrible packing up at Glossop and he was in a black, black place.

The move itself happened over two days. Marilyn's friend Colleen helped Aub for the first day. He was fond of Colleen, and she made sure he got cups of tea and food, and she seemed to understand how he felt and helped him get to know his new room. It was large and light and his furniture was moved in and set up first. He had a new three-quarter bed and mattress, a bookcase with lots of his books, his desk and chair, an easy chair, his television and sound system, and a large built-in wardrobe. There was plenty of room for him to get around with his walking frame and it was only a few steps to the big bathroom.

They slept in the house from the first night, although the movers didn't finish until mid-afternoon of the second day. He felt a bit lost, and for some reason he had difficulty getting the hang of the layout. He woke in the night and couldn't work out where he was, and Val wasn't there, and he couldn't wait for the night to be over.

He'd had a few trips (Marilyn said they were falls) but a bloke can trip a bit when he's older, can't he? They seemed to have trouble getting him up again, but in his day, he could have lifted a bloke up easily. He just felt tired, and sometimes a bit lonely. It was no one's fault; he just reckoned he'd outlived his time.

One morning, three weeks after moving, he couldn't stand up. His legs just wouldn't hold him. Everything was too much, and for once he said, 'You'd better call the doctor.'

A few hours later, he was in hospital, just wanting to sleep. Marilyn had given them all the information, but they kept asking silly questions like what his name was, who was the prime minister, what year was it, and all that baloney.

After getting a bed on the ward, he got some sleep, and when he woke up again he didn't know if it was daytime or night. There were bells and noises in his head, and occasionally a face in front of his, talking to him, but he couldn't be bothered answering.

When he started to put things together again, the doctor told him he'd had an 'event' (whatever that was), but one of the nurses said it was a mild stroke. It was difficult to make his body do what he wanted, and to his complete and absolute disgust and embarrassment, they'd put a pad like a child's nappy on him.

He'd signed the form to say he didn't want to be resuscitated, and he was very definite about it. It was in his file and on the doctor's notes. There was no way they were to take action if that occasion arose. 'God, let me die.'

Unbelievably, Marilyn received a call from the emergency doctors one Sunday afternoon, to say he had been comatose and they had resuscitated him, and given him a shot of atropine. She was dumbfounded. When the doctor then said that they thought he needed a pacemaker, she asked, 'Would you do that for a ninety-eight-and-a-half-year-old?' and received the answer, 'Of course. It's a simple operation.'

She could never tell Aub what they had done, but they got the message. Their lack of respect for his instructions cost him dearly. Having ignored his specific directive, and consequently causing him to live the years in front of him, they should have hung their heads in shame.

The days were long, and there were too many of them. The aged care team talked to him about going into a nursing home. But he was going home, so he wasn't signing any forms. He flatly refused. They said he couldn't go home yet, and he would be sent out to Fullarton on a transitional care package. Marilyn apparently agreed, and he wasn't impressed with her either. Obviously, they didn't want him in their new house. He just wanted to get out of it all.

The hospital sent him out to the place, and he hated it. He didn't like the room, he didn't like the staff, and he didn't like the meals. Apparently, he had to stay for three months.

As the exit time got closer, Marilyn talked to him about needing to go into a nursing home to live. They couldn't take him home to live because the aged care assessment team had decided that it was not safe. She held enduring power of guardianship and attorney, but because he could understand, it was still required that he should sign the agreement form. He wasn't going to agree, and he wasn't going to sign. He knew that she'd just bought a house that had no room for him and was putting him out like old rubbish.

Marilyn got very distressed each day as the three months ran out, and finally, in tears, she told him he had to sign the forms because he was going to be out on the day after tomorrow. So, in absolute disgust, he signed the bloody thing, and then he went into a monumental sulk and wouldn't talk to her. He didn't know that this had left her with two days to find a nursing home bed, and he wouldn't have understood if he had. What it was to have thankless children. And David probably had a hand in it too for all he knew.

Two days later. he was moved to the Campbelltown Nursing Home. He had a room with an attached bathroom, but it had no view. (Marilyn fretted over that but said nothing.) There had been no time to worry about anything but good care for him and she was so grateful they had taken him. It was friendly and well run and he had a few of his own things. Still, he was very upset with her for getting a house without room for him, and he wasn't going to let her forget it. They said he'd moved in with them, and had a special room of his own, but he didn't remember that, so he knew it wasn't true.

He could walk a bit now, but his legs were shaky and he was slow, and he still had to use the frame. He demanded they bring in his walking stick and sulked when they said it wouldn't be safe for him.

They wouldn't let him have his scissors either, so that was another sulk. He wouldn't eat in the dining room with the others but did make it down to the lounge on some afternoons so that he could see people come and go.

Gradually he got to know the staff, and he gave them all nicknames and they looked after him well. He particularly liked one of the tall Sudanese carers, who was the best of all at showering him, and there were a few others whose personalities he began to enjoy, but it wasn't home, and he disliked it with a passion.

Why couldn't a bloke decide for himself what would happen to him at this stage of life? He felt anger that he had always paid his dues, and felt that in return he should be the master of his fate. In the old farming days, he wouldn't have found himself in a place like this. Old Whiskers had been quite senile at the end but had still been looked after by various ones in the family. Nowadays, the powers that be didn't consider home to be a safe place for him any more. Phat!

Jen and Geoff came each week, and he liked to see them. He would ask lots of questions about what was happening with the boys, and Jen would talk non-stop from the time she got there. He was grateful that they came each time, as he knew it was an effort for them, but he fretted and worried a lot about Jenny and what would happen to her as she got older.

He felt he never saw anyone but, in truth, he had a lot of visitors and just didn't realise it. Ron and Ruth (neighbours from the old house) called, cousins and grandchildren called, friends from the Riverland and some extended family all called on him at various times, and some of them regularly. No matter how long they were there, none of them ever stayed long enough.

Marilyn and David came to see him each day, mostly in the late afternoon, and while chatting, they'd pour him a brandy or a glass of red. He liked this and called it happy hour. They always found things to talk about. She was retiring and selling her business, and it was a bit interesting hearing about the process of sale and handover. It was different from selling the block.

Sometimes he would be sulky, and would 'dish a fair bit out', then after they'd gone, he'd wonder if they would come in next day. When they'd go to leave, he'd say, 'That's right, you just go off and do your own thing like you always do,' in a snarky way. He knew why he did it – she shouldn't have put him out, and he wasn't going to let her forget it. He was hurt and he felt abandoned.

He had a cordless phone, and it took him a while to get the hang of it. When he did, he would ring his cousins or friends and greet them with his trademark 'How's your knees and things?' and finish with 'See you Christmas,' or 'Hope all your fowls die.' It couldn't be anyone else but Aub. It was his link with the outside, and it meant he could talk with Meryl in Melbourne, and to other distant friends.

He remembered Auntie Dot taking him to the telephone exchange for the first time, and he thought about how much his dad never got to see. One day when the nurse was helping him, he noticed she had something tucked in her belt at the back. When he worked out it was her phone, he quipped, 'Humph, not many people can talk with that part of their body.' She laughed. His wit hadn't deserted him yet.

In fact, there were never enough people to talk with. He wanted to talk about anything and everything, and all sorts of things. The carers on the staff never had time for a good chat. No one who came to see him stayed long enough for a real good yarn. And then it hit him like a bombshell. Poor Val had been unable to talk, and she couldn't write. She had been three years like that. How on earth had she managed to smile like she did, living with strangers? And his heart broke to think about it.

That brought him back to voluntary euthanasia. He had outlived Val, and family and friends. They were all gone. He'd done his best. Now he was stuck in God's waiting room hoping for his end every day. Why should anyone else have the right to deny him that? They were playing God every day by doing so. Why couldn't he have an exit pill?

The Tally

58

Everyone was talking about him turning a hundred. What about it? He hadn't asked for it, didn't want it, nor the rubbish telegram from the Queen. As far as he was concerned, there was no great merit in it. If they wanted to be excited, that was up to them.

At ninety-nine, he'd learned the value of his excellent memory. He could remember all the country towns that had been busy with horses, carts, farriers, blacksmiths, bakers and butchers and the like. Now they were ghost towns, passed by, and often only the old institute still stood. He would think of a route and add up the long-gone towns along it that he could remember.

He would choose a place or a person and follow those thoughts for the rest of the day. He could visualise easily and could still even see the mole on his friend's chin. He could smell, and the new-cut hay would be in the room with him while he dozed, thinking about an afternoon at the farm. He could feel the cool water smooth over him as he dived into the river. Val was there with her great big smile, and her clear green eyes, but he tried not to think about her because it brought up the awful ache. The experiences of his life time filled his days, and his nights.

He was grateful for this because despite all his years of reading he now found it difficult to read much at all. He still loved his poetry books and read them knowing most of the poems by heart. Marilyn had given him a Good News version of the Bible, and he read that. Of course, he still remembered so many parts of it from his early years of Bible study, and that made it easier for him to follow. He had had a very strong Christian upbringing but, after living so long, his views were quite conflicting.

Young Trevor Harris, who had grown up next door on the block, came in to see him regularly. Trevor was a devout Christian. He was an architect who had travelled extensively in the places of the Bible and the faith. Aub found him very interesting to talk with. They could have an intelligent conversation, and he would find himself thinking on it later. He was always pleased to see Trevor come in, as he was different from the other visitors, being the only one who discussed such matters with him. Without realising or admitting it, he was in a way accepting Trevor's pastoral care.

He had no fear of death, and frequently said in frustration, 'God, why can't I die?'

Marilyn would tell him he was not bad enough for them to take him 'down there', and not good enough for them to take him 'up there', and that he was 'stuck in the middle'. He wasn't amused.

He liked the staff, particularly anyone who had a few minutes to talk with him. The care was good, but he disliked his situation. He disliked that he couldn't read much any more. He disliked that his balance was poor. He wouldn't go out in the car for a drive (and he missed that badly), as the old parasite from the tropics had now ravaged his bowels and taken control.

Sue was a weekly visitor with her cheery 'Hi, Grandpa.' She always made him feel better and would chat away with him about all sorts of things. Sometimes when his legs were really swollen and sore, she'd treat them, and it would hurt, but they always felt better later. There

was another physio who came in to see him and do that, but she wasn't as good as Sue. One day, he couldn't remember the words of an old song, and quick as a flash she looked them up on her phone. For goodness sake, how did she do that?

As his century drew near, he began to realise that other people really did think it was a big deal. He had lived for eighty-four years after his dad had died, and sixty-six years since his brother Ivor's death, and he didn't like to add up the years since anyone else's passing.

He wondered why he had lived so long, and Marilyn would say his job was not obviously yet done, and there was something special he was yet to pass on to his children and grandchildren.

He couldn't see it, but it set him off thinking about the generations of people he had known from his great grandfather down. The first family of Edward Jury, who had come out from England in 1840, had spread widely and almost without exception they had been good living community minded people. His Moody grandfather and grandmother had come from Ireland, and his Hilton and Chapman forebears had arrived from England. He was the end of his line, but he was beginning to understand that this was in name only.

As a younger man, he'd never thought about how women used to change their name when they got married, but the genes still carried on. It seemed to him now that the name wasn't as important as who you really were, and whether you knew and appreciated the ancestors you had come from. In these later years, he was less upset about not having had a son.

He wasn't going to have a party just because he was a hundred, and he wasn't going to have a fuss, but as usual, Marilyn ignored him and said they'd have it anyway. She sent out invitations to an open house to celebrate his century and explained that Aub himself would not be there. Knowing he could no longer cope with a lot of people at once, she said that people from away would be rostered to see him during the day (he was only five minutes down the road), giving them each time to talk with him, and asked that people who lived locally come to the party but please visit him on another day. There was a great response. Family and friends came from as far as Western Australia, Victoria, Tasmania and all over South Australia. It was a good roll-up, and a great testament to how well Aub was liked and respected. They had a good time, and so did Aub. There were lots of photos, plenty of food, stories, and even furniture pertaining to Aub, including the rocking chair he had been nursed in.

Even the letter from the Queen wasn't bad. There was a photo of an elderly lady in a printed cotton dress smiling in the garden, and he realised for the first time that she was no spring chicken either.

The nursing home staff and administration people made him feel special and he held court in his room. He had plenty to think about, with many more visitors over ensuing days, and although it made him tired, he felt a good deal of satisfaction knowing he was not just old and forgotten.

The Last Bid

'Turn the lights down nurse, and leave me, while I hold my last review,
For the Bush is slipping by me, and the town is going too.
Draw the blinds. The streets are lighted, and I hear the tramp of feet-
And I'm weary, very weary, of the Faces in the street.'

Henry Lawson, 'The Last Review'

59

Over the next few months, he got a bit mixed up with things, and he couldn't seem to manage the same. When he would demand that the staff get his daughter now, she would be down in a few minutes to help him sort out whatever the issue was.

He had no sense of time any more and had no concept that he had been there for three years, which was probably just as well. Now, being over a hundred and one, his mind dwelt mostly back in his childhood, with his father and mother and people like Aunt Julia whom he hadn't thought of for years.

He was dreaming his nightmares again and told Marilyn that he would wake in the night 'scared like a little kid'. He was shaken and upset by how vulnerable he felt, and he didn't know where his confidence had gone. It was another thing he'd lost.

He must have had a bit of a trip in the doorway of his bathroom because he was on the floor looking at a couple of blokes who were trying to pick him up. He was hot, and he felt like he couldn't breathe – perhaps he could just stop?

They put him in bed, and next time he looked up, Marilyn was there. He could hear her arguing with the nurse about him not going to hospital. 'It's not what he wants.' And she was right there. The argument went on, and somewhere among it he heard Sue's voice, and then it was just all noise and he wanted them to all just leave him alone. He reached out to touch a face and visibly shrank back shocked, as it wasn't who he thought it was; the hair was wrong.

The ambulance man seemed to 'float' around, and the argument was still on. He was gasping for breath but could hear Sue quietly explaining that he had had enough. He struggled with his brain to get it together, and just managed to say loudly and clearly, 'I can't do this any more.' Then he stopped struggling and closed his eyes.

The nurse and the ambulance officer heard his message, and called in the palliative care team, and he went to sleep.

Marilyn and Sue sat with him for two days. David came, and Kris and Geoffrey and the palliative care nurse. Jen and Geoff visited, and the doctor explained to Jen that Aub's time had come, and she needed to let him go. She didn't grasp it, though.

They played his favourite music and sometimes quietly spoke to him, but they never knew if he was aware that they were there or not. After over a hundred years, his active, intelligent brain had taken him somewhere they couldn't follow, and only he could know now if there were answers to his questions.

Epilogue

Aub's wish for death was granted at one-thirty in the morning on 19 July 2008. It is a great testament to him that, at the age of one hundred and one and a half, and having outlived his friends and the senior family, well over a hundred people attended his funeral.

I spent five days working on his eulogy. Everything was backed up, and I had finished and selected some music.

On the sixth morning, I went to print the file, but when I opened it, it was blank. I tried everything, but still could find nothing. Properties on the file showed that the contents were there, in megabytes, but all I could see was nothing, just a blank. I even checked the font colour to make sure it hadn't just gone white!

The computer man I called could not help, and said he'd never seen anything like this, where the contents were there but could not be viewed.

I had to start again and will always wonder if in some strange way it was a signal that Dad had found that there was something after death, or if it was a sign of protest against what I was writing.

The dead file is still on my old computer, and I haven't parted with it for that reason.

Dad, I sincerely hope you like the book.

Acknowledgements

Writing a book takes many, many hours, and I have been absorbed with my own train of thought, often unaware of what was going on around me. This book could not have been achieved without a great deal of family support.

David, thank you for your continual thoughtfulness and unwavering support, the cups of tea, household tasks and shopping that you so willingly took on. This is your book too, and without you it could never, would never, have been finished.

Kristin, as you know, the computer and I do not speak the same language. You have been a wonderful translator, never telling me that you didn't have time to sort my problems, still loving me through my erratic journey. You saved my sanity several times and coaxed me into the digital age. Your input appears unseen in every chapter and my debt to you is huge.

Susan, the personal support you gave Aub in the last years of his life was invaluable not just to him but also to me. There were times that were very difficult. I knew when you first read this book that your comments came from the heart. Your feedback and your description of how you felt while reading it were warming. Thank you for your feedback and your love.

Geoffrey, I am so grateful for the hours you spent on first proof-reading for me, and in helping me with advice on some of the tedious questions around publishing. Your careful analysis helped clear my mind on several issues. Thank you for your love, generosity and time.

Glen, you are such a valued member of our family, always ready to help us all, despite your many time commitments. You knew Aub as an interesting and engaging character, and I loved your comment 'When the film gets made, Russell Crowe to play Aub.' Such confidence in my telling of the story without even having read the book! Thank you for your ever positive and consistent support.

Author's Note

To you as reader, those of you who knew Aub will have your own memories and stories and feelings, and they may not match what you read in the book. I have related the story as he told it, how he felt, and what he thought, as closely as I can from the many discussions, arguments, laughs and heart to hearts that we shared in his twilight years. I have been careful not to put my own (often differing) views on the page. If you are a reader meeting him for the first time, I hope that I have managed to portray what a fascinating character he was.

www.ingramcontent.com/pod-product-compliance
Lightning Source LLC
Chambersburg PA
CBHW071809080526
44589CB00012B/733